BEDFORD COUNTY, VIRGINIA

BIRTH RECORDS

VOLUME 1
1853–1856

৵৽৶

Ann Chilton

Heritage Books
2024

HERITAGE BOOKS

AN IMPRINT OF HERITAGE BOOKS, INC.

Books, CDs, and more—Worldwide

For our listing of thousands of titles see our website
at
www.HeritageBooks.com

Published 2024 by
HERITAGE BOOKS, INC.
Publishing Division
5810 Ruatan Street
Berwyn Heights, MD 20740

Heritage Books by the author:
Bedford County, Virginia Birth Records, Volume 1, 1853–1856
Bedford County, Virginia Birth Records, Volume 2, 1856–1866

International Standard Book Number
Paperbound: 978-0-7884-7783-6

BIRTH RECORDS

BEDFORD COUNTY,VIRGINIA

1853 - 1856

Bedford County was formed in 1753 from the County of
Lunenburg.
It became effective May 10,1754.
The name Bedford was chosen by the Virginia Assembly
to honor the Fourth Duke of Bedford,John Russell who
was at that time the Secretary of State of Great
Brittian.
Bedford County is nestled in a range of Mountains that
include Twin Peaks of Otter,Headforemost,No Business,
Big and Little Onion,Taylors,Porters and many other
smaller ones .
Creeks and rivers flow through this beautiful country
side making it an ideal place to live and retire.
The early records have been well cared for and are a
source of pride for those in charge.
Court Records,Deeds,wills and Marriages were well re-
corded from 1753.
Birth records did not begin until 1853.
The only source before that time being family Bibles
and personal records.

This book lists the name of the child,date of Birth,
Parents name and father's occupation.

If the child was Slave it is listed as such with the
Mother's name and that of the Owner.

The initials FN indicated the Parent or Parents were
Free Negroes.

As you can see the first part of Page #1 is missing
but I have included what is available.This small
part may help someone in their research.

Good Luck in your search.

Ann Chilton
1992

BEDFORD COUNTY VIRGINIA BIRTH RECORDS
1853-1866

The first half of page one is missing but the remaining information may be of help in searching for one's Ancestor.

No date,No name,Parents were E.and Barbara Ann Agee. Father was a farmer.

No date,No name,Parents were William and Eliza Ann Arrington,Father was a farmer.

No date,No name,Parents were Richard and Frances Arrington.Father was a farmer.

No date,No name,Black Slave,Motherwwas Nancy,Owner was Edmon Arrington

No date,No name,Parents Matthias and Mary Jane Agee. Father was a farmer.

No date,No name,Parents were Robert M.and Frances E.M. Abbott.Father was a farmer.

No date,No name,Parents were Chesley and Margaret Ann Andrews.Father was a Carpenter.

No date,No name,Parents were W.N. and Penelope E.Anderson.Father was a farmer.

No date,No name,Parents were Robert and Frances R.Allen Father was a farmer.

No date,No name, ,Black,Slave, Mother was Ester. Owner was Robert Allen.

No date,No name,Slave, Mother was Arena.Owner was Robert Allen.

No date,No name,Mother was Martha Burkholder

No date,No name,Parents were William R.and Susan C. Blankenship.Father was a farmer.

No date,No name,Parents were William R.and Mary Boblits Father was a farmer.

No date,No name,Parents were Isham and Mary Ann Blake. Father's occupation listed as Ditches.

No date,No name,Slave, Mother was Judy.Owner's son Simon Buford gave information.

No date,No name,Parents were David F.and Ann Beard. Father was a farmer.

No date,No name.Parents were Jesse L.and Phiby Ann Bryant.Father was a farmer.

No date,No name.Parents were Francis H.and Musidora Beel.Father was farmer.

No date,No name.Slave,Mother was Mary.Owner,Rev.F.M. Barber.

No date,No name.Parents were John D.and Dolly Waller Burks.Father was farmer.

No date,No name.Slave,Mother was Frances.Owner,Martin P.Burks.

No date,No name. Slave, Mother was Eliza.Owner,Martin P.Burks.

No date,No name. Parents were John F.and Martha Ann Boley.Father was farmer.

No date,No name.Mother was Catherine.Information given by Mrs Turpin(friend).

No date,No name.Mother was Ann.Information given by Mrs Turpin(friend).

No date,No name.Mother was Emmily.Information given by Mrs Turpin(friend).

No date,No name.Slave.Mother was Jane.Owner,Dr.A.Bowling.

No date,No name.Slave.Mother was Dicy.Owner,Spottswood Brown.

No date,No name.Parents were J. and Sarah Ann Bussey.

Page 2.

CHILTON,Harvey Richard,Nov.29,1853.Parents George N. and Martha jane Chilton.Father was farmer.

CARTER,Texanah,July 18,1853.Parents were Jefferson and Mary Ann Carter. Father was farmer.

CARTER,James Alexander,Nov.18,1853.Parents were William S. and Tabitha Carter,Father was farmer.

CARTER,Frederick.June 9.1853.Parents,James W. and Susannah Carter.Father was farmer.

CLARK,Mary Elizabeth.Dec.11,1853.Parents,Isham and Mariah Speed Clark.Father was farmer.

CHILTON,No name,Oct.1,1853.Slave.Mother Jane.Owner John P.Chilton.

CAMPBELL,June 1853.No names.Mother,Ellen. Owner Thomas Campbell.

BIRTH RECORDS

CAMPBELL,Frances.March,1853.Slave,Mother,Ellen.Owner
Thomas Campbell.

JERRY,Feb.1,1853.Slave.Mother, Miranda.Hiram Cheatwood,Agent.

CAMPBELL,James William.May 14,1853.Parents,James W.
and Elizabeth Campbell.Father was a Carpenter.

McDANIEL,Walker.Sept.15,1853.Parents,Richard W. and
Elizabeth Craig.Father was Carpenter.

CLARK,Allen.FN. Dec.10,1853.Parents,John and Adeline
Clark.Father was Shoemaker.FN

CARUTHERS,Veola.Dec.11,1853.(Male).Parents,William H.
and Ann Henry Caruthers.Father was farmer.

COPPEDGE,John Gilbert.Sept.2,1853.Parents,Lievallen
and Martha Ann Coppedge.Father was Tobacco Factory
Worker.

CHILDRESS,Spottswood.Nov.1853.Parents,Thomas B.and
Eliza Childress.Father was a Miller.

CARROLL,Ida Washington.July 4,1853.Parents,Charles C.
and Martha Jane Carroll.father was farmer.

COCKE,Susan lee.June 12,1853.Parents William B.and
Frances Atoway Cocke.Father was farmer.

CLARK,George Etter.July,1853.Parents,Woodson and Doro-
tha richardson Clark.Father was a farmer.

McCLINTOCK,William Lee.Jan.7,1853.Parents,Lee and
Catherine McClintock.father was a Tanner.

CHEATWOOD,Mary Wilson.July 31,1853.Parents,Daniel B.
and Sally Patterson Cheatwood.Father was a farmer.

COFER,Sallie Nelson.April 12,1853.Parents,James M.and
Mary Etta Cofer.Father was a farmer.

CHILDRESS,William.Dec.,1853.Parents,William and Eliz.
Childress.Father was a farmer.

CARR,George William.Oct.16,1853.Parents,Abiel S. and
Elizabeth Carr.Father was a Stonecutter.

CROUSE,margaret.Feb.28,1853.Parents,Charles and Elmira
Crouse.Father was a farmer.

CALLAWAY,Thomas William.Aug.6,1853.parents, John W.
and Ariana Mariah Callaway.Father was a farmer.

CHEATWOOD,Eliza.Dec.1853.Slave.Mother Fanny.Owner
Hiram Cheatwood.

CLAY,Tolbert.Jan.18,1853.Slave.Mother Lucinda.Owner
Gen.Oden G.Clay.Edward Crumpacker,Overseer.

BIRTH RECORDS

CLAY,Richard.Dec.1853.Slave.Mother Martha,Owner Gen. Oden G.Clay.

CRAIG,Richard Hopkins.Nov.6,1853.Parents, Archabald G. and Henryetta Craig.Father was a farmer.

CRADDOCK,Elvira Morton.Aug.6,1853.Parents,David and Mary Tucker Craddock. Father was a farmer.

CREASY,Francis Marion.March 23,1853.Parents,Claibourn and Ann Creasy.Father was a farmer.

CARTER,James Napoleon.Sept.10,1853.Parents,James M.and Frances Carter.Father was a farmer.

Page 3,

DEWITT,Charles Scott. Jan.29,1853.Parents,James M.and Elizabeth DeWitt.Father was a farmer.

DAVIS,__?__, Slave,(Male).Mother,Charlott.Owner Micajah Davis Jr. Bannister Coffee,Overseer.

DAMERON,Texas,(Female),Aug.15,1853.Parents,Malachi and Angeline Dameron. Father was a farmer.

DUNCAN,John James.March 2,1853.Parents,George W.and Mary Elizabeth Duncan.Father was a farmer.

DAMERON,Charles Joshua.Jan.18,1853.Parents,Zachariah and Margaret Wills Dameron.Father was a Tanner.

DAWSON,Sarah Emmily.June 3,1853.Parents,Roderick D.and Lucy Dawson. Father was farmer.

DONALD,Lucy.Dec.1853.Slave.Mother Caroline. Owner,Benjamin A.Donald.

DAVIS,George.Oct.21,1853.Parents,Micajah and Ellen Elizabeth Davis.

DAVIS,James.June,1853.Slave. Mother Caroline.Owner Micajah Davis.

EUBANK,John James.March,1853.Parents,Ambrose and Sarah Wright Eubank.Father was a farmer.

EVERETT,Robert.May,1853.Slave. Mother Martha.Owner Joseph H.Everett.Information by Zachariah Everett.(brother of owner).

EWING,William Edward.May 1,1853.Parents William and lydia Ewing.Father was a farmer.

Page # 4

Folden,Maryann Gasper and Sarah Elizabeth Rebekah,(Twins) Aug.22,1853.Parents,Jesse Y. and Mary Folden.Father a farmer.

BIRTH RECORDS

FREEMAN,___?___,Female,May 27,1853.Parents Edwin H.and Elizabeth Frances Freeman.Father was a farmer.

FORGIE,___?___,Female,June 18,1853.Parents, Daniel K. and Nancy Anderson Forgie.

FERGIE,___?___, Male,Aug.1853.Slave.Mother,Rhoda.Owner Daniel K.Fergie,

FERREL,Charles Price.May 2,1853.Parents,Milton P. and Lucy Hobson Ferrel.Father was a farmer.

FISHER,Charles Bright.Oct.1853.Parents, James T.and Mary Ann Fisher.Father was a farmer.

FALLS,Fendal,Feb.13,1853.Slave. Mother Peggy. Owner Benjamin Falls.

FALLS,William B. April,1853. Slave. Mother,Emmaly. Owner Benjamin Falls.

FALLS,Elmira, Oct.1853. Slave. Mother,Winny.Owner, Benjamin Falls.

Falls,Mariah. Nov.1853. Slave. Mother Luisa. Owner, Benjamin Falls. Information given by Alexander Hatcher.

FREEMAN,Lucian Overton.Feb.12,1853. Parents,Garland H. and Thormutis Freeman.father was a farmer.

FREEMAN,Sarah Alice, Feb.1853.Parents,James O. and Minerva Freeman.Father was a Carpenter.

GOOD,Roberta Ann, Jan.11,1853. Parents,Edmond and Ann Mary Good. Father was a farmer.

GWATKINS,Isaac, March 10,1853.Slave.Mother, Mary.Infomation given by Saml H.Gwatkins(owner's son).

GWATKINS,William, Aug.10,1853. Slave.Mother,Caroline. Owner,Mary J.Gwatkins.

GROSS,___?___,Dec.1853. Parents,Richard H.and Selinda Gross.Father was a farmer.

GOOD,Anne, Dec.1853. Slave. Mother,Violet. Owner,John Good.

HODGES,Andrew D.,Oct.5,1853.Parents, Benjamin W.and Judy A.Hodges. Father was a farmer.

HOLLY,Mariah,March,1853.Slave. Mother Mariah. Owner Elijah Holly.

HIGGINBOTHAM,Altha Jane,Oct.7,1853.Parents,Joseph C. and Angeline Elizabeth Higginbotham.Father was a farmer.

HATCHER,Emerline,May 5,1853. Slave.Mother, Mary.Owner, Caleb Hatcher.

BIRTH RECORDS

HAWKINS,Spencer,1853. Slave. Mother, Charlott.Owner,
George W.Hawkins.

HASTEN,Martha Christenah,Aug.7,1853.Parents,William
M. and Margaret Hasten.Father was a farmer.

HARDY,William Henry, Jan.15,1853. Parents,James A.
and Lucinda Hardy.Father was a farmer.

HAWKINS, __?__ ,Feb.1853. Parents,Edward W.and Adeline
hawkins.Father was a farmer.

HURT,Mary,June 29,1853.Slave. Mother, Betsy.Owner,John
P.Hurt.

HAYNES,Sara Catherine,April 12,1853.FN. Parents,Braxt-
on and Writter M.Haynes.FN. Father was a farmer.

HARDY,Eliza Jane,June 28,1853. Parents,Capt. Joseph S.
and Paulina Ann Hardy.Father was a farmer.

HATCHER, __?__ ,Aug.1853. Parents, Thomas and Elizabeth
Noel Hatcher.Father was a farmer.

HATCHER,Robert Marion,Feb.25,1853. Parents,Alexander
M. and Mary Amanda.Father was a farmer.

HAWKINS,Celina Ann, Aug.7,1853. Parents,Robert C.and
Mary Frances Hawkins.

Page #5.

HOBSON,Edward, July 20,1853.Parents,Benjamin N.and
Editha Susan Hobson.Father was a farmer.

HENDERSON,Sallie Elvira,Aug.10.1853. parents,Rubin D.
and Rebecca Henderson.Father was a farmer.

HAWKINS,Berry McDaniel,April 15,1853. Parents,Alford
and Elizabeth Hawkins.Father was a farmer.

HARRIS,Jim Henry,March,1853.Slave,Mother,Judy.Owner,
James W. Harris.

HARRIS,John Albert,1853. Slave. Mother, Polinah.Owner,
James W.Harris.

HARRIS,Francis, Jan.1853. Slave. Mother,Patsy. Owner,
Hanibal Harris.

HUTTER,Solomon, Feb.12,1853. Slave. Mother, Harriett.
Owner, E.S.Hutter.

HUTTER,Coleman, March 29,1853. Slave. Mother, Susan.
Owner, E.S.Hutter.

HARRIS,Betsy, March,1853. Slave. Mother, Polly. Owner,
Dr.Hector Harris.

HOPKINS,John,Jan.1853.Slave. Mother, Marinda. Owner,
Jesse T.Hopkins.

BIRTH RECORDS

HOPKINS,Alice, Jan.1853. Slave. Mother, Margaret.
Owner, Jesse T.Hopkins.

HOLT,Lucy, 1853. Slave. Mother, Nancy. Owner,John W.
Holt.

HOLT,Lewis,1853. Slave. Mother, Fillis. Owner,John W.
Holt.

HARDY,Major Rieley,June 23,1853. Slave.Mother,Amanda.
Owner, James A. Hardy.

HARRIS,Hariott,May,1853.Slave. Mother, Amanda,Owner,
Doct.Hector Harris.

HARRIS,James,Nov.1853. Slave. Mother, Mary. Owner,
Doct.Hector Harris.

HENRY,Edward Mournin,FN,Feb.1853.Mother,Betsy Henry FN
Information given by Milly Henry FN grandmother.

HOFFMAN,Allis Jane,Nov.1853.Parents,John and Angeline
Augustus Hoffman.

JONES,Frank,Sept.2,1853. Parents,John W. and Elizabeth
J.Jones. Father was a Merchant.

JOPLING,Antony, Sept.3,1853.Slave. Mother, Fanny.Owner
Thomas B. Jopling.

JOPLING,Jane,March 12,1853.Slave. Mother, Mary.Owner
Thomas B.Jopling.

JONES,Eliza Jane,Jan.6,1853. Parents,Thomas M.and
Elizabeth Jane Jones. Father was a farmer.

JONES,Emerline,Jan.13,1853. Slave. Mother,Milly. Owner
Thomas M. Jones.

JONES,Tillis,March,1853.Slave. Mother, Syloy. Owner,
George Jones.

JOPLING,Julia Anna,Jan.6,1853. Parents,William W. and
Julia Ann Jopling. Father was a farmer.

JETER,Charles,Feb. 3,1853.Slave. Mother,Louiza.Owner,
Capt.Jesse Jeter.

JETER,James,Nov.11,1853.Slave. Mother Julia,Owner,
Capt.Jesse Jeter.

JONES,___?___, Nov.25,1853.Male,Parents,Samuel Lee and
Mary Virginia Jones.Father was a farmer.

JONES,Franklin Pierce.Sept.9,1853.parents,Jesse and
Ellen Catherine Jones.Father was a farmer.

JONES,Alexander Lafayett,Aug.15,1853. Parents,William
and Elizabeth Ann Jones.Father was a farmer.

JOHNSON,William Witton,Jan.8,1853. Parents,James F.and
Susan E.Johnson.Father was a Lawyer.

BIRTH RECORDS

JOHNSON,William Henry,1853. Slave,Mother, Charlott. Owner,James F.Johnson.

JONES,Mary Ann,Oct.1853. Slave.Mother,Harriott.Owner, Mr Sally Jones.Information by Robert C.Jones,Owner's son.

Page # 6

KERNES,Spottswood Lee,March22,1853.Parents,Abraham and Ann Kernes.Father was a farmer.

KEY,James Maddison,March 6,1853.Parents,james H.and Mildred Frances Key.Father was a farmer.

KABBLER,Malinda,Nov.8,1853.Slave.Mother,Polina.Owner, Mrs Catherine Kabler.

KELSO,Henry,Jan.1853.Slave. Mother,Nancy.Owner,Robert Kelso.

KELSO,Andrew,March,1853.Slave.Mother,Lucy.Owner,Robt. N.Kelso.

KELSO,Kitty,Oct.1853.Slave. Mother,Ann.Owner, Robt. N.Kelso.

KELSO,Susan,B.Dec.1853. Slave. Mother,Lucy. Owner, Robert N.Kelso.

KIRKPATTRICK,Samuel,July 29,1853.Parents,Phillip and Margaret Ann Kirkpattrick.Father was Tinner.

LINDSAY,Elizabeth,Feb.10,1853.Parents,Robert and Jenetta Lindsay.Father was a Wheelright.

LEE,Roberta Virginia,April 2,1853.Parents,Thomas N.and Frances Susan Jane Lee.Father was a farmer.

LOWRY,Susan,Oct.1,1853.Slave. Mother,Lucy.Owner,Lunceford Lowry.Information by John Lowry(friend).

LUCK,John Bumpass,April 23,1853.Parents,George P.and Nancy Luck.Father was a farmer.

LUCAS,Martha Jane,May 20,1853.Parents,Robert and Ann Eliza Lucas.Father was a farmer.

LACKIE,Jeff,Dec.26,1853.Slave. Mother,Harriet.Owner, Mrs Emmelie S.Lackie.

LOWRY,Eliza,April,1853.Slave. Mother,Fillis.Owner,Mrs. Matilda C.Lowry.Information by Spottswood Brown(owners brother).

MOOSLEY,Andrew Whitlock,April 24,1853.Parents,George C.and Mary Daniel Moosley.Fahter was a farmer.

MOOSLEY,____?____,April 4,1853.Male,Slave.Mother,Julia. Owner,George C.Moosley.

BIRTH RECORDS

MARSHALL,Edward Henry,April 27,1853.Parents,Robert W. and Ann M. Marshall.Father was a farmer.

McDANIEL,Fill,Jan.4,1853.Slave. Mother,Nilly.Owner, Samuel McDaniel.

McDANIEL,George,March,1853.Slave.Mother,Martha. Owner, Samuel McDaniel.

McDANIEL,Addison,Oct.20,1853.Slave.Mother,Betsey.Owner, Mrs Nancy McDaniel.

MILLNER,Eliza Margaret,June,1853.Parents,Jeremiah D. and Catherine Millner.Father was a farmer.

MENNIS,Lucy,July,1853.Slave.Mother,Mary Eliza.Owner, William C.Mennis.

MANSON,Mary,March,23,1853.Parents,R.E.and Sophiah Manson.Father was a Lawyer.

MASON,Seline Mary,Nov.1853.Parents,John J.and Mahaley Mason.Father was a farmer.

METCALFE,John,Jan.1,1853.Slave.Mother,Dolly. Owner, James Metcalfe.

METCALFE,Laura,May 11,1853.Slave.Mother,Mary.Owner, James Metcalfe.

McGHEE,Burwell,Feb.9,1853.Slave.Mother,Martha.Owner, Samuel H.McGhee.

McGHEE,Parthena,June,1853.Slave.Mother,Patsey.Owner, Samuel H.McGhee.

McDANIEL,William,June 13,1853.Slave.Mother,Louisa. Owner,Allen McDaniel.

Page # 7

NOEL,Stephen,April 20,1853.Slave.Mother,Emmaly.Owner, Alexander I.Noel.

NORCROSS,William Nelson,Feb.1853.Parents,Samuel and Frances Norcross.father was a wheelright.

NELSON,___?___,Sept.1853.Slave,Male.Mother,Hannah.Owner. Doct.Thomas H.Nelson.

NELSON,Edward,Aug.1853.Slave.Mother,Nancy.Owner,Doct. Thomas H.Nelson.

NELSON,Julia,Nov.1853.Slave.Mother,Martha.Owner,Doct. Thomas H.Nelson.

ODEN,Mary Frances,Sept.18,1853.parents,Elisha E.and Catherine Starr Oden.Father was farmer.

OTEY,Leander Harrison,July,1853.Slave.Mother,Kitty. Owner,John W.Otey.

BIRTH RECORDS

ONEY,Isabella Edgar,Aug.2,1853.Parents,James W. and Mary Frances Oney.Father was a farmer.

OGDEN,___?___, Feb.2,1853.Male,Slave.Mother,mary.Owner, John Ogden.

OGDEN,___?___,Oct.10,1853.Female.Slave.Mother,Rhoda. Owner,John Ogden.

OGLSBY,Dick,Dec.1853.Slave.Mother,Elizabeth.Owner, Ledowick Oglsby.

OGDEN,Winny,June,1853.Slave.Mother,Winney.Owner,Henry M.ogden.

OGDEN,Walter,March 31,1853.Slave.Mother,jane.Owner, Henry M.Ogden.

OGDEN,Julia,Nov.1853.Slave.Mother,Harriett.Owner,Henry M.Ogden.

OWENS,Martha Frances and Mary Agnes(twins)Nov.21,1853. Parents,James F.M.and Agnes Harriet Owens.Father was a farmer.

OTEY,Mary William,July,5,1853.Parents,Doct.John A.and Frances William Otey.Father was Physician.

OTEY,Julia Ann,Dec.1,1853.Slave.Mother,Fanny. Owner, Doct. John A.Otey.

PARKER,Mary Arnold,June,23,1853.Parents,George C. and Hester Ann Parker.Father was a farmer.

POWELL,Laura Ellen,July 1,1853.Parents,Lucas and Frances Powell. Father was a farmer.

PAGITT,Beverly,Aug.27,1853.Parents,Beverly and Permelia Pagitt.father was a farmer.

PAGITT,James Melvin,Sept.17,1853.Parents,james A. and Lucy Pagitt.Father was a farmer.

PAGITT,John William,Sept.20,1853.parents,John R.and Sarah Frances Pagitt.Father was farmer.

PERKINS,Robert Emmit,March 18,1853.Parents,Joseph and Jane Perkins.Father was a Wheelright.

PAGE,___?___,May 15,1853.Male.Parents,John G. and Mary Reynolds Page.Father was a farmer.

PENN,___?___,Dec.1853.Slave. Mother,Harriett.Owner,Moses Penn.

PERROWS,___?___,May 10,1853.Male,Slave.Mother,Martha. Owner,James S.Perrows.

POINDEXTER,Frances Stark,April 10,1853.Parents,Richard W.and Mary Whitlow Poindexter.Father was a farmer.

PAGE,Ann,Aug.1853.Parents,Robert and Parthena Page. Father was a farmer.

BIRTH RECORDS

PHILLIPS,Alice Spottswood,1853,Parents,Lindsey and
Catherine Frances Phillips.Father was a farmer.

POINDEXTER,Frank,Feb.29,1853.Slave.Mother,Matilda.
Owner,Eliza M.Poindexter Est.

POINDEXTER,Sam,Jan.4,1853.Slave.Mother,Agnes.Owner,
Thomas Poindexter Est.

POINDEXTER,Sarah Jane,March,1853.Slave.Mother,Susan.
Owner,Thomas Poindexter Est.

POINDEXTER,Thomas,July,1853.Mother,Louisa.Owner,
Thomas Poindexter Est.

Page # 8

PALLESON,Priscilla,1853.Slave.Mother,Martha.Owner,
Nelson A.Palleson.

PEARCY,Mary Frances,July 24,1853.Parents,Thomas and
Frances Pearcy.Father was a farmer.

POINDEXTER,Kilee,Dec.1853.Slave.Mother,Eliza.Owner,
Anderson Poindexter.

POINDEXTER,Milton,Jan.1853.Slave,Mother,Judy.Owner,
John S.Poindexter.

RULE,Mary Rebeckah,Aug.15,1853.Parents,Adam and Mary
Rule.Father was a farmer.

ROSEBROUGH,John,March 23,1853.Slave. Mother,Ann.Owner,
Robert Rosebrough.

ROSE,John Edward,May 27,1853.Parents,Thomas E.and
Catherine Rose.Father was a farmer.

RUCKER,Harriott,Sept.11,1853.Slave.Mother,Amanda.
Owner,James M.Rucker.

REYNOLDS,Mildred Albany,April 2,1853.Parents,Joel P.
and Catherine Reynolds.Father was a Wheelright.

RADFORD,James,April,1853.Slave. Mother,Eliza. Owner,
Winston Radford.

RADFORD,Charles,April,1853.Slave. Mother,Rozetta.
Owner,Winston Radford.

REECE,George Washington,April 2,1853. Slave.Mother,
Lucy. Owner,Joseph T.Reece.

ROBINSON,Henry,Aug.1853.Slave. Mother,Mariah. Owner,
Benjamin N.Robinson.

ROBINSON,Vina,April,1853.Slave. Mother,Malinda.Owner,
Edward N.Robinson.

RICHEY,John Richard,June 29,1853.Parents,Harvey F.and
Sarah Jane Richey.

BIRTH RECORDS

Page # 9,

SHARP,Jim,Dec.20,1853.Slave.Mother,Charlott.Owner,
Capt.Sampson Sharp.

SHARP,Mitchel,Dec.29,1853.Slave.Mother,Patsey.Owner,
Capt.Samson Sharp.

SAUNDERS,___?___, Male,Slave.Mother,Aylesey.Owner,Cor-
delia Saunders.

SHELTON,Jane Watts,Aug.8,1853.Parents,Wesley and Eliza
Margaret Shelton.Father was a Merchant.

SHELTON,Richard,Jan.2,1853,Slave,Mother,Catherine.
Owner,Wesley Shelton.

SALES,Malinda,Feb.1853.Slave. Mother,Milly.Owner,Sally
P.Sales Est.

SLEDD,Sarah,July 1,1853.Slave.Mother,Betsey. Owner,
William E.Sledd.

SLEDD,Ann,Sept.1,1853.Slave.Mother.Mary.Owner,William
E.Sledd.

SLEDD,Winny,Dec.20,1853.Slave.Mother,Milly.Owner,
William E.Sledd.

SLEDD,William Robert,June,28,1853.Parents,William E.
and Arabella Sledd.Father was a farmer.

SPINNER,Jesse,Aug.7,1853.Parents,Doct.J.F. and Martha
Ann Spinner.Father was a Physician.

SMITH,John Calvin,1853.Parent,Robert Smith.Father was
a farmer.Information given by Thomas Wright(friend).

SEAY,Sarah Ann,may 14,1853.Parents,David P.and Amanda
N.Seay.Father was a Blacksmith.

STRONG,Laura,Jan.1853.Parents,Clifton and Patsy Strong.
Father was a Farmer.

STALEY,John Booker,Aug.9,1853.Parents,James S.and
Martha Marshall Staley.Father was a Miller.

STEPTOE,Watt,July,1853.Slave.Mother Rhoda.Owner,Robert
C.Steptoe.

STEPTOE,Frank,July,1853.Slave,Mother,Violet.Owner,
Robert C.Steptoe.

STEPTOE,Mary,Aug.1853.Slave.Mother,Lucy.Owner,Robert
C.Steptoe.

THAXTON,Milly Ann,Feb.22,1853.Slave.Mother,Ginny.Owner,
David F.Thaxton.

THOMAS,Mary Charlott,Nov.5,1853.Parents,Samuel M.and
Amanda Pope Thomas.

BIRTH RECORDS

THOMAS,Mary Elizabeth,march 22,1853.parents,John C. and Eliza Brookin Thomas.Father was a farmer.

TANNER,James Rodigal,FN,Nov.12,1853.Parents Joel and Rhoda Tanner FN.Father was a farmer.

THOMPSON,John,April,1853.Slave. Mother,Susan.Owner, Nelson A.Thompson.

THEMBS,John Frederick,Jan.27,1853.Parents,John B.and Sarah Ann Thembs.Father was a Miller.

TURPIN,Martha,July,1853.Slave. Mother,Mariah.Owner, Roland G.Turpin.

THOMAS,__?__,Feb.28,1853.Female. Parents,Proscer P. and Susan Porride Thomas.Father was a farmer.

THOMAS,__?__, June 10,1853.Parents,James and Sally Thomas.Father was a farmer.

TANKISLEY,Paulis Good,May 12,1853.Parents,Richard A. and Mary jane Tankisley.Father was a farmer.

TURPIN,Joshua,Jan.1853,Slave.Mother,Eliza.Owner,John Turpin.

TAYLOR,James Peterson,May 20,1853.Parents,Adam and Frances Jane Taylor.Father was a farmer.

Page # 10.

WOOD,Talitha Florentine,Feb.17,1853.Parents,Thomas C. and Rebeckah Wood.Father was a Miller.

WILKERSON,William Oliver,Sept.7,1853.Slave.Mother, Tabby.Owner,Nicholas Wilkerson.

WILLKS,Roena,march 29,1853.Parents,Leyburn and Elizabeth J.Willks.Father was a farmer.

WOOD,__?__,Female,Dec.10,1853.Parents,Charles A. and Lydia Wood.Father was a farmer.

WILKERSON,Sarah Catherine,July 4,1853.Parents,William L. and Keziah S.Wilkerson.Father was a farmer.

WILLIAMS,Brackenridge,Nov.1853.Slave.Mother,Marsella. Owner,Albert William Est.

WILLIAMSON,Elizabeth,Aug.12,1853.Slave.Mother,Nancy. Owner, Solomon Williamson.

WATSON,Mitton Clark,Nov.3,1853.Parents,William D.and Sarah Jane Watson.Father was a farmer.

WILSON,Susan Webster,July 7,1853.Parents,Vincent and Elizabeth Wilson.Father was a farmer.

WILSON,Samuel,June 7,1853.Parents,James W. and Susan Wilson.Father was a farmer.

BIRTH RECORDS

WATTS,Nancy,March.1853.Slave.Mother,Susan.Owner,Mrs
Isabella Watts.

WATTS,Wiatt,Jan.1853.Slave. Mother,Winney.Owner,Rich-
ard D.Watts Heirs.

WHITE,Susan,Feb.1853.Slave.Mother Ann.Owner,Jacob S.
White.

WILSON,Henry,Jan.1853.Slave,Mother Betsey.Owner,Peter
H.Wilson.

WATTS,Eliza,May,1853.Parents,William and Elvira Watts.
Father was a farmer.

WEBBER,James Edward,Feb.1853.Parents,James B. and
nancy Webber.

WIGGENTON,Creasy,Jan.31,1853.Slave.Mother,Polina.
Owner,Benjamin Wiggenton.

WIGGENTON,Cora,March 10,1853.Slave.Mother,Polina Mor-
ning.Owner,Benjamin Wiggenton.

WIGGENTON,Ben,June 22,1853.Slave. Mother,Jenny. Owner,
Benjamin Wiggenton.

WATSON,Charles Joseph,Oct.19,1853.Parents,Uriah A. and
Mary Ann Rebeckah Watson.Father was a farmer.

WILSON,Elizabeth Frances,Sept.1853.Parents,George W.
and Eliza Ann Wilson.Father was a farmer.

WHITELEY,Eugene,April,1853.Slave.Mother,Elizabeth.
Owner,Mrs Ann C.Whiteley.

WHITLEY,Duke,April,1853.Slave,Mother,Sylva.Owner,
Mrs Ann C.Whiteley

WHITLEY,Elbert,May,1863.Slave.Mother,SArah.Owner,
Mrs Ann C.Whitley.

WHITLEY,Phill,June,1853.Slave,Mother,Ginny.Owner,Mrs
Ann C.Whitley.

Page # 11,

AYERS,John N.July 3,1853.Parents,John M. and Mary H.
Ayers..Father was a farmer.

ASHWELL,___?___, Dec.1853.Slave.Male.Owner,Mary Ashwell.

ADAMS,Mary C.,Nov.3,1853.Parents,Abram and Frances M.
Adams.

AYERS,___?___, Female,March 14,1853.Parents,james W.
and Sarah P.Ayers.Father was a farmer.

ARTHUR,Catherine,Jan.14,1853.Parents,Albon A.and
Mariah M.Arthur.Father was Clerk of COunty Court.

BIRTH RECORDS

ANTHONY,William Thomas,FN,Oct.1853.Parent,Ann Anthony

ANDREWS,Sandy and Amanda,(twins)1853.Slaves.Mother, Molly. Owner,Mark Andrews.

AYERS,Elizabeth M.,April 15,1853.Parents,Sebert and Henretta Qyers.

ALIFF,___?___,May 10,1853.Male,Parents,Alex B.T. and Clementine Aliff.

Ayers,Missouri F.,March 15,1853.Parents,Maston J.and nancy Ayers.

ANDREWS,Marilla,Aug.1853,Slave. Mother,Frances.Owner, Thomas Andrews.

ANDREWS,Maria,July,1853.Slave.Mother,Jinny.Owner, William W.Andrews.

ANDREWS,___?___,Female,Aug.1853.Slave.Mother,Celia. Owner,William W.Andrews.

AYERS,BishopA.April,1853.Parents,Talbot and Jane Ayers

AYERS,___?___,Male,July 18,1853.Parents,Ishmael and Frances Ann Ayers.

ADKINSON,Mildred Ann,April,1853.Parents,Burwell and Nancy Adkinson

AGEE,___?___, Female,Aug.7,1853.Parents,Reason G.and Matilda Agee.

ANDERSON,Lewis G.,Dec.20,1853.Parents,Joel C.and Betsey Anderson.

ANDERSON,James T.,Oct.27,1853.Parents,William H.L. and Frances Ann Anderson.

ANDERSON,Martha S.,march 14,1853.Parents,Richard H. and Mary Jane Anderson.

ARTHUR,Henry,Aug.1853.Slave. Mother,Betsey.owner, Lewis C.Arthur.

AUSTIN,Emma,Nov.21,1853.Slave.Mother,Martha.Owner, William N.Austin.

ALLEN,Jeremiah R.,Nov.21,1853.Parents,Robert S.and Nancy Allen.

BOARD,Jim,1853.Slave.Mother,Milly.Owner,John Board.

BOARD,Maria,1853.Slave,Mother,Mary.Owner,John Board.

BARTON,Wingfield,Feb.9,1853.Parents,Reed and Jane E. Barton.Father was a farmer.

BOARD,___?___,1853.Male.Slave.Mother,Milly.Owner,Saml H.Board.

BIRTH RECORDS

BUTTERWORTH,Frances,Sept.1853.Parent,James Butterworth.
Father was a farmer.

BURNETTE,Margaret V.J.,July 4,1853.Parents,Williamson
and Celia Ann Burnette.Father was a farmer.

BATES,Henry Mahlen,Sept.4,1853.Parents,Lewis and Betsy
bates.Father was a farmer.

BETZ,William Henry,Nov.17,1853.Parents,William And
Belinda Betz.Father was a farmer.

BOND,Nicholas,Jan.1,1853.Slave.Mother,Fanny.Owner,
Pleasant Bond.

Fisher,Eleanor,May 15,1853.parents,Saml and Elizabeth
Fisher.

BELL,M.O.,Dec.15,1853.Parents,Orville P.and Nancy B.
Bell.Father was a Merchant.

BOARD,Sam,1853,Slave,Mother,Ester.Owner,Thomas B.Board.

BUFORD,Alfred,W.,May 1,1853.Parents,John W.and Sarah B
Buford.Father was a farmer.

BARTON,Martha Ann,Sept.29,1853.Parents,William and
Frances Jane Barton.Father was a farmer.

BURROUGHS,Amanda S.,April 2,1853.Parents,Thomas and
Catherine Burroughs.

BURROUGHS,Jane,Nov.1853.Slave.Mother,Emily.Owner,Thomas Burroughs.

BUTLER,James R.FN.March 5,1853.Parents,William Butler,
FN and Ruth Butler FN

Page # 12,

BOARD,___?___,Male,July,1853.Slave.Mother,Ann.Owner,
S.M.Board.

BURNETTE,Mildred C.,Nov.1853.Parents,Elisha C.and
Sarah Ann Burnette.

BANDY,Celona Ann,Aug.9,1853.Parents,Saml and Harriet
Bandy.

BANDY,Nancy Ann,Dec.28,1853.parents,Richard H.and Mary
Elizabeth Bandy.

BOARD,Mary Prescilla,Oct.1853.Slave.Mother,Mary.Owner,
Maria Board.

BONDURANT,Sandy R.,Jan.1853.Parents,William W.and Sarah M.Bondurant.

BECKNER,Mary E.,Sept.6,1853.Parents,John S.and Elizabeth Beckner.

BIRTH RECORDS

BOWLING,Martha S.,May,1853.Parents,William H. and Julia H.Bowling.

BURKHOLDER,Henrietta,W.,Dec.1853.Parents,Joel and Mary Ann Burkholder.

BEARD,___?___,1853,Female.Parents,Robert M. and Elizabeth Beard.

BURNETTE,Lockey Jane,Nov.4,1853.Parents,Christ A.and Orphey Burnette.

BATES,Henry M.,Oct.8,1853.Parents,Lewis and Elizabeth Ann Bates.

BURNETT,Sarah E.,Oct.6,1853.Parents,William w.and Mary E. Burnett.

BOND,William G.,1853.Parents,Andrew J. and Mary Bond.

BROWN,William M.July 2,1853.Parents,Doctor S. and Sandona Brown.

BROWN,Catherine J.July 27,1853.Parents,Thomas J. and Adaline Brown.

BROWN,___?___,Female,March 10,1853.Slave.Mother,Mary. Owner,James Brown.

BATES,Mary M.,Feb.1,1853.Parents,William and Charlotte Bates.

CARTER,John James, July 9,1853.Berry S.and Charlott Carter.

COBBS,__?__,Jan.1853.Female.Slave. Mother,Maria.Owner, Tighleman A.Cobbs Jr.

CLAYTOR,___?___,Feb.1853.Female,Slave.Mother,Mary.Owner, William G.Claytor.

CLAYTOR,James M.,Feb.5,1853.Parents,Saml H. and Eliza Jane Claytor.

CREASY,Roseley,Aug.28,1853.Slave.Mother,Chanty.Owner, Rob Creasy Est.

CREASY,Cordis,Dec.1853.Slave.Mother,Paulina.Owner, William Creasy.

CREASY,William Robert,April,1853.Parents,Leonard S. and Pauling jean Creasy.

CUNDIFF,John M.,Aug.1853.Parents,George W. and Sarah E. Cundiff.

CAROLL,Susan,March 3,1853.Parents,Henry and Catherine Caroll.

CHEWNING,James B. Nov.7,1853.Parents,Callohill and Eliza Jane Chewning.

BIRTH RECORDS

CHEWNING,David,April,1853.Slave,Mother,Susan.Owner,
Dicey Chewning.

CROUCH,Rolley,March 26,1853.Parent,Molly Crouch.

CORLEY,Texanna,March 15,1853.Parents,James B.and
Judith Corley.

CRAIGHEAD,__?__,July 20,1853.Parents,Rob A.and Frances
Craighead.

CUNDIFF,Hezekiah,Feb.1853.Slave.Mother,Amanda.Owner,
Christopher Cundiff.

CARDER,Thomas P.,Sept.1853.Parents,James M. and Sarah
Carder.

CARNER,Osier,July,1853.Slave. Mother,Amanda.Owner,
Elias Carner.

CLAYTOR,Rose,Aug.30,1853.Slave. Mother,Sophia.Owner,
Rob.M.Claytor.

CHEWNING,Henry,June,1853.Slave. Mother,Paulina.Owner,
James Chewning.

CLAYTOR,Bob,1853.Slave.Mother,betsey.Owner,Saml G.
Claytor.

HUNDLEY,Henry,May 2,1853.Parents,Peter and Sally Hundley.

CRAFT,George N.,Feb.21,1853.Parents,George W.and
Susan Craft.

CUNNINGHAM,Susan B.,Dec.21,1853.Parents,James and
lavina F.Cunningham.

Page # 13,

CRUMP,Lucy,Sept.18,1853.Slave.Mother,Darcus.Owner,
Beverly Crump.

CRUMP,Mary,Sept.20,1853. Slave.Mother, Clarisa.Owner,
Mary Crump.

COBB,Oscar,Jan.1853. Slave. Mother,Betsey.Owner,Tilyh-
mand Cobb Sen.

CRUMPACKER,John E.,Oct.15,1853.Parents,Richard A. and
Mildred Crumpacker.

CLAYTOR,Maria,Nov.1853. Slave.Mother,sally.Owner,Tho-
mas R.Claytor.

CLAYTOR,Susan,Nov.1853.Slave. Mother,Fanny.Owner,Edw-
ard M.Claytor.

CARNER,LUCY,Dec.1853.Slave. Mother,Let. Owner,Elizah
Carner.

BIRTH RECORDS

CRENSHAW,Sam,May,1853. Slave. Mother,Ellen. Owner, Prescilla Crenshaw.

CRENSHAW,Frank,May,1853.Slave. Mother,Elvira.Owner, Prescilla Crenshaw.

CARNEY,Rob S.,July 1,1853.Parents,Abram and Nancy E. Carney.

CROUCH,Mary S.,June,1853.Parents,Levies O.and Mary Crouch.

CROUCH,Jeremiah,June 20,1853.Parents,Dennis and Joicey Crouch.

CREASY,Amanda B.,Dec.11,1853.Parents,Saml and Cath- anda Crouch.

CREASY,Charles A.,Feb.26,1853.Parents,Charles and Sarah Creasy.

CORLEY,James William,Oct.15,1853.Parents,James and Polly Corley.

DICKERSON,Daniel,July,15,1853.Slave.Mother,Amanda. Owner,William Dickerson.

DEARDORFF,Susan E.,Feb.12,1853.Parents,Charles H.and Mary E.Deardorff

DREWRY,Elijah W.,Feb.24,1853.Parents,James C.and Julia Ann Drewry.

DEARING,Florilla,C.,Sept.22,1853.Parents,William W. and Rachel Sarah Dearing.

DENT,__?__, June,1853.Female.Owner,Marbel N.Dent.

DENT,Solomon,March,1853.Slave.Mother,Susanna.Owner, Peter Dent.

DENT,Harrison,Feb.1853. Slave.Mother,Rebecca.Owner, Marbel N.Dent.

DOWDY,Parry Franklin,march 22,1853.Parents,Walter B. and Mildred L.Dowdy.

DEARING,Frances,Sept.5,1853.Parents,Green and Rhoda Jane Dearing.

DOWDY,James E.,May 10,1853.Parents,Jesse and Susan Dowdy.

DOOLEY,Sarah A.E.,Sept.1853.Parents,Thomas E. and Mary Nancy Dooley.

DREWRY,William,Sept.1853.Parents,Joseph C.and Mary Drewry

DAVIS,Mary Susan,Sept.30,1853.Slave.Mother,Harriett. Owner,Lucy Davis.

BIRTH RECORDS

DAVIS,George,March,1853.Slave,Mother,Emily.Owner,
Lucy Davis.

DEARING,__?__, 1853,Slave.Mother,Cecelia. Owner,
Silas Dearing.

DICKERSON,Jane,May,1853.Slave.Mother,Kitty.Owner,
James Dickerson.

DREW,Mary,FN, 1853.Parent,Jane Drew F.N.

DEBO,John F.P.,Feb.9,1853.Parents,Michael and Wil-
mouth Debo.

PAGE # 14,

ENGLISH,Judith,1853.Slave.Mother,edna.Owner,Parnrnas
English.

EARLY,__?__,Male,1853.(Born dead).Slave.Mother,Char-
lott.Owner,James A.Early.

ELLIS,Abner,Aug.1853.Parents,Thomas and Mary Ellis.

FIZER,__?__,Dec.15,1853.Male,Slave.Mother,Emily.Owner,
Charles B.Fizer.

FIELD,Virginia,(Female) and Virginus(Male)Twins.April
27,1853.Parents,John B.and Elizabeth Field.

FRANKLIN,William Abner,Aug.1853.Parents,Saml and
Elena Franklin.

FIELDS,Daniel W.,July,1853.Parents,William and Matilda Fields.

FRANKLIN,__?__, Male,Dec.16,1853.Parents,Abner H. and
Mary Ann Franklin.

FIZER,Lydia A.Sept.2,1853.Parents,Richard and Sarah
Frances Fizer.

FRANKLIN,__?__, Dec.24,1853.Male,Parents,James C.and
Angelien D.Franklin.

FUQUA,John H.June 20,1853.Parents,Martin and Martha
J.Fuqua.

FEATHER,Laura Jane,May 7,1853.Parents,Richard B.and
Mary Ann Feather.

FARRIS,Edward Bruce,May,1853.Slave. Mother,Clara.
Owner,John J.Farris.

FARRIS,John J.,Dec.28,1853.Parents,John J.and Mary
Farris.

FRAZIER,William,June 4,1853.parents,Robert and calista Frazier.

BIRTH RECORDS

FEATHER,Alexander,July,1853.Parents,Joseph and Julia Ann Feather.

FITZPATRICT,Archer,Aug.20,1853.Slave.Mother,Suckey. owner,Thomas Fitzpatrict.

FITZPATRICT,Thomas,Aug.3,1853.Parents,Hirams A.and Lucinda Fitzpatrict.

FELLERS,Mary O.,Aug.6,1853.Parents,Peter and Angeline M.Fellers.

FRANKLIN,Henry C.,April 18,1853.Parents,Elias J.and Sarah jane Franklin.

Page # 15,

GOGGIN,Pleasant,Jan.2,1853.Parents,William L.and ELiza L.Goggin.Father was a Lawyer.

GOGGIN,__?__, Oct.1853.Slave.Mother,Heinretta.Owner, William L.Goggin.

GILL,Alexander,April 1,1853.Slave.Mother,Sarah.Owner, Charles W.Gill.

GILL,Scott,Jan.1,1853.Slave.Mother,Harriet.Owner, Charles W.Gill.

GIBBS,Elizabeth,Feb.1853.Slave.Mother,Betsey.Owner, George L. Gibbs.

GILLS,__?__,July 7,1853.Parents,Asa and Caroline Gills

GOGGIN,James L.Aug.14,1853.Parents,Thomas C.and Elizabeth Jane Goggin.

GIBBS,__?__, Feb.29,1853.Parents,Wyatt and Nancy Gibbs.

GULPIN,William G.,March 7,1853.Parents,John O. and Ann Minerva Gulpin.

GIBBS,Mildred Lewis,Feb.1853.Slave.Mother,Matilda. Owner,Asman A.Gibbs.

GRIGHLEY,John,Feb.23,1853.Slave.Mother,Mary.Owner, James T.Grighley.

GRAHAM,Nancy Jane,March 3,1853.Parents,Lawson and Elizabeth Graham.

GOODE,Susan Agnes,May,1853.Slave.Mother,Milly.Owner, Stephen Goode.

GOAD,James G.Nov.3,1853.Parents,Lewis and Julia Ann Goad.

GWATTNEY,Mary Ann,1853.Parents,Albert and Mary Gwatney

HOGAN,Frances,Oct.29,1853.Parents,Obediah D. and Malinda Hogan.

BIRTH RECORDS

HUDDLESTON,Ann Maria,March 8,1853.Parents,Richard and Eliza Huddleston.

HUDDLESTON,__?__,Oct.1853.Slave,Mother,Ann.Owner,Richard Huddleston.

HARRIS,George Washington,May,1853.Slave.Mother,Harriett. Owner,Saml Harris.

HARRIS,Henry Clay,June 1853. Slave.Mother,Mary.Owner, Saml Harris.

HOLT,Fanny S.,Nov.12,1853. Parents,William L. and Sarah Ann Holt.

HOLT,Mary,May,1853.Slave. Mother,Emily. Owner,William Holt.

HANCOCK,Jesse,June 17,1853.Parents,Simon and Betsy A. Hancock.

HUGHES,Twins,No names.June 15,1853.Slaves.Mother, Caroline. Owner,Saml Hughs

HOPKINS,Caleb,Dec.22,1853.Slave,Mother,Rose.Owner, Frances G.Hopkins.

HURT,__?__, Jan.1853.Male.Slave.Mother,Sarah. Owner, Joel Hurt.

HURT,Henry,Dec.1853.Slave.Mother,Narcissa. Owner, Joel Hurt.

HURT,John Wesley.June.1853. Slave.Mother, Sally.Owner, Joel Hurt.

HANCOCK,Royal,April,1853.Slave.Mother,Martha.Owner, Christopher Hancock.

HOPKINS,Nancy,Aug.1853.Slave. Mother,Amelia. Owner, Charlotte Hopkins.

HANNABAS,James M.Dec.13,1853.Parents,David and Marcella Hannabas.

HOLDREN,George G.,June 29,1853.Parents,Jackson B.and Mary Holdren. Page 16

HICKS,Eliza Ann,april,1853.Slave.Mother,Charlott. Owner,William Hicks.

HALE,Harvey,FN. Aug.31,1853.Parent,Lucy Ann Hale FN.

HODGES,Mary As.Oct.11,1853.Parents, Milton and Sarah Ann Hodges.

HUNT,George C.,Nov.12,1853.Parents,Charles K. and Frances Hunt.

HURT,Leroy W.,May,1853.Parents,Joshua and Narcessa Hurt.

BIRTH RECORDS

HIX,__?__, Sept.1853.female.Parents,Drewry and Ann Henry Hix.

HIX,Prince Albert,Feb.12,1853.Parents,Phillip and Judith Hix.

HALE,__?__,April,1853.Female,FN. Parent,Betsy Hale.

HOLDREN,Charles C.,Feb.1853.Parents,Abram and Frances Holdren.

HACKWORTH,Arackna Maude,Aug.14,1853.Parents,Washington and Melinda Hackworth.

HORN,David,Nov.17,1853.Parents,John and Sophia Horn.

HOPKINS,Rob.K.,May 18,1853.Parents,Tilghman and Mary Ann Hopkins.

HARRIS,John E.,1853.Parents,Saml M. and Eliza Ann Harris.

HOWELL,Amanda,July 30,1853.Parents,Washington and Martha Jane Howell.

JONES,Rob William,March 8,1853.Parents,Edward C.and Martha Jones.

JAMES,Virginia L.,May,1853.Parents,Isaac and Harrat S. James.

JORDAN,__?__,Aug.1853.Female,Slave.Parents,Alexander and Anni Jordan.

JORDAN,Booker,1853.Mother Rebecca.Owner,Jubal Jordan.

JORDAN,__?__, 1853.Slave. Mother,Jane.Owner,Jubal Joran.

JORDAN,__?__,1853.Female,Slave.Mother,Rhoda. Owner, Jubal Jordan.

JETER,__?__,Dec.27,1853.Male.Parents,Henry E. and Chilnessa Jeter.

JOHNSON,__?__,Oct.1853.Parents,Thomas and Sarah Johnson

JORDAN,__?__,1853.Male.Slave.Mother,Mason. Owner,Jubal Jordan.

JORDAN,__?__,1853,Female.Slave.Owner,Jubal Jordan.

JOHNSON,__?__,July,1853.Male.Parents,George and Florentine Johnson.

JAMES,__?__,July,1853.Parents,Isaac Sen.and Nancy James

JAMES,Sarah F.,July 3,1853.Parents,Isaac Jun.and Adaline James.

JENKINS,Catherine,Feb.1,1853.Parents,Obediah and Tabitha Jenkins.

BIRTH RECORDS

IRVINE,Susan,Jan.1853. Parents, Alex and Felecia Irvine.

IRVINE,__?__, Sept.1853.Female,Slave. Mother,Mary. Owner,Alex Irvine.

IRVINE,__?__, Feb.1853,Females(born dead).Mother, Mary, (Twins) Owner,Alex Irvine.

JETER,____?____,Feb.1853.Male. Parents,Fielden and Ann B. Jeter.

JONES,Jackson,March 1,1853.Slave,Mother,Arrena.Owner, Elizabeth Jones.

JONES,Lucy Ann,Aug.1853.Slave.Mother,Lucy.Owner, Elizabeth Jones.   Page 17

JOHNSON,John,May,1853.Parents,George and florentine Johnson.

KRANTZ,___?___,Dec.1853,parents,Thomas and Rebecca Krantz.

KASEY,__?__,1853.Female,Slave.Mother,Jane.Owner,Thomas Kasey.

KASEY,__?__,1853 Female.Slave. Mother,Hannah. Owner, John   Kasey.

KASEY,___?___,1853,Female.Slave.Mother,Jane.Owner,Thomas Kasey.

LAZENBY,Robert,Dec.1853.Slave.mother,Minerva.Owner, Edward Lazenby.

LAZENBY,Mary,Dec.1853.Slave. Mother,Rebecca. Owner, Edward Lazenby.

LAZENBY,Attilia,Nov.23,1853.Parents,William R. and Anni E.Lazenby.

LEFTWICH,Octavia,march 3,1853.Parents,Granderson and Lucy Ann Leftwich.

LEFTWICH,Julia E.,March 14,1853.Parents,Etchison G. and Massey Leftwich.

LAUGHON,Ann B.FN,Jan.11,1853.Parent,Ann Laughon.

LAUGHON,Eliza,Feb.1853.Parent,Paulina Laughon.

LOYD,John Anthony,Feb.17,1853.Slave.Mother,Chelsey. Owner,Henry Loyd Jr.

LEFTWICH,Mark A.,May 28,1853.Parents,Thomas and Moreah Leftwich.

LEFTWICH,Rhoda,,1853.Slave.Mother.Patsy.Owner,Thomas leftwich.

LAUGHON,Charles E.,Aug.29,1853.Parents,Isham and Mary Jane Laughon.

BIRTH RECORDS

LEFTWICH,John William,Aug.18,1853.Parents,John Q.and Mary Ann Leftwich.

LOWRY,Irvine,Sept.1853,Slave.Mother,Celia. Owner, Elliott Lowry.

LEFTWICH,___?___,Dec.1853.Female. Slave.Mother,Tina... Owner,William Leftwich.

LEFTWICH,___?___, July,1853.Female.Slave.Mother,Mary. Owner,William Leftwich.

LEE,___?___,July,1853.Female.Parents,Richard A.. and Mary jane Lee.

Leftwich,Lucy Ann,April 15,1853.Slave. Mother, Charlott. Owner, James Leftwich Est.

LEFTWICH,Laura,Oct.5,1853.Slave. Mother,Susan. Owner, James Leftwich Est.

LOYD,John A.,Nov.1853.Parents,Joseph G. and Margarett Loyd.

LOYD,Deanna V.,1853.Parents,Mason and Mary S. Loyd.

LAUGHON,Alonzo,Oct.16,1853.Parents,Joshua and Mary E.Laughon.

LEFTWICH,Alfred D.,July 16,1853.Parent, Ann Leftwich.

LUCAS,Joseph,Jan.1853.Parent, Chlow Lucas.

LEFTWICH,Martha,1853.Slave.Mother,Candice.Owner,Alex Leftwich.

LEFTWICH,Gray,1853.Slave. Mother,Frances.Owner,Alex leftwich.

Page 18,

McCLAIN,Marcia E.,Nov.27,1853.Parents,Jesse and Mary Ann McClain.

MEADOR,Mary G.,Sept.17,1853.Parents,Edward A. and Agnes A.Meador.

MINTER,Frances,Sept.1,1853.Slave. Owner,Billy Minter.

MARTIN,___?___,Sept.8,1853.Male.Parents,Saml and Elizabeth Martin.

MANSFIELD,___?___,Sept.1853.Female,Slave.Mother,Nancy. Owner,William L.Mansfield.

MARSHAL,Nancy A.,Oct.1,1853.Parents,Poindexter and Mary Jane Marshal.

McDANIEL,Winston,March 27,1853.Slave,Mother, Emily.

MITCHELL,Cary L.,March,1853.Parents,John P. and Martha Jane Mitchell.

BIRTH RECORDS

MEADOR,John O.,June,11,1853.Parents, Green B. and
Mary Ann Meador.

MARTIN,Daniel J.,Jan.19,1853.Parents,Charles and
Lydia Martin.

MITCHELL,Saml R.,March 8,1853.Parents, William C. and
Lucy M.Mitchell.

MITCHELL,Elley,Aug.1853.Slave. Mother,Caroline. Owner,
William C. Mitchell.

MITCHELL,Melina,Dec.1853.Slave. Mother,Lucy.Owner,
William C.Mitchell.

MANSFIELD,Margaret,Nov.19,1853.Parents,Thomas S. and
Ann E.Mansfield.

STRATTONS,__?__,1853.Slave.Mother,Eliza. Owner,Frazier
Strattons Est.

MEADOR,Thomas R.,June 4,1853.Parents,Thomas C.and
Catherine Meador.

MORGAN,__?__,Male,July 8,1853,Parents,William B.and
Nancy J.Morgan.

MORGAN,Solo M.,March 13,1853.Parents,Alex and Adaline
Morgan.

MORGAN,__?__,April,1853.Slave. Mother,Fie. Owner,Alex
Morgan.

MERRYMAN,Fanny Mae,1853.Parents,Edward and Eleanor
Merryman.

MERRYMAN,__?__ & __?__,(Twins)Females,Slaves.Mother,Aggy.
Owner,Edward Merryman.

MITCHELL,Mary Jane,Nov.29,1853.Parents,Joel D. and
Frances Mitchell.

MOORE,Louisa,1853.Parents,William Sen. and Nancy Moore.

MORGAN,William M.,Aug.1853.Parents,Jubal A. and Arr-
ena Morgan.

MEADOR,Martha E.S.,May 27,1853.Parents, Sparrel H.and
Mary Ann Meador.

MAYS,Dickerson,May 25,1853.Slave. Mother,Adeline.
Owner,Joseph W.Mays.

MOREMAN,__?__,March,1853.Female,(Born Dead).Slave.
Mother,Charlott.Owner, Saml P.R. Moreman.

MOTLEY,_?_,Oct.31,1853.Parents,John and Martha Motley.

MAYHEW,Margaret Ann,Dec.23,1853.Parents,William M.and
Rebecca Mayhew.

MANUEL,Mary C.,May 22,1853,Parents,jeremiah E.and
Martha Ann Manuel.

BIRTH RECORDS

MITCHELL,Carolin,Nov.1853.Slave.Mother,Sarah.Owner, Rob. C.Mitchell.

MITCHELL,Summerville,Dec.1853.Slave. Mother,Hannah. Owner, Rob. C.Mitchell.

MITCHELL,Milly,Oct.1853.Slave.Mother, Eliza.Owner, Rob.C.Mitchell.

MITCHELL,___?___,May,14,1853.Male. Parents,Rob W.and Catherine Mitchell.

MINOR,Alis C.,June,1853. Parents,Rob.C.and Susan Minor.

MORGAN,Richard,June 13,1853.Parents,David C.and Susan Morgan.

MONROE,John T.,Aug.31,1853.Parents,John M. and Mary jane Monroe.

MARTIN,Mary,Sept.1853.Parents,William and Emily Martin.

MARTIN,Sandy,Dec.29,1853.Parents,William D. and Frances Martin

MITCHELL,James S.,Oct.1853.Parents,Jordan and Eliza Mitchell.

Page   19,

MARTIN,James N.,May 13,1853.Parents,John and Frances Martin.

MUSGROVE,Julia A.,June 5,1853.Parents,D.P. and Martha Musgrove.

MILES,James S.,1853. Parents,John C.and Sarah Miles.

MATTHEWS,Mildred S.,July 13,1853.Parents,William H. and Mary Jane Matthews.

NICHOLS,Sandy B.,April 19,1853.Parents,Isaac H. and Julia Ann Nichols.

NEIGHBORS,___?___,Aug.31,1853.Male,parents,Henry and Susan Neighbors.

NELMS,Louisa,1853, Slave.Mother,Ester.Owner,Eben Nelms

NELMS,Jane,1853, slave.Mother,Suckey. Owner,Eben Nelms

NELMS,___?___,1853.Slave. Owner,Eben Nelms.

NEWMAN,Sarah J.,Nov.11,1853.Parents,Bailey and Mildred Newman.

NEIGHBORS,Elizabeth,Sept.4,1853.Parents,William and Marinda Neighbors.

NEIGHBORS,Mary Lucy,May 15,1853.Parents,Chris C.and Lucy Ann Neighbors.

NEWMAN,Charlott,Oct.16,1853.parents,William and Harriet Newman.

BIRTH RECORDS

NEWSOM,Frances Ellen,Nov.1853,Parents,John N.and Mary
F.Newman.

NEWMAN,Sally D.,July 2,1853.Parents,William and Betsy
Newman.

MOWLIN,__?__,May 29,1853.Male. Parents, James H. and
Jane Mowlin.

Page   20,

ORE,Aleline,March 10,1853.Parents,James A.and America
Ore.

OVERSTREET,James R.,Aug.30,1853.Parents,Granville and
Mary Overstreet.

OVERSTREET,Eliza A.U.,Oct.22,1853.Parents,Joshua and
Mary Jane Overstreet.

OAKS,___?___,May 31,1853.Female.Parents,Rice L.and Susan
Oaks.

ORE,George,Oct.1,1853.Slave. Mother,mary. Owner,
William Ore.

OVERSTREET,Charles Wesley,Feb.24,1853.Parents,Benjamin
and Martha Overstreet.

PETERS,Isham,1853,Slave.Mother,Sally.Owner,Clifton C.
Peters.

PETERS,Mildred M.,May,1853.Parents,Clifton C.and Susan Peters

PERCELL,___?___,1853,Female,Slave.Mother,Phillis.Owner,
Thomas Percell.

POLLARD,___?___,July,1853.Slave.Mother,Mary. Owner,Fran-
ces Pollard.

POLLARD,___?___,Female,Sept.1853.Parents,Saml C.and Sarah
C.Pollard.

PARKER,Sarah Catherine,Dec.9,1853.Slave.Mother,Phoebe.
Owner,Ammon H.Parker.

PULLEN,Maria,March,1853.Slave.Mother,Dicy. Owner,
Charlott Pullen.

PULLEN,Julia Ann,Jan.1853.Slave.Mother,Susan. Owner,
Charlott Pullen.

PULLEN,Thomas Henry,Jan.1853.Slave.Mother,Mary.Owner,
Charlott Pullen.

PHELPS,Mary,Dec.27,1853.Slave.Mother, Rachel. Owner,
Ammon Phelps.

PENDLETON,Elizabeth,1853.Parents,henry and Nancy Pendleton.

29

BIRTH RECORDS

PREAS,Elizabeth,July 6,1853.Parents,Joseph and Mahala Preas.

PENDLETON,Nancy E.,June 5,1853.Parents,James M.and Jane Pendleton.

PRESTON,Scott & Wesley,(Twins)March 3,1853.Slaves., Mother,Sophia. Owner,Christopher Preston.

PRESTON,Richard P.Slave.Mother,Milly. Owner,Thomas J. Preston.

POWERS,__?__,Aug.9,1853.Male. Parents,Lafayett and Ang- eline Powers.

PENN,Letta,Dec.1853.Slave. Mother,Maria.Owner,Lucinda Penn.

PENN,Maria & Fanny,(Twins),Dec.1853.Mother,Ellen. Owner,Lucinda Penn.

POLLARD,Ann Elizabeth,Aug.31,1853.Parents,John A.and Mary Pollard.

PEARCY,Mary Jane,Dec.28,1853.Parents, William and Sinah Pearcy.

PATTERSON,____,& ____,(Twins)Male and Female.May,1853. Parents,Maltree and Susan Patterson.

PAYNE,Martha S.,July,1853.Parents,James H. and Ann Payne.

PREAS,Henry F.,Aug.1853.Parents,William H. and Mary Jane Preas.

PRESTON,Mary,Sept.1,1853.Slave.Mother,Sarah. Owner, William Preston.

PRESTON,James A. ,July 7,1853.parents,james S. and Mariah Preston.

Page # 21,

PEARCY,Ann Eliza,Nov.20,1853.Parents,William and Frances O.Pearcy.

PEARCY,Matthew,Oct.5,1853.slave. Mother,Betsey. Owner, William Pearcy.

PLATT,Morton,S.,Aug.3,1853.Parents,Andrew L.and Fran- ces Platt.

PEARCE,James F.T.,Aug.31,1853. Parents,Josiah and Amand C.Pearce.

PRESTON,William J.,May 31,1853.Parents,Jesse B. and Eliza Preston.

PLYMALE,William T.,June 9,1853.Parents,Saml and Mary C. Plymale.

BIRTH RECORDS

QUARLES,Elizabeth A. June,1853. Parents, John B. and Elizabeth Quarles.

QUARLES,Henry W.,Jan.30,1853. Parents, John and Cornelia Quarles.

QUARLES,Mary,July,1853.Slave, Mother,Elizabeth,Owner, John Quarles.

RUCKER,Joseph R.,Aug.10,1853. Parents, Ambrose C. and Sarah Jane Rucker.

RUCKER,mahala,March,1853.Slave.Mother,Sarah. Owner, Ambrose Rucker.

RAMSEY,Marinda,July,1853.Parents, James M. and Martha Ramsey.

ROBERTSON,__?__,Aug.,1853.Male.Slave.Mother,Milly. Owner,John J.Robertson.

ROBERTSON,____?,July,1853.Slave.Mother,Phillis. Owner, Francis W.Robertson.

RAINS,Mary E.,May 26,1853. Parents, Richard and Mary M.Raines

RADFORD,_?__,1853. male,Slave. Owner,Munford Radford.

RADFORD,___?_,1853,Male, Slave.Owner,Munford Radford.

RADFORD,__?_,1853,Male. Slave, Owner,Munford Radford.

RADFORD,__?_,1853, Female,Slave,Owner,Munford Radford.

READ,____,1853, Female,Slave.Owner,Elizabeth Read.

REESE,__?_,1853,Female,Parent,Mary Reese.

ROBERTS,Amand,Oct.1853, Slave.Mother,Bieca. Owner, William H.Roberts

ROBERTS,Winny,Aug.1853, Slave. Mother,Nancy. Owner, William H.Roberts.

ROSE,Martha Jane,Jan.24,1853. Parents,William H. and Martha E. Rose.

ROBERTS,__?_,May 25,1853. Parents,Littleberry and Frances L.Roberts.

REECE,__?_,Oct.1853.Slave. Mother, Mary. Owner,William W.Reece.

Page # 22,

SPRADLIN,Franklin P.,Jan.27,1853.Parents,James and Lucinda Spradlin.

SAUNDERS,Burwell,Sept.1853. Slave. Mother,Frances. Owner,George G.Saunders.

STONE,__?_,1853,Female,Slave. Owner,Martha Stone.

BIRTH RECORDS

SMITH,Saml,1853,Slave. Mother, Martha. Owner,Stephen
P.Smith.

STRATTON,Ann,Aug.1853. Salve. Mother,Milly. Owner,
Frazier O.Stratton Est.

SAUNDERS,Ava May,May 30,1853. Parents,Truston L.and
Eliza Saunders.

SAUNDERS,__?__,Dec.1853. Male,Slave. Mother,Judy.
Owner, Truston Saunders.

STINNETT,__?__,Sept.11,1853. Male, Parents,Lindsay and
Judith Stinnett.

SNIDER,William R.,Nov.7,1853, Parents, William F. and
mary Jane Snider.

STEPHENS,Frances O.,Nov.15,1853. Parents,William H.
and Mary E.Stephens.

STINNETT,Leanner Jane,Aug.15,1853. Parents, Alex and
Catherine Stinett.

SWAIN,__?__,1853. Female. Slave. Owner, Elizah Swain.

SAUNDERS,Texanna,1853. Slave. Mother, Nancy.Owner,
Joseph Saunders.

STINNETT,William R.,Aug.25,1853. Parents,John L. and
Martha Jane Stinnett.

SMELSOR,Nancy Ed,Feb.6,1853.Parents,Paschal an Frances
Smelsor.

SMELSOR,Nancy Jane,Jan.2,1853. Parents,Henry and
Catherine Smelsor.

SCRUGGS,Eliza & Lucy,(Twins),Aug.16,1853.Slaves. Mother, Cinthia. Owner, Huophilis C.Scruggs.

SCRUGGS,John,JUne,1853.Slave. Mother, Rachel. Owner,
Reeves S.Scruggs.

SCRUGGS,William,Oct.1853.Slave. Mother, Hennrietta.
Owner, Reeves S.Scruggs.

StCLAIR,__?__,Oct.24,1853.Male. Parents,Burwell C. and
Sarah Frances StClair.

SINER,Julina,1853. Parents,Jonathan and Martha Ann
Siner.

SINER,Susan,April 12,1853.Slave. Mother,Lavinnia.
Owner, Lucy Siner.

SETTLE,Sarah Ann,Aug.9,1853.Parents,John S. and Barb-
ary Settle.

StCLAIR,Mary C.,Oct.17,1853.Parents, John P. and
Frances StClair.

BIRTH RECORDS

SMITH,Julia,July 31,1853.Slave. Mother, Celine. Owner, William C.Smith.

STEWARD,Mary Ellen,Sept.8,1853. Parents, Berry and Parthena Steward.

STONE,William D. Sept.23,1853. Parents, George and Elizabeth Stone.

SAUNDERS,Thomas D.,Aug.4,1853. Parents, Thomas and Sabra Saunders.

SAUNDERS,Bob,Feb.7,1853. Slave. Mother,Martha. Owner, Thomas Saunders.

SCRUGGS,Virginia,1853. Slave. Mother,May. Owner,Eliz. Scruggs.

STINNETT,John J.,1853.Parents,John T.and Margaret Stinnett. Father was an Overseer.

Page # 23,

TUCK,Nancy Ann,June 20,1853. Parents, George W. and Mary Tuck.

TATE,Henry F.,June 9,1853. Parents,Hugh H.and Mary P. Tate.

TURNER,Charles H.,July 1,1853. Parents, Charles E.and Nancy Turner.

TATE,Malissa Jane,1853. Parents,Caleb and Ann Elizabeth Tate.

TURNER,George,1853,Slave. Mother, Ann. Owner, Admire Turner.

TURNER,Charlott,1853. Slave. Mother, Lucinda. Owner, Admire Turner.

THAXTON,William,Sept.5,1853. Parents, William and Sophia Thaxton.

TOMPKINS,John Taylor, 1853. Parents,Daniel and Lydia Tompkins. Father was a Physician.

THURMAN,Robert J.,Feb.16,1853. Parents, Austin L.and Ann Maria Thurman.

TERRY,Frances, Nov.29,1853. Parents, Sanford W. and Mary Jane Terry.

TINSLEY,___?___, June 4,1853.Male,Slave. Mother, China. Owner, Saml G. Tinsley.

THURMAN,___?__,July 27,1853.Female, Parents, Alex L.and Susan Thurman.

THURMAN,Mary Ann B.,May,1853. Parents,John and Nancy Thurman.

BIRTH RECORDS

THURMAN,___?___, May 1853. Slave. Mother, Mary. Owner, Sophia Thurman.

TERRY,Elisha,May,1853. Slave. Mother, Sally. Owner, Henry Terry.

THOMAS,Eliza,Jan.1853. Slave. Mother, Louisa. Owner, Harvey Thomas.

TYLER,Tilghman,Oct.31,1853. Parents, Joseph W. and Martha Tyler.

TURNER,William A.,April 24,1853. Parents,Hardaway A. and Sophia B. Turner.

UPDIKE,Thomas J.,July,1853. Parent, Saml Updike.

UPDIKE,Mary Jane, June,1853. Parents, Anson and Caroline Updike.

Page # 24,

WILLIAMS,___?___,May 24,1853. Female,(Died). Parents, James F. and Cornelia Williams.

WEBB,Sallie M.,Feb.11,1853. Parents,William and Lucy Webb.

WILSON,McHenry,Jan.14,1853. Parents, James and Eliza Wilson. Father was a Millwright.

WADE,James M.,May 24,1853. Parents, Silas G. and Nancy Wade.

WILDMAN,___?___,Dec.18,1853. Male. Parents, Elisha S.and Mary Wildman.

WITT,___?___,July,1853.Male, (Died).Parents, William W. and Nancy Witt.

WALKER,Henry S.,April 28,1853.Parents, David H. and Caroline Walker.

WALKER,Edgar, Aug.4,1853. Slave. Mother, Polly Ann. Owner, James A.Walker.

WALKER,Andrew,Feb.27,1853. Slave. Mother, Louisa. Owner, James A. Walker.

WALKER,Stephen,Sept.18,1853.Slave. Mother, Kinissa. Owner, James A.Walker.

WHITTEN,___?___,Nov.3,1853. Male. Parent, Mildred Whitten.

WADE,___?___,March,1853. Slave. Owner, Thomas Wade's Heirs.

WRIGHT,Robert S.,Feb.11,1853. Parents, James O. and Maria Louise Wright.

BIRTH RECORDS

WRIGHT,Jim Henry,April,1853. Parents, Joel and Susan Wright.

WILLIAMSON,Dillard S.,March 21,1853. Parents,Thomas J. and Mahalia A. Williamson.

WITT,Martha & Mary,Dec.1,1853. (Twins).Slaves. Mother, Biddy. Owner, Alex Witt & others.

WADE,Davis P.,Nov.1853. Parents, William A. and Mary Wade.

ROBERTSON,Jim Henry, April 23,1853. Slave. Mother, Emily. Owner, Jeffrey Robertson.

WELLS,Richard W.,April 23,1853. Parents, Richard M. and Harriett Wells.

WILKERSON,Martha J.,Feb.1853. Parents, David M. and Virginia Wilkerson. Father was a Physician.

WILLIAMS, Edmund,Nov.1853. Slave. Mother, Jinretta. Owner, Saml Williams.

WILSON,Mary J.D., Sept.1,1853. Parents, Elizah and Martha S. Wilson.

WIGGENTON,__?__,Female, 1853. Slave. Mother, Frances. Owner, Isral Wiggenton.

WIGGENTON,__?__,1853. Female, Slave. Mother, Susan. Owner, Isral Wiggenton.

WRIGHT,__?__,April,1853. Female,Slave. Mother, Martha. Owner, Joseph P.Wright.

WEEKS,Sarah S.,may 15,1853. Parents, William D. and Ellen Weeks.

WHITE, martha Jane, Aug.29,1853. Parents, Samuel G. and Catherine Jane White.

WADE,George,Oct.1853. Slave. Mother, Judith. Owner, Alex Wade

WRIGHT,__?__,May 25,1853. Male. Parents, Wright H. and Mary Jane Wright.
WRIGHT,__?__,Nov.13,1853. Female. Parents, John Q.A. and Mary G.Wright.

WORLEY,Eliza V.,Dec.28,1853. Parents,Francis W. and Eliza Worley.

WORLEY,Ann Marie, Feb.1853. Slave. Mother, Sidney. Owner, Francis W.Worley.

WHITTEN,Matilda, 1853. Slave. Mother, Catherine. Owner Joseph Whitten.

WALKER,Saml T.,Jan.17,1853. Parents, Joel and Nancy Ann Walker.

BIRTH RECORDS

WILSON,Minerva S.,Dec.12,1853. Parents, James M. and Emaline Wilson.

WRIGHT,Sophia,Jan.1853.Slave. Mother, Amy. Owner, James Wright.

WRIGHT,mary S.,Feb.26,1853.Parents, Peter M. and Sarah Jane Wright.

WRIGHT,Susan S.E.,Jan.6,1853. Parents, James M. and Mary L.Wright.

WALKER,Ellen,1853. Slave. Owner, William J.Walker.

WHITE,___?___,March 7,1853. Parents,George and Susan White.

Page # 25, No Mothers listed on this page.

WILSON,Edward D., Dec.5,1853. Parent,John N.Wilson

WEST,Charles G.,June 17,1853. Parent, Joel West.

WINGFIELD,Letty, April 1,1853. Slave. Owner, G.A. Wingfield.

WINGFIELD,Louisa,July 15,1853.Slave. Owner, G.A.Wingfield.

WALDREN,___?___,Dec.10,1853. Parent, Thomas D.Waldren.

Page # 26, 1854.

ALLEN,George,Dec.1854. Slave. Mother, Ellen. Owner, Robert Allen.

ALLEN, Charlott, May,1854. Slave. Mother, Mary. Owner, Robert Allen.

ARRINGTON,Martha Frances,Dec.28,1854. Parents, Parham and Mary C.Arrington. Father was a farmer.

AGEE,___?___,June 7,1854. Female. Parents, Arkless E.and Barbara A. Arrington.

ANDERSON,John Harvey, Sept.25,1854. Parents, William A. and Penelope E. Anderson .Father was a farmer.

ARRINGTON,James E.,July 29,1854. Parents, Hampton and Mary Arrington.Father was a farmer.

ARRINGTON,William Hampton,June,1854. Parents, Richard and Frances Arrington. Father was a farmer.

ANDERSON,Louisa,Sept.1854. Slave. Mother, Martha. Owner,John N.Anderson.

ACREE,Thomas Oliver, Nov.30,1854.Parents, Allan J.and Ann E.Acree.

ARRINGTON,Nancy Ann,July,1854.Parents, Hampton and Lila Ann Arrington.Father was a farmer.

BIRTH RECORDS

BILBRO,Andrew,Dec.1854. Slave, Mother, Lucy. Owner, Benjamin Bilbro.

BILBRO,Julus,Nov.1854. Slave. Mother, Matilda. Owner, Benjamin Bilbro.

BILBRO,Mary Lucy,March 21,1854. Parents,William and Mary M. Bilbro.Father was a farmer.

BURNETT,John Christopher,July 8,1854. Parents, Calvin and Mary B.Burnett. Father was a farmer.

BLAKE,Edward Steptoe,FN,July,1854. Parents,William and Mildred Ann Blake.

BALLARD,Mary Elizabeth,May 4,1854.Parents, Clarbourn L. and Mary Ann Ballard.Father was a farmer.

BROWN,Mary James & Job W.,(Twins). Sept.6,1854. Parents, Alfred A. and Ann L. Brown.Father was a Shoe-maker.

BELL,Robert Halloway,June 13,1854.Parents,Francis H. and Musidora A. Bell. Father was a farmer.

BROWN,Lucinda,Dec.13,1854.Slave. Mother, Cinda.Owner, Granville L.Brown.

BONDURANT,James Alexander,Aug.1,1854. Parents,John P. and Mary B. Bondurant. Father was a Merchant.

BURKS,Mitton,July.1854. Slave. Mother, Nancy. Owner, Jesse S.Burks.

BURKS,Isaac, June,1854. Slave. Mother, Mahala. Owner, Martin P.Burks.

BURROUGHS,Eliza Roberta,July,1854. Parents, James B. and Sarah F. Burroughs.Father was a Tanner.

BILBRO,Charles,Oct.1854. Slave. Mother, Lucy. Owner, William M.Bilbro.

Page # 27,

CARROLL,John William,April,1854. Parents, M.A. and Martha C. Carroll. Father ran a Steam Sawmill.

CARTER,Fleming Moses, March 24,1854. Parents, Little-berry and Eliza Carter. Father was a farmer.

COLEMAN,Mary Ann, June 5,1854. Parents, Samuel and Mariah Coleman.Father was a farmer.

COFER,Ann Eliza,Sept.3,1854. Parents, John C. and Sarah B. Cofer. Father was a farmer.

COFER,Mary Jane, May 13,1854. Slave. Mother, Ursula. Owner, Pleasant D.Cofer.

COBB,Frances Rebecca,April 12,1854.Parents, James V. and Sarah Jane Cobb.Father was a farmer.

37

BIRTH RECORDS

COTTREAL,Victoria Ellen,June 15,1854.Parents, James and Mary Ann Margaret Cottreal.Father was a farmer.

COLEMAN,Harriet,June 1,1854. Slave. Mother, Lucy. Owner,Leroy Coleman.

COFFEE,Oshaelen,Sept.15,1854. Parents, Holcomb L.and and Eliza Ann Coffee.Father was a farmer.

CARNIFIX,Robert Benjamin,Feb.22,1854. Parents, Edward M. and Mary Jane Carnifix.Father was a farmer & Millright.

CARNIFIX,George,June 10,1854. Slave. Mother, Eliza. Owner,Edward M. Carnifix.

CLEMENT,Margaret Jane,Jan.24,1854. Parents, James M. and Eliza A. Clement.Father was a carpenter.

CALLOWAY,Fillis,Jan.9,1854.Slave. Mother,Emerline. Owner,John Calloway.

CALLOWAY,Adda,March 17,1854. Slave. Mother, Sarah. Owner, John Calloway.

CALLAWAY,Louiza, Oct.24,1854. Slave. Mother, Queen. Owner, John Callaway.

CRANK,Nancy, May 21,1854. Parents,William J. and Sejies Crank. Father was a farmer.

CLAY,Lucy Ann,March 5,1854. Slave. Mother, Theodocia. Owner, Paul A.Clay.

CLAY,Pattrick,March 17,1854. Slave. Mother, Judy. Owner, Paul A.Clay.

COBBS,Nicholas Hamner,July 31,1854. Parents, John c. and Martha B. Cobbs. Father was a farmer.

CLAY,Mariah,Aug.1854. Slave. Mother, Fanny. Owner, O.G.Clay.

CLARK,Samuel, July,31,1854. Slave. Mother, Sally. Owner, Woodson Clark.

CHAPPELL,Adam, Dec.1854. Slave. Mother, Prudence. Owner, Richard Chappell.

CRANK,Sallie Ann,July 29,2854. Parents, James L. and Susan J.Crank.Father was a farmer.

CHILDRESS,William Newton, Jan.1854. Parents, William T. and Elizabeth Childress. Father was a farmer.

CHEATWOOD,Charlott Sale, Oct.23,1854.Parents, Daniel B. and Sallie P.Cheatwood.Father was a farmer.

CHEATWOOD,Ann, Aug.1854. Slave. Mother, Milly. Owner, Daniel B.Cheatwood.

BIRTH RECORDS

COX,Jane, Feb.,1854. Parents, Wiatt and Ann Cox.

CRUMPACKER,Robert,Aug.1,1854. Parents, Edward and Mary Crumpacker. Father was a farmer.

CLAY,Emmer, Dec.1854. Slave. Mother, Lucinda. Owner, O.G.Clay.

COBBS,James Walter, Dec.1854. Parents, Benjamin F.and Landonia E.Cobbs. Father was a carpenter.

CLAY,Frances. Dec.1854. Slave. Mother, Sarah. Owner, J.A.Clay.

CAMPBELL,Charlott, Sept.1854. Slave. Mother, Angeline. Owner, Thomas Campbell.

CAMPBELL,Susan, June 1954. Slave. Mother, Ann. Owner, Thomas Campbell.

COCKRAN,Mary. Aug.31,1854. PARENTS, Thomas and Louiza Cockran. Father was a Farmer.

CARTER, Sarah Ann and Edward James,(Twins) Sept.1854. Parents, James C. and Susanna Carter.

CLEMENT, John,March,1854. Slave.Mother, Emerline. Owner, Robert A. Clement.

CHILTON,Henry Lee, June 17,1854. Parents, James and Sarah E.Chilton. Father was a farmer.

COLEMAN,Cyrus, 1854. Slave. Mother, Fillis. Owner , Robert Coleman.

Page # 28,

DOOLEY,Martha Susan,Oct.27,1854. Parents, Alexander J. and Ann Eliza Dooley. Father was a farmer.

DOOLEY,Andrew, April 8,1854. Parents, John and Ann Dooley. Father was a farmer.

DOOLEY,James Alexander, April 23,1854. Parents, John C. and Frances A. Dooley. Father was a farmer.

DEWITT,Eliza Dennis, July 28,1854. Parents, Elisha D. and Susan Dewitt. Father was a farmer.

DAVIS,Mary Ann,Jan.17,1854. Slave. Mother, Caroline. Owner, Mrs B.Davis.

DAVIS,Charlott,Nov.2,1854. Slave. Mother, Delphia. Owner, Mrs. B.Davis.

DAVID,___?__,July,1854. Slave. Female, Mother, Matilda. Owner, Micajah Davis Jr.

EWING,Charles Leslie, June 11,1854. Parents, Charles H. and Eliza F. Ewing. Father was a farmer.

BIRTH RECORDS

EDGAR,_?__,Jan.23,1854. Male,(Died). Parents, John H. and Catherine Edgar. Father was a farmer.

EUBANK, John,Aug.5,1854. Slave. Mother, Harriett. Owner, Joseph Eubank.

EUBANK,Rachel, Nov.20,1854. Slave. Mother, Matilda. Owner, Joseph Eubank.

EWING,Lewis Henry, July 23,1854. Parents, William and Lydia Ewing. Father was a farmer.

EARLY, Charles Edward, Nov.2,1854. Parents, John W. and Sarah A. Early. Father was a farmer.

EARLY,Samuel, Feb.22,1854. Slave. Mother, Lucinda. Owner, John W.Early.

ELLIS,Lelia Willa, Aug.1854. Parents, William and Lucy C.Ellis. Father was a farmer.

EVERETT,John, July 21,1854. Slave, Mother, Martha. Owner, Joseph Everett.

EVERETT,Solomon,Sept.13,1854. Slave. Mother, Vilett. Owner, A.N.Everett.

EUBANK,John Thomas, Dec.28,1854. Parents, Richard B. and Susan Eubank. Father was a farmer.

EVERETT,Andrew Jackson, April,1854. Slave. Mother, Elvira. Owner,John F.Everett.

ELLIOTT,Robert Giles & Frances Charlott.(Twins).March 27,1854. Parents, Adam and Susan Ann Elliott.Father was a wheelwright.

FARIS,Stephen Lewis, Oct.20,1854. Parents, William and Catherine Faris. Father was a farmer.

FARMER,James Lewis, May 30,1854. Parents, James A. and Eady Ann farmer. Father was Blacksmith.

FUQUA,Agness, Oct.1854. Slave. Mother, Fancy. Owner, Mrs Sallie M.Fuqua.

FOSTER, Thomas Walker, Nov.23,1854. Parents, Faris and Louiza Foster. Father was a farmer.

FORQUERON,Joseph,Jan.11,1854. Parents, Little Berry and Mary Jane Forqueron. Father was a farmer.

FREEMAN,Amanda,July 31,1854. Parents, John H. and Martha Freeman. Father was a farmer.

FIZER,Giles, March,1854. Slave. Mother, Milly Ann. Owner, William H.Fizer.

FIZER,_?__,March,1854. Parents, William H. and Mary Fizer.

BIRTH RECORDS

FARNHAM,Nelly, July 23,1854. Slave. Mother, Jenett. Owner, Baldwin Farnham.

FALLS, James Thomas,Dec.1854. Parents, George P. and Malinda Falls. Father was a Blacksmith.

GIBBS,John Edwin, Aug.26,1854.Parents, William W. and Angeline Gibbs. Father was a farmer.

GOOD,Sally,Jan. 1854. Slave. Mother, Kitty. Owner, John Good.

GOODMAN,Amanda,Aug.1854. Parents, John and Martha Goodman. Father was a farmer.

GILLS,Susan Henryetta, Oct.6,1854. Parents, William H. and Sarah W. Gills. Father was a farmer.

GILLISPY,__?__,Feb.4,1854.Male, Parents, E.B. and Mary Frances Gillispy. Father was a farmer.

GLASS,__?__ Aug.1854.Male, Parents, James E. and Lucy Glass. Father was a Shoemaker.

HATCHER,Judson Logwood, Feb.4,1854. Parents, jeremiah G. and Angeline Hatcher.Father was a farmer.

HARRIS,__?__,Aug.1854. Slave, Mother, Sarah. Owner, Rev. William Harris.

HARRIS,__?__,Aug.1854. Female. Slave. Mother, Ann... Owner, Rev. William Harris.

HATCHER,Malinda Ann, May 9,1854. Slave. Mother, Mary. Owner, Caleb H.Hatcher.

HATCHER,Anna Hurt, Nov.5,1854. Parents, Caleb H. and Florintine Hatcher. Father was a farmer.

HORSLEY,Nicholas Cabell, April 9,1854. Parents,Nicholas and Elizabeth L. Horsley.Father was a farmer.

HATCHER,__?__,Sept.1854. Parents, A.P. and Mary M. Hatcher. Father was a farmer.

HOLLY,Eliza Thomas, Nov.1854. Parents, Richard B. and Sarah E. Holly. Father was a farmer.

HATCHER, Edward Perkins,July 9,1854. Parents, John C. and Rebecca S. hatcher, Father was a farmer.

HODGES,Ferlander Jefferson, May 5,1954. Parents, Samuel and Sarah E. Hodges. Father was a farmer.

HECK,__?__,Dec.15,1854. Male, Parents, Daniel and Elizabeth Heck.

HATCHER,Jesse Orella,Dec.25,1854.Slave. Mother, Mary. Owner, Thomas H. Hatcher,

HARRIS,William Wirt, June 4,1854. Parents, C.J. and Cassandra Harris. Father was a Teacher.

BIRTH RECORDS

HARRIS,Richard,Sept.1854. Slave. Mother, Mariah.Owner, Hanibal Harris.

HATCHER,Benjamin Brown,April 14,1854. Parents, Alex M. and Mary Ann Hatcher. Father was a farmer.

HATCHER, Warrick, Nov.1854. Slave. Mother, Mary. Owner Henry Hatcher.

HATCHER, Caleb. May 1,1854. Slave. Mother, Polina. Owner, Thomas Hatcher.

HATCHER,Ava Alice. Oct. 1854. Parents, Granvill and Celista hatcher. Father was a farmer.

HATCHER, Fanny, Dec.1854. Slave. Mother, Mary. Owner, Granvill Hatcher.

HOWARD,Louiza Ann, March 2,1854. Parents, John W. and Cleopatra A. Howard. Father was a farmer.

HAWKINS,Malissa, April 27,1854. Parents, Fleming and Alis Ann Hawkins. Father was a farmer.

HATCHER,Ginnie, Sept.21,1854.Slave. Mother, Martha. Owner, Allen D. Hatcher.

HARRIS, Charles, Aug.1854. Slave. Mother, Polina . Owner, Doc Hector Harris.

HEWITT,___?___,Dec.27,1854.Male. Slave. Mother, Lucy. Owner, Henry H.Hewitt.

HARRIS,Ludwell, May 19,1854. Slave. Mother, Margaret. Owner, James M.Harris.

HARRIS, James Walter, June 30,1854. Parents, James and Louiza Harris.Father was farmer.

HARRISON,PATRICK,May 9,1854. Slave. Mother, Sophia. Owner, Richard P.harrison. Father was a farmer.

HARRISON,Paulis, June 20,1854. Parents, Paulis and Virginia Harrison. Father was a farmer.

HATCHER,Roberta Lewis, March 9,1854. parents, Albert M. and Elizabeth E. Hatcher. Father was a farmer.

HUNTER,Harvey,March 31,1854. Slave. Mother, Mariah. Owner, Aeneas Hunter.

HARRIS, Sulvia,March,1854. Slave, Mother, Harriett. Owner, James W.harris.

HARRIS,Emily, April,1854. Slave. Mother, Nancy.Owner, James W.Harris.

HARRIS,Mary Eliza, may.1854. Slave. Mother, Louiza. Owner, James W.Harris.

HARRIS, Mary Cole, Sept.1854. Slave. Mother, Polina. Owner. James W. Harris.

BIRTH RECORDS

Page # 30

HOBSON, Ellen, 1854, Slave, Mother, Emily. Owner,
Samuel Hobson.

HOBSON,Claibourn, 1854. Slave, Mother, Harriet.
Owner, Samuel Hobson.

HOBSON, William, 1854. Slave. Mother, Fanny. Owner,
Samuel Hobson.

HOBSON,Mariah, 1854. Slave. Mother, mary. Owner,
Samuel Hobson.

HOBSON, Edditha & Edna,(Twins).Slaves. Mother, Sarah.
Owner, Samuel Hobson.

HOLT,Mary Allis,May 16,1854. Parents, Josiah W. &
Elizabeth F. Holt. Father was a Machinest.

HAWLEY,Mary Emmily, April 3,1854.Parents, L.J. and
Elizabeth Ann Hawley. Father was a Lightning R.Dealer.

HUTTER,Joseph, Aug.29,1854. Slave. Mother, Lydia.
Owner, Edward S.Hutter.

HUTTER, Phil Anderson, Oct.6,1854.Slave. Mother,
Matilda. Owner, Edward S.Hutter.

JONES,Eliza, Aug.1854. Slave, Mother, Molly. Owner,
Thomas M. Jones.

JONES,Harvey, Jan.1854. Slave. Mother, Sarah. Owner,
A.A.Jones.

JOPLING,Morton,Aug.14,1854. Parents, Thomas B. and
Sarah E. Jopling. Father was a Farmer.

JOPLING,Robert Kelso,March 29,1854. Parents, James W.
and Emily Jopling. Father was a farmer.

JETER,George Harrison, march 11,1854. Slave. Mother,
Martha. Owner, Jesse Jeter.

JETER,Wittshire,Sept.18,1854. Slave. Mother, Julia.
Owner, Jesse Jeter.

JETER,Horace,Oct.1854. Slave. Mother,Rose. Owner,
Jesse Jeter.

JENNINGS,Harvey,Aug.1854. Slave. Mother, Vina. Owner,
James C.Jennings.

KARNES,William Randolph, Nov.2,1854. Parents, Michael
and Sarah Karnes.

KARNES, ? ,March 31,1854. Parents,William and Nancy
Karnes. Father was a farmer.

KIDD,John Jefferson,Jan.30,1854.Parents, Henry D. and
Mary C.Kidd. Father was a farmer.

KABLER,Margarett,Nov.1854. Slave. Mother, Ann. Owner,
William C.Kabler.

BIRTH RECORDS

KABLER,Allice,1854. Slave. Mother, Lucy. Owner,William C.Kabler.

KNIGHT,Henry, Dec.25,1854. Slave. Mother, Ann. Owner, J.J.Knight.

KELSO,John, Nov.1854. Slave. Mother, Lucy. Owner, Robt. N.Kelso.

KELSO,Annah,March,1854. Slave. Mother, Mary. Owner, Robert N.Kelso.

KELSO,Jack, June,1854. Slave, Mother, Betty, Owner, Robert N.Kelso.

KELSO,Julia, Jan. 1854. Slave. Mother, Judy. Owner, Robert N.Kelso.

Page # 31,

LEE,William, Sept.30,1854, Slave, Owner, Thomas N.Lee.

LUCK,Laura Lee, May,1854. Slave. Mother, Clora. Owner, George P.Luck.

LUCK,Hillery, May,1854. Slave. Mother, Mary. Owner, George P.Luck.

LOWRY,Manervy,Dec.25,1854. Slave. Mother, Betsey. Owner, John Lowry.

LOGWOOD,Thomas Burrell, Aug.24,1854.Parents, Alexander H. and Theodocia Ann Logwood. Father was a farmer.

LOGWOOD,Walter Henderson,April 17,1854. Parents,Robert and Mary E.Logwood. Father was a farmer.

LOWRY,Caroline, Jan.1854. Slave. Mother, Emmerline. Owner, Nelson Lowry.

LEFTWICH,__?__,April 9,1854.Male, Parents, John S. and Elizabeth Leftwich.

LEFTWICH,Lucinda, Jan.4,1854. Slave. Mother, Nancy. Owner, John S. Leftwich.

LOWRY,Margaret,March,1854. Slave, Mother, Phillis. Owner,Matilda C.Lowry.

LEE,Samuel Clay,Feb.15,1854. Parents,William H. and Susan A. Lee.Father was a farmer.

LEE,John,May,1854. Slave. Mother, Deannah. Owner, William H. Lee.

LEFTWICH,Missouri Emmerline, Sept.9,1854.Parents, Joel and Sallie W. Leftwich. Father was a farmer.

LOWRY,Payton,April,1854.Slave, Mother, Sarah. Owner, Milton Lowry.

MARSH,Elizabeth Eller, July 12,1854.Parents, Thomas E. and Lydia C.Marsh. Father was a farmer.

BIRTH RECORDS

MOSELEY,Louiza,June,1854. Slave. Mother, Julia. Owner, George C.Moseley.

MOORE,David William Henry,Feb.3,1854.Parents, Goodrich and Catherine Moore. Father was a farmer.

MEADOR,John Calvin,Dec.1854. Parents, John J. and Susan E. Meador. Father was a Carpenter.

MOORMAN,Toney,April,1854. Slave. Mother, Betsey. Owner, Lodowick A.Moorman.

MOORMAN,Malinda,June,1854. Parents, Lodowick A. and Ann Moorman.

MILLNER,__?__,April,1854.Female. Parents, Madison F. and Elizabeth Millner. Father was a farmer.

MEADOR,Allice,March,1854. Parents, John W. and Eliza Meador. Father was a Miller.

MILLENER,__?__,Dec.29,1854.Male. Parents, Albert G.and Nancy Millener. Father was a farmer.

MILLENER,Charles, Oct.1854. Slave. Mother, Martha. Owner, Albert G.Millener.

METCALFE,Landonia,March 14,1854.Slave. Mother, Eliza. Owner, James Metcalfe.

MELTON,Mary Isabella Judy,April 8,1854. Parents,Samuel and Mariah W. Melton. Father was a farmer.

MINNIS,__?__,May,1854.Male. Slave. Mother, Martha. Owner, William C.Minnis.

MERRIWETHER,Betsey,Sept.1854. Slave. Mother,Berinda. Owner,Charles I.Merriwether.

MAJOR,Emmet Dudley,Oct.2,1854. Parents, Harwood and Cleotria Major. Father was a farmer.

MAJOR,Walter,Pendleton,Nov.1854.Parents,Spottswood and Catherine K.Major.Father was a farmer.

MERRIWETHER,George,Nov.1854.Slave. Mother, Polina. Owner, James A.Merriwether.

McGHEE,Sarah Eller,Sept.30,1854.Slave. Mother, Frances. Owner,William T.McGhee Est.

MOSBY,Mary Frances,July 23,1854.Parents,Powhatan and Margaret E.Mosby. Father was a farmer.

MAJOR,Alley,March 1,1854. Slave. Mother, Mary Jane. Owner, William Major.

MAKEPEACE,Sarah Elizabeth,Oct.25,1854. Parents,Alvin S. and Ruhamah Makepeace.

BIRTH RECORDS

MARKHAM,Robert, April 7,1854. Slave. Mother, Lucy.
Owner, Miss Patsey Markham.

Page # 32,

NEIGHBORS,Samuel Henry, Sept.1,1854. Parents, Samuel
and Susan Neighbors. Father was a farmer.

NOEL,Hillery Alexander,Nov.14,1854. Parents, Alexander
I. and Catherine A. Noel. Father was a farmer.

NOEL,Luvenia & Arrenia,(Twins),April1,1854. Slaves,
Mother, Rachel. Owner, John C. Noel.

NOEL,St. Paul,March,1854. Slave. Mother, Martha. Owner,
John C. Noel.

NOEL,John, Aug.1854. Slave. Mother, Adah. Owner,
Polestine W. Noel.

NELSON,Emily,July 4,1854. Parents, Thomas H. and Emily
Nelson. Father was a Physician.

NELSON,Julia Ann, Sept. 1854. Slave. Mother, Martha.
Owner, Thomas H. Nelson.

NELSON,Lewis, Dec.,1854. Slave. Mother, Caroline.Owner,
Thomas H.Nelson.

NOEL, Virginia, MAy 7,1854. Parents, Erasmus D. and
Catherine Noel. Father was a farmer.

OVERACRE,George,June,1854. Parents, George W. and
Emily N. Overacre. Father was a farmer.

OWNBY,Hillerey,Aug.1854. Slave. Mother, Elvy. Owner,
Mrs Nancy Ownby.

OVERSTREET,James Harrison, Aug.16,1854. Parents,
Tilman I. and Nancy F.Overstreet.Father was a farmer.

OTEY,Polina, July.1854. Slave. Mother, Catherine.
Owner,Charles C.Otey.

OGLESBY,Martha,April,1854.Slave. Mother, Mariah.
Owner, Joshua B.Oglesby.

OGDEN,Sallie Robert,Dec.14,1854. Parents, William and
Susan Ogden. Father was a farmer.

ORRANGE,Sarah Elizabeth,Dec.23,1854.FN, Parents, Edward N. and Eliza I. Orrange.Father was a farmer.

POWELL,Morris,Jan.1854. Slave. Mother, Charlott. Owner,
William Powell.

POWELL,Edwin,April,1854. Slave. Mother, Lucinda. Owner,
William Powell.

PECK,Joseph Thomas, Sept.20,1854. Parents, Edward
and Eliza Peck. Father was a farmer.

BIRTH RECORDS

PREBLE,George W.,Dec.24,1854. Parents, William and Nancy Preble. Father was a Blacksmith.

PIERCE,John Pleasant, Dec.1854. Parents,Moses and Elizabeth Pierce. Father was a farmer.

HARRIS,Rebecah,June, 1854. Parents, Thomas and Delila Powers. Father was a Blacksmith.

PAGETT,Ann Booker,Aug.4,1854. Slave. Mother, Jane. Owner, Beverly Pagett.

POINDEXTER,Martha, June,1854. Slave. Mother, Dosha. Owner, Richard W.Poindexter.

PAGETT,Mary Jane,Nov.16,1854. Parents, Richard and Polly Pagett. father was a farmer.

POINDEXTER,James.Aug.1854. Slave. Mother, Susan. Owner, Martha G.Poindexter.

POINDEXTER,Susan, Dec.1854. Slave. Mother, Sylva. Owner, Eliza D.Poindexter.

PAGITT,Mary Elizabeth,May 31,1854. Parents, Beverly H. and Elizabeth M. Pagitt.

PAGE, Selia,Oct.26,1854. Parents,Robert W. and Parthena Page. Father was a farmer.

PAGE, Thomas Garland,Oct.23,Parents,Edmund G. and Elizabeth Page. Father was a farmer.

PETERS,Mathena Ann, May 9,1854.Parents, William and Martha Ann Peters. Father was a Lock keeper.

PENN,Eliza, Jan.1854. Slave. Mother, Harriet. Owner, Moses Penn.

PENN,Sanford, March 1854. Slave. Mother, Mary. Owner, Moses Penn.

PHELPS,Mariah, Dec.25,1854. Slave. Mother, Matilda. Owner, Peter W. Phelps.

Page # 33,

QUARLES,Mary Cameron,June 6,1854. Parents,Giles T.and Elizabeth Quarles.

QUARLES, ? ,Sept.1854. Male, (Died). Parents,Samuel H. and Elizabeth R. Quarles. Father was a farmer.

ROY,Mariah, Sept.1854. Slave. mother, Sally. Owner, David M.Roy.

RILEY, ? ,Aug.14,1854.Female. (Died). Parents, George and Elizabeth Riley.Father was a farmer.

RUSHER,Martha Susan,July 5,1854. Parents,Jesse T. and Judith Ann E. Rusher. Father was a farmer.

BIRTH RECORDS

READ,___?__,Dec.12,1854.Male. Parents, Edward T. and Eliza Amanda Read. Father was a farmer.

ROSE,Nancy Jane, April 11,1854.Uriah and Sarah Ann Rose. Father was a farmer.

ROBINSON,___?__,Sept.1854. Slave. Mother, Mary. Owner, James H. Robinson.

REYNOLS,Nelson, April,1854. Slave. Mother, Louiza. Owner, Charles B.Reynols Jr.

RUCKER,Marinda, Dec.7,1854. Parents, James M. and Marinda Rucker. Father was a farmer.

ROBINSON,Ellen,Sept.1854. Parents, Benjamin T. and Jane Robinson. Father was a farmer.

ROBINSON,Virginia,Jan.7,1854. Parents, James W. and Ann E. Robinson. Father was a farmer.

ROBINSON,John, July 14,1854. Parents, John H. and Mary Robinson. Father was a farmer.

ROBINSON,Mary Ann, April,1854. Slave. Mother, Elizabeth. Owner, Benjamin N.Robinson.

REESE,Ben, Aug.1854.Slave. Mother, Mariah. Owner, Joseph T.Reese.

REECE,Anna, Nov.1854. Slave. Mother, Lucinda. Owner, Joseph T.Reece.

RICE,Lewis,1854. Slave. Mother, Leannah. Owner, Bailey Rice.

RICE,Mary Frances, March 4,1854.Parents,William C. and Amanda Virginia Rice. Father was a farmer.

ROBINSON,Lelia Allice. Feb.10,1854.Parents, Edward N. and Martha M. Robinson. Father was a farmer.

ROBINSON,Doctor, Dec.1854. Salve. Mother, Malinda. Owner, Edward N.Robinson.

RUFF,John James,Nov.6,1854. FN, Parents, David Ruff,FN. and Nancy.

SHEPHERD,___?__,Oct.20,1854.Male. Parents, B.H.F. and Mary J.Shepherd. Father was a farmer.

SAUNDERS,Winston, Feb.1854. Slave. Mother, Martha. Owner, Anzoletta Saunders.

SAUNDERS,Edward Hagermon,Aug.1854. Slave. Mother, Frances. Owner,Anzoletta Saunders.

SCOTT,Cooper,May,1854. Slave. Mother, Caroline. Owner, Saml M.Scott.

SLEDD,Yarmer, June,1854. Slave. Mother, mary Ann. Owner, William E.Sledd.

BIRTH RECORDS

SAUNDERSON,George E.,May 24,1854. Parents, George E. and Elizabeth A. Saunderson. Father was a farmer.

SALE, Albert,Feb.14,1854. Slave. Mother, Mary. Owner, Rev.Nelson Sale.

SALE,Lindsay, April,1854. Slave. Mother, Rachel. Owner, Rev. Nelson Sale.

STEPTOE,Martha, Nov.28,1854. Slave. Mother, Rhoda. Owner, Robert G.Steptoe.

SCOTT,Patsey, May,1854. Slave. Mother, Hariott. Owner, Mrs E.R.Scott.

SCOTT,Arthur, May,1854. Slave. Mother, Jane. Owner, Mrs E.R.Scott.

SCOTT,__?__,May 7,1854. Slave. Mother, Mariah. Owner, Mrs E.R.Scott.

SHELTON,Chester,July 4,1854.Slave. Mother, Nancy. Owner, Wesley Shelton.

Page # 34,

THAXTON,Ellen,Dec.15,1854. Slave. Mother, Amanda. Owner, David T.Thaxton.

THAXTON,William, Sept.1854. Slave. Mother, Harriet. Owner, Nathaniel F.Thaxton.

THOMAS, Isaac,Nov.1854. Slave. Mother, Soniza. Owner, Saml M.Thomas.

TAYLOR,__?__,July,26,1854. Female. Parents, Albert H. and Mary Jane Taylor. Father was a Farmer.

TARDY,Thomas Elihue,Oct.23,1854. Parents, Paul J. and Martha Ann Tardy. Father was a farmer.

TURPIN,Thomas, Feb.1854. Slave. Mother, Margaret. Owner, Phillip Turpin.

TURPIN,__?__,Oct.27,1854.Female. Parents, Elisha G. and Amanda Turpin. Father was a farmer.

THOMASON,Samuel Edward, Sept.5,1854. Parents, John N. and Mary D. Thomason.Father was a Factory worker.

TAYLOR,Marshall P.Scott,May 16,1854. Parents, William N. and Martha Jane Taylor.Father was a farmer.

THOMAS,Mary Elizabeth,sept.16,1854. Parents, L.H. and Susan Thomas.

THOMAS,Nancy Me,Aug.27,1854. Parents, James and Sally Thomas. Father was a farmer.

THOMAS,Eliza Ann, Dec.29,1854. Parents, Thomas M. and Mary Jane Thomas. Father was a farmer.

ᴴIRTH RECORDS

TURPIN,Emma Veloria,April 10,1854. Parents, Willis C. and Mary F.Turpin. Father was a farmer.

TURPIN,Davy, Sept.1854. Slave. mother, Louiza. Owner, Thomas Turpin.

TURPIN,Flora, July,1854. Slave. Mother, Genetta. Owner, Thomas Turpin.

TINSLEY,Alfred, Sept.1854. Slave. Mother, Milly. Owner, Mrs Lucy Tinsley.

THOMAS,Sarah Elizabeth, Aug.4,1854. Parents, George W. and Henryetta Thomas. Father was a farmer.

VAUGH,Joseph Wingfield, Aug.18,1854. Parents, Bedford and Mary J.Vaugh. Father was a farmer.

VARNER,William Frances, June 1,1854. Parents, John W. and Mary F. Varner. Father was a farmer.

FRANCES,Martha, Sept. 1854. FN. Mother, Frances.

WILLIAMS,__?__, Female.Jan.1,1854. Parents,John A. and Sarah E.Williams. Father was a farmer.

WILLIAMS,Emmer, June,1854. Slave. Mother, Sarah. Owner, Mrs Matilda Williams.

WOOD,Sarah Virginia, Feb.24,1854. Parents, John and Genette Wood. Father was farmer.

WATTS,Harvey,March 3,1854. Slave. Mother, Jane. Owner, Mrs Isabelle Watts.

WATTS,Allice,Nov. 10,1854. Slave. Mother, Sophia.Owner, James W. Watts.

WILCH,John Wesley,July,1854. Parents, James and Adaline Wilch.

WILSON,John Thomas, July 18,1854. Parents, Thomas J. and Elizabeth Wilson.Father was a farmer.

WHITE,Rosser, Feb.22,1854. Slave. Mother, Martha. Owner Henry M. white.

WHITE,Malinda,March 26,1854.Slave. Mother, Clara. Owner Henry M.White.

WHITE,Albert,Sept.10,1854. Slave.Mother, Sarah. Owner, Henry M.White.

WATSON,John,May 20,1854. Slave. Mother, Tenah. Owner, Barnet A.Watson.

WATSON,Wiatt,Dec.6,1854. Slave. Mother, Catherine, Owner, Mrs Nancy Watson.

WHITLEY,Ransum,July,1854. Slave. Mother, Elizabeth. Owner, Mrs Ann Whitely

BIRTH RECORDS.

WHITELEY,John, July,1854. Slave. Mother, Watsey.
Owner, Mrs Ann Whiteley.

WRIGHT,Wesley Martin,Dec.11,1854. Parents, Gustavus
and Agness B.Wright.Father was a farmer.

WILSON,Bettie Frances,Dec.1854. Parents, Thomas C.and
Polina Wilson. Father was farmer.

WILSON,Judy Emer, Nov.6,1854. Parents, George H. and
Elizabeth Wilson.Father was a farmer.

WIGGENTON, Moses, July,1854. Slave. Mother, Rose.
Owner, Benjamin Wiggenton.

WRIGHT,David Henry, March 24,1854. Parents, John D.
and Jane E. Wright.Father was a farmer.

WADE,Caliste Ann, Oct.7,1854. Parents, William H. and
Elizabeth R. Wade. Father was a Taylor.

Page 35,

WORLEY,Samuel L.Goggin,March 15,1854.Parents, John and
Emily Worley. Father was farmer.

WILKES,James & John (Twins),May,1854. Slaves, Mother,
Sophiah. Owner, Benjamin Wilkes.

WILKES, Lucinda, Dec.1854. Slave. Mother, Eliza. Owner,
Benjamin Wilkes.

WILKERSON,Ann, may,1854. Slave. Mother, Betsey. Owner,
Thomas M.Wilkerson.

WHITE,Sarah, Nov.1854. Slave. Mother, Ann. Owner,
Jacob S.White.

WHITE,Wiatt. Dec.1854. Slave. Mother, Dilsey. Owner,
John M.White.

WILLIAMS,__?__,June,1854. Slave. mother, Caroline.
Owner, James M.Williams.

WILLIAMS,Samuel,March,1854. Slave. Mother,Hannah.
Owner, James M.Williams.

WATSON,Stephen Richard, Feb.2,1854.Parents, Wiatt J.
and Mariah L.Watson.Father was a farmer.

WILKERSON,William, July,1854. Parents, William O.and
Margaret Wilkerson.

WILKERSON,Dibrel,Oct.1854. Slave. Mother, Patsey.
Owner, William O.Wilkerson.

WILKERSON,Early,Nov.1854. slave. Mother, Aggy. Owner,
William O.Wilkerson.

WILKERSON,Rachel, may,1854. Slave. Mother, Polly.
Owner, Mrs Rachel Wilkerson.

BIRTH RECORDS

HOLCOMB,John, Feb.1854. Slave. Mother, Lucy. Owner, Mr Holcomb.

WILKERSON,Mary Ann Keziah, Nov.5,1854. Parents, Joseph B. and Julia J. Wilkerson.

WILKERSON,Elizabeth, March 1,1854. Slave. Mother, Susan Owner, William L.Wilkerson.

WILKERSON,Simon,Aug.1,1854. Slave. Mother, Mariah. Owner, William L.wilkerson.

YOUNG,Christian, may 18,1854. Parents, John and Lucy Young. Father was a farmer.

Page 36,

ADAMS,Ruth, Oct.1854. Slave. Owner, Grief Adams.

AUSTIN,Thomas A., Parents, Abram and Anuncia C.Austin. Father was a farmer.

ANDERSON,Lewis G.,Dec.17,1854.Parents, Joel C. and Betsey.Anderson. Father was a farmer.

ANDERSON,Judith E.L.,May 22,1854. Parents,Jubal L.B. and Agnes M.Anderson.Father was a farmer.

ATKINSON,Eliza Ann,1854, Parents,Joseph and Elizabeth Atkinson. Father was a farmer.

ANDREWS,__?__,Oct.13,1854.Parents, William M. and Sarah E.Andrews.Father was a farmer.

ANDREWS,Munford, April,1854. Slave. Owner, William M. Andrews.

ANDREWS,Violet, June 10,1854. Slave. Owner, Mark Andrew

ARRINGTON,Abner, July 14,1854. Slave. Owner, Catherine G.Arrington.

AYERS,Robert W.,Nov.20,1854. Parents, Elijah Q. and Elizabeth J.Ayers.Father was a farmer.

ASHWELL,Beldire A.E., Oct.15,1854. Parents, Pleasant L. and Emeline Ashwell. Father was a farmer.

ARTHUR,Henry. April,1854. Slave. Owner, Albon A.Arthur.

ADAMS,Jim. April 22,1854. Slave. Owner, Saml Adams.

AYERS,Thomas J. Oct 20,1854. Parents, Saml J. and Mary Jane Ayers. Father was a farmer.

ANTHONY,Abner. Nov.10,1854. Parents,Abner and Almira Anthony.

BOARD,Bob. Jan.1854. Slave. Owner,Saml H.Board.

BRAMBLETT,William Irvine, May 7,1854.Parents, John S. and Mary C. Bramblett. Father was a Bricklayer.

BIRTH RECORDS

BRADLEY,Mary S.,Feb.11,1854. Parents, James H. and Ann B. Bradley. Father was a farmer.

BEARD,___?___,Male. Dec.7,1854. Parents, Robert M. and Elizabeth Beard. Father was a farmer.

BEARD,Sarah V.F.,1854. Parents, John O. and Martha Ann Beard. Father was a farmer.

BOWLS,Frances,J.,April 30,1854. Parents, William A. and Mildred Bowls. Father was a farmer.

BELL,Bob, Feb.,1854. Slave. Owner, Orville P. Bell.

BURKS,Betty B.,Sept.,1854. Parents, Edward C. and Elizabeth Burks.Father was a Lawyer.

BURKS,Burton, 1854. Slave. Owner, Edward C.Burks.

BANDY,Richard F.,Parents, Cornelius and Sally Bandy. Father was a farmer.

BURROUGHS,___?___, 1854. Slave.Died. Owner, John Burroughs

BROWN,___?___, 1854. Male. Slave. Owner, Saml T.Brown.

BROWN,___?___, 1854, Female. Slave. Owner, Saml T.Brown.

BROWN,___?___, 1854. Female. Slave. Owner, Saml T. Brown

BROWN,Bates, Dec.30,1854. Parents, Saml T. and Violet Brown.

BURROUGHS,___?___, Dec.1854. Female.Slave. Owner, Thomas Burroughs.

BLANKENSHIP,William P.,March 10,1854. Parents, John and Christeanna Blankenship.

BATES,California, Sept.26,1854. Parents, William and Charlotte Bates. Father was a farmer.

BURNETT,William W. Nov.6,1854. Parents, John and Mary A. Burnett. Father was a farmer.

BURROUGHS,James L. Feb.14,1854. Parents, Joseph and Sarah Burroughs. Father was a farmer.

FRANKLIN,June, Feb.1854. Slave. Owner, Benj.___(Franklin)

BUFORD,___?___, Oct.1854,Male. Owner, Pascal Buford.

Page 37,

BUFORD,Charlotte,Dec.23,1854. Slave. Owner, Pascal Buford.

BOND,David, 1854. Slave. Owner, Pleasant Bond.

BOND,Jim. Dec.24,1854. Slave. Owner, Pleasant Bond.

BAKER,William B. Jan 12,1854. Parents, Burwell,W. and Margaret Jane Baker. Father was a farmer.

BIRTH RECORDS

BONDURANT,William, May 10,1854. Parents, Silas F. and Elizabeth Jane Bondurant. Father was a farmer.

BURNETT,Mary S.,Sept.1854. Parents, James H. and Lavina Burnett. Father was a farmer.

CROWDER,James T.,April 19,1854. Parents, John H. and Elizabeth F.Crowder. Fahther was a farmer.

CAMPBELL,Charles, Sept.30,1854. Slave. Owner, Susan Campbell.

CRAIGHEAD,Virginia R.,Dec.11,1854. Parents, William B. and Martha A. Craighead. Father was a farmer.

CLARK,Josiah, Dec.27,1854. Parents, George W. and Malinda Clark. Father was a farmer.

CUNDIFF,Mary S.,Sept.1854. Parents, Isaac and Elizabeth Cundiff. Father was a farmer.

CREASY,Sarah C.,Nov.12,1854. Parents, Jefferson and Louisa Jane Creasy. Father was a farmer.

CARDER,Lucy Ann, April 18,1854. Parents, James M. and Sarah Carder.

CHEEK,___?___, Nov.21,1854. Parents, William H. and Susan F.Cheek. Father was a farmer.

CUNDIFF,Lelia B.,Jan.1854. Parents, William B.and Sarah Jane Cundiff. Father was a farmer.

CREASY,Harriett L.,July 16,1854. Parents, David H. and Charlotte Creasy. Father was a farmer.

CRENSHAW,John. Dec.20,1854. Slave. Owner, John Crenshaw

CLAYTOR,McHenry, Aug.11,1854. Parents, William G. and Mary P.Claytor.

CAMPBELL,___?___, 1854.Female. Slave. Owner, Nancy Campbell.

CRAIGHEAD,___?___, March,1854. Male. Parents, Thomas B. and Julia A. Craighead.

CRENSHAW,Alex. Feb.9,1854. Slave. Owner, Richard Crenshaw.

CRENSHAW,Emily,Jan.12,1854. Slave. Owner, Richard Crenshaw.

CRENSHAW,Joanna,Nov.10,1854. Slave. Owner, Richard Crenshaw.

CRUMP,Susan M.,March 21,1854. Parents, Ben and Frances M.Crump.Father was a farmer.

COBBS,___?___, July,1854. Male. Slave. Owner, Tilghiman CObbs.

BIRTH RECORDS

COBBS,Nelly Ann, May 1,1854. Slave. Owner, Tilghiman Cobbs.

COBBS,Minna, July 1,1854. Slave. Owner, Tilghiman Cobbs

COBBS,Sarah Ann, July 1,1854. Slave. Owner, Tilghiman CObbs.

COBBS,Seßt,1,1854.Male. Slave. Owner, Tilghiman Cobbs.

CALLAHAN,Thomas J. April 10,1854. Parents, William and Melvina F.Callahan. Father was a farmer.

Page 38,

Claytor,Adaline,July,1854. Slave. Owner, Edward M. Claytor.

CLAYTOR,__?__, Dec.1854.Male. Slave. Owner, Thomas R. Claytor.

CLAYTOR,Betsey,July,1854. Slave. Owner, Thomas R. Claytor.

COBBS,Doctor, Jan.1854. Slave. Owner, Tilghman A.Cobbs.

CHEWNING,Bob, Nov.23,1854. Slave. Owner, Callahill D. Chewning.

CARTER,Alex. Dec.5,1854. Parents,Berry L.and Charlott Carter. Father was a farmer.

CROUCH,Martha Ann, Oct,1854. Parents, Joel and Sarah Crouch. Father was a farmer.

CARTER,Berry J.,Nov.20,1854. Parents, Benjamin F. and Martha Ann Carter. Father was a farmer.

CARROL,Martha J.,Dec.9,1854. Parents, Thomas D. and Hannah Carrol.

DICKERSON,Frances Elizabeth,June. 1854. Parents, James and Eviline Dickerson. Father was a farmer.

DICKERSON,__?__,1854.Slave. Female. Owner,William Dickerson.

DENT,Edmond,Feb.10,1854. Parents,Morganly and Martha Dent. Father was a farmer.

DEARING,Eliza,Feb.6,1854. Parents, Edward W. and Frances Dearing. Father was a farmer.

DREWRY,James. Sept.1854. Parents, Joseph C. and Mary F. Drewry. Father was a farmer.

DICKERSON,Sarah Jane, May 19,1854. Parents, Clemmons and Mary Ann Dickerson, Father was a farmer.

DICKEY,Harriet,T.R.,March 12,1854. Parents, Rufus L. and Catherine A. Dickey. Father was a Miller.

BIRTH RECORDS

DENT,Ann Booker,Sept.3,1854. Slave. Owner, Marbell N. Dent.

DENT,Arbuter. April 3,1854. Slave. Owner, Joel Dent.

DEBO,Mary, Dec.17,1854. Parents, John and Jane Debo.

DICKERSON,__?_, Sept.1854. Female. Slave. Owner, William Dickerson.

DICKERSON,__?_, 1854. Female. Slave. Owner, William Dickerson.

DICKERSON, Stephen,July,1854.Slave. Owner, William Dickerson .

DICKERSON,__?_, Sept.1854. Slave. Owner, William Dickerson.

DICKERSON,Robin,Dec.6,1854. Slave.Owner, William Dickerson.

DICKERSON,__?_,Dec.28,1854. Slave.Male. Owner, William Dickerson.

DOOLEY,John, Dec.23,1854. Parents, Jabez and Harmony Dooley.

DENT,Charles,June 16,1854.Parents, John J. and Mary Dent.

Page 39,

EARLY,Helen B.,April 17,1854.FN. Parent, Eliza R.Early.

ELLIOTT,Rothnell,M.,Oct.4,1854. Parents, Charles H. and Frances Elliott. Father was a Carpenter.

ENGLISH,Mary Jane, Aug.26,1854. Parents, John W. and Sarah E. English.

FUQUA,Eliza B.,Aug.1,1854. Parents,Granville and Martha M. Fuqua. Father was a farmer.

FIZER,Abram, June,1854. Parents, Charles B. and Frances J. Fizer. Father was a farmer.

FRANKLIN,__?_,Aug.,1854. Parents, William and Martha B. Franklin. Father was a farmer.

FARISS,Mary, May,1854. Slave. Owner, Anderson C. Fariss.

FRAILING,Ladilia,W.,June 14,1854. Parents, Robert A. and Sarah F. Frailing. Father was a farmer.

FEATHER,Medora J.,Nov.5,1854. Parents,Henry P. and Ann Elizabeth Feather. Father was a Carpenter.

FOUTZ,Yelverton,L. Feb.1854. Parents, Green B. and Martha A. Foutz. Father was a Shoemaker.

BIRTH RECORDS

FUQUA,Mary E.,Oct.7,1854. Parents, Benjamin B. and Bermelia J. Fuqua. Father was a farmer.

FOSTER,Patrick L. Aug.6,1854. Parents,Rich A. and Nancy Foster.Father was a farmer.

FUQUA,Caleb. July 31,1854. Parents, Martin L. and Martha Jane Fuqua. Father was a farmer.

FUQUA,___?___, Jan.25,1854. Slave. Owner, Joshua Fuqua.

FALLS,Mary E. June 14,1854. Parents,Daniel and Cynthia Falls. Father was a farmer.

FUQUA,___?___, Jan.25,1854. Male. Slave. Owner,Thomas Fuqua.

FISHER,Lindsay, Oct.15,1854. Parents, Thomas Jr. and Mary Frances Fisher. Father was a farmer.

FUQUA,Saml F.,Feb.14,1854. Parents, John H. and Eliza Fuqua. Father was a farmer.

FRANKLIN,___?___, 1854. Male. Parents, Jesse H. and Locky Franklin. Father was a farmer.

GARRETT,Emma C. March,1854. Parents, Elijah and Margaret B. Garrett.

GIBBS,James D. Nov.26,1854. Parents, William A. and Mary A. Gibbs. Father was a farmer.

GIBBS,Mary,June 21,1854. Slave. Owner, Joel Gibbs.

GILL,Jinny Lind. June,1854. Slave. Owner, Charles Gill

GOAD,Richard P.,June 19,1854. Parents, James M. and Elizabeth Goad. Father was a farmer.

GARRETT,___?___, Oct.2,1854.Female. Parents, Absalon and Sarah C. Garrett. Father was a farmer.

GIBBS,Rob Henry, Feb.1854. Parents, Jesse R. and Frances A. Gibbs.

GOGGIN,Martha C.,July 26,1854. Parents, william L. and Elizabeth L. Goggin. Father was a farmer.

GOGGIN,___?___, Feb.1854. Female. Slave. Owner, William L Goggin.

GIBBS,Celia, April,1854. Slave. Owner, Esman A. Gibbs

GIBBS,Sarah, Dec.1854. Parents, Paschal N. and Betty Gibbs. Father was a farmer.

GOAD,___?___, Aug.13,1854. Parents, William R. and Martha F. Goad. Father was a Mechanic.

GOODWIN,William, July 20,1854. Parents, Jesse B. and J Jane Goodwin. Parent was a farmer.

BIRTH RECORDS

Page 40,

GRAY,Ann H.,Aug.,1854. Parents, Alex and Lucinda Gray. Father was a farmer.

GWALTNEY,Julia E.,Dec. 23,1854. Parents, Albert and Mary Gwaltney. Father was farmer.

BOARD,George, April,1854. Slave. Owner, Frances Board

GRISBY,Cary, Jan.27,1854. Slave. Owner, James Grisby.

GRAY,James A.,Oct.10,1854. Parents, james and Rachel Gray.

GOGGIN,Martha, Feb.14,1854. Slave. Owner,Stephen Goggin

GOGGIN,Henreitta,March 10,1854. Slave. Owner, Stephen Goggin.

HENSLEY,James A.,Aug.1,1854. Parents, Saml W. and Mary A. Hensley. Father was a farmer.

HOPKINS,___?___, 1854.Male. Slave. Owner, Frances G.Hopkins.

HUGHS,_____ &_____,Twins,Died. June,1854.Slave. Owner, Saml Hughs.

HUGHS, Daniel, 1854. Slave. Owner,Saml Hughs.

HOLDREN,___?___, Dec.23,1854.Male. Parents, Jackson B.and Mary Holdren. Father was a farmer.

HOLDREN,___?___, 1854. Parents, John and Patsy Holdren. Father was a farmer.

HOFFMAN,Mary F.,Nov.14,1854. Parents,Saml and Frances L.Hoffman. Father was a Merchant.

HAYNES,___?___, Dec.1854. Male. Parents, Jacob and Adaline Haynes. Father was a farmer.

HURT,Ellen, Aug.24,1854. Parents, Joel L. and Sally Hurt. Father was a farmer.

HURT,Simon Peter, Jan.1854. Slave. Owner, Joel L. Hurt

HERNDEN, Ally,Jan.20,1854. Slave. Owner, Elizabeth Hernden.

HICKS,___?___, Oct.7,1854. Female. Slave. Owner, William Hicks.

HEPENSTALL,___?___, 1854. Female. Slave. Owner, Caleb Hepenstall.

HACKWORTH, Betsey Ann, Jan.1,1854.Parents, Wesley and Martha Hackworth. Father was a farmer.

HUBBARD,Mary F.,May,1854. Parents, Bangasland and Sarah M.Hubbard . Father was a farmer.

BIRTH RECORDS

HUBBARD, __?__ , June,1854. Female. Parents, John and Emsey Hubbard.

Hancock, William D.,May 17,1854. Parents, John H. and Martha Jane Hancock.

HOGAN,George W.,July 23,1854. Parents, Washington.and Nancy J.Hogan.

HOWELL,Alex W., Dec.1854. Parents, Pleasant and Silina Howell.

HATCHER,Mary L.,May 30,1854. Parents, Spencer and Jo-annah Hatcher.

HUDDLESTON,__?__ , June 7,1854.Slave. Owner, John Huddl-ston.

HEULL,William C. Feb.14,1854. Parents, John and Malinda Huhll.

HULL,Octavia,July 7,1854. Slave. Owner, Samuel Hull

HULL,Pleasant, March 15,1854. Slave. Owner, Samuel Hull

Page 41,

JOHNSON,Henry, 1854. Slave. Owner, William Johnson

JOHNSON,John, 1854. Slave. Owner, William Johnson

JORDAN,George,June,1854. Slave. Owner, John Jordan

JAMES, Matson, July 6,1854. Parents, Elias and Agness L. James.

JORDAN,Ann E.,April 10,1854. Parents, Alex and Lucy Ann Jordan. Father was a Tobacconist.

JETER,Amanda, Aug.,1854. Slave. Owner, Henry E. Jeter

JONES,Oscar W. June 7,1854. Parents, Rob E. and Lydia Jones. Father was a farmer.

JONES,Milligan, Dec.9,1854. Slave. Owner, Henry Jones

IRVINE, Henry, Nov.1854. Slave. Owner, Alex Irvine

IRVINE,Carter, Dec.1854. Slave. Owner, Alex Irvine.

JONES,Lewis,March,1854. Slave. Owner, Elizabeth Jones.

JONES,Anthony, may,1854. Slave. Owner, Elizabeth Jones

MORRIS, __?__ , Dec.,1854. Male. SLave. Mother, Nancy Morris.

JONES, __?__ , Dec.1854. Male. Slave. Owner, Daniel Jones

JONES,George, Aug.30,1854.Male. Slave.Owner, Daniel P. Jones.

JONES,Fletcher,May 15,1854. Parents, Rob.C. and Emily E. Jones. Father was a farmer.

BIRTH RECORDS

JONES,Pleasant,May 12,1854.Slave. Owner, Rob Jones.

JOHNSON,Thomas,Feb.8,1854. Parents, George W. and Sarah Ann E. Johnson. Father was a farmer.

JOHNSON,Edward J. Aug.7,1854. Parents, William W. and Ruth Ann Johnson. Father was a farmer.

JORDAN,___?__,1854.Slave. Owner, Jubal Jordan.

JORDAN,___?__, 1854. Slave. Owner,Jubal Jordan

JORDAN,___?__, 1854. Slave. Owner, Jubal Jordan

JORDAN,,___?__, 1854. Slave. Owner, Jubal Jordan

JORDAN,___?__, 1854, Slave. Owner, Jubal Jordan

JETER,Susan,Aug.1,1854. Parents, Beverly R. and Mary Ann Jeter.

JACOBS,___?__, Aug.1,1854. Slave. Owner, Aaron Jacobs

KASEY,___?__, Oct.18,1854. Parents, James S. and Mary F. Kasey. Father was a Merchant.

KASEY,_____,Aug.14,1854. Parents, John G. and Elvira F. Kasey. Father was a CLerk.

KASEY,David, 1854. Slave. Owner, Thomas Kasey.

KIRBY,___?__, May,1854. Parents,Wyatt and Magdaline Kirby. Father was a farmer.

KASEY,Texannah,Aug.1854. Parents, James C. and Mary Louisa Kasey. Father was a farmer.

KASEY,Mary,Aug.27,1854. Parents,Newlon and Mary Kasey. Father was a farmer.

___?__, ___?__, May,1854. Female,Slave. Owner, John ___?__, (Page torn)

KIDWELL,John, June,1854. Parents, Hezekiah and Elizabeth F. Kidwell.Father was a farmer.

KEATTS,Saml H. Nov.10,1854. Parents,James and Sallie W. Keatts. Father was a farmer.

Page # 42,

LEFTWICH,Alfred,may 30,1854. Slave. Owner, James Leftwich Est.

LOYD,Lewis,Dec.,1854. Slave. Owner, James Loyd Jr.

LAUGHLIN,John,Oct. 1854. Parents, James and Elizabeth J. Laughlin.

LEFTWICH,___?__, 1854. Male. Slave. Owner, Alex Leftwich

LEFTWICH,___?__, 1854. Female. Slave. Owner, Alex Leftwich.

BIRTH RECORDS

LEE,___?___, July 4,1854.Male. Parents, James G. and Susan Lee. Father was farmer.

LEFTWICH Casseius,L.,March 25,1854. Parents, Valentine and Eveline Leftwich. Father was a farmer.

LACY,Alvira F. & Wilsa Ann,(Twins) march 17,1854.Parents, Thomas J. and Alvira Lacy.

LUGAR,___?___, & ___?___, (Twins)Females. Slaves. Owner, Thompson Lugar.

LUMPKIN,Taswell,Nov.1854. Slave. Owner, Robert W. LUmpkin.

LYLE,Judah M. July 2,1854. Parents, William and Lucinda Lyle. Father was a farmer.

LAUGHON,Landona,Oct.13,1854. Parents, Noah and Elizabeth Laughon.

MOORMAN,___?___, 1854. Female. Slave. Owner, Saml P.R. Moorman.

MOORMAN,___?___, 1854,Female. Slave. Owner, Saml P.R. Moorman.

MEADOR,Booker,Aug.1854. Slave. Owner, Wilson Meador.

MAUPIN,John R. April 10,1854. Parents, Carr M. and Frances Maupin. Father was a farmer.

MEADOR,Rosannah,Oct.1854. Parents, Edward A. and Agnes E. Meador. Father was a farmer.

MAEDOR,Sarah, Aug.3,1854. Parents, Whitfield and Sarah A. Maedor.

MARSHAL,Mary E.,Nov.16,1854. Parents, John R. and Mary E. Marshal. Father was a farmer.

MARSHAL,Gilbert & ___?___, (Twins),April,1854. Slaves. Owner, John R. Marshal.

MATTON,Robert A. April 27,1854. Parents, Robert P. and Martha M. matton. Father was a farmer.

MEAD,_William,June.1854. Slave. Owner, William Mead

MEAD,William, 1854. Slave. Owner, William Mead.

MEAD,Virginia,Oct.1854. Slave. Owner, William Mead.

MILSON,___?___, Dec.9,1854. Parents, John D. and Mary Milson. Father was a farmer.

MOULTON,Mary Ellen,June,1854. Parents, Benjamin and Mary Moulton. Father was a Physician.

METTS,John W.,March 10,1854. Parents, John R. and Matilda V. Metts.

BIRTH RECORDS

MITCHELL,Mildred E.,Aug.1854. Parents, John and Parthena Mitchell.

DANIEL,Nancy,July 12,1854. Slave. Owner, Loudon McDaniel

McDANIEL,Laura,Aug.30,1854. Slave. Owner, Loudon MCDaniel.

MITCHELL,William C.,June 1,1854. Parents, Thomas C. and
Mildred Ann Mitchell.

Page # 43,

MATTON,Medora T.,May 16,1854. Parents, Michal T. and
Mary Jane Matton. Father was a farmer.

MORGAN,Taswell,Dec.25,1854. Parents, Jesse and Julia
Morgan. Father was a farmer.

MAXY,Victoria F.,Sept.1,1854. Parents,Isaac and Elizabeth Maxy. Father was a farmer.

KEALLAYS,John, Jan.1,1854. Slave. Owner,James D.Keallays

MORRIS,Sarah S.,May 26,1854.Parents,Micajah G. and
Lively Morris. Father was a farmer.

MITCHELL,Billy,Jan.26,1854. Slave. Owner, William C.
Mitchell.

MUSGROVE,Filmore,Dec.1854. Slave. Owner, John H.Musgrove

MILLER,__?__, Dec.,1854.Male,Slave. Owner, William S.
Miller.

MILLER, James W.,July 4,1854. Parents, William S. and
Sarah Jane Miller. Father was a farmer.

MARTIN, Green M.,March 9,1854. Parents, Green B. and
Naomah C.Martin, Father was a farmer.

MITCHELL,Gustavus J.,Nov.17,1854. Parents, Robert and
Sallt Mitchell. Father was a farmer.

MITCHELL,__?__, Dec.24,1854.Male. Parents, Edward O.P.
and Martha E. Mitchell.

MITCHELL,Ann,April,1854. Slave. Owner, Saml M.Mitchell

MORGAN,Whitfield, April 30,1854. Slave. Owner, Christopher Morgan.

MORGAN,Alex, Sept.9,1854. Slave. Owner, Christopher
Morgan.

MORGAN,Ann, Sept.1854. Slave. Owner, Christopher Morgan

McCLAIN,John L., May 26,1854. Parents, William and
Lettitia McClain.

McCLAIN,Pleasant, 1854. Slave. Owner, James McClain.

BIRTH RECORDS

McCABE,James Harvey, Feb.1,1854. Slave. Owner, Malinda McCabe.

McCABE,John Robert,Nov.1854. Slave. Owner,Malinda McCabe.

MARTIN,Gilly Ann,July 7,1854. Parents, Jobe and Cynthia Martin.

Page # 44,

NEWSOM,Ann O.,Oct.26,1854. Parents, Nathaniel and Lucy Ann Newsom.

NEWSOM,__?_, Jan.1854. Female. Slave. Owner, Nathaniel Newsom.

NEIGHBORS,__?_, Oct.1854. Female. Parents, Chris and Lucy Ann Neighbors.

NANCE,Sarah M.,March 23,1854. Parents, Thomas W. and Elizabeth Nance.

NANCE,Henry,Aug.1854.Slave. Owner, Thorp H.Nance.

NEIGHBORS,Eliza Ann, Aug.1854. Parents, Anderson and Mary Ann Neighbors.

NANCE,__?_, June 30,1854.Male. Parents,Albert L. and Jane Nance.

NELMS,Florilla M.,Sept.1854. Parents, Charles D. and Mary E. Nelms.

NELMS,Jac Ben.Jan.1854. Slave. Owner, Charles D.Nelms

NOWLIN,__?_, May,1854. Male. Owner, James H. and Jane Nowlin.

NEWMAN,Mary Ann J.,Oct.8,1854. Parents, James W. and Mary Ann Newman.

NEWSOM,March 10,1854. Slave. Owner, Elizabeth Newsom.

OVERSTREET,__?_, March 29,1854.Male. Owner, Thomas Overstreet.

OVERSTREET,__?_, 1854. Female. Slave. Owner, Thomas Overstreet.

OWNSBY,Charles L.,March 25,1854. Parents, Charles P. and Catherine J. Ownsby.

OVERSTREET,Robert W.,Jan.25,1854.Parents, William B. and Catherine Overstreet.

OVERSBTREET,Tabitha J. March 19,1854. Parents, Alex and Tabitha Overstreet.

OVERSTREET,John S.,July 2,1854. Parents, Jesse and Ann E. Overstreet.

OVERSTREET,Maria V.,July,1854. Parents, John G. and Lucy Overstreet.

BIRTH RECORDS

OAHS,Amanza,Oct.6,1854. Parents, Rice T. and Susan Oahs. Father was a Cabinetmaker.

Page # 45,

PATTERSON,Clara H.,Feb.13,1854. Parents, Thomas and Phebe Jane Patterson. Father was a Blacksmith.

PREAS,John Henry,May 9,1854. Slave. Owner, Henry Preas

PENDLETON,Ann H.,Jan.22,1854. Parents, Henry and Nancy Pendleton. Father was a Blacksmith.

PRESTON,Lucy,AUg.12,1854. Slave. Owner, John S.Preston

PATE,___?___, Oct.20,1854. Slave. male. Owner, Cornelius Pate.

PATE,___?___, Dec.1854. Female.Slave. Owner, Cornelius Pate.

PULLEN,___?___, Nov.1854. Female.Slave. Owner, Charlotte Pullen.

PULLEN,_Sally,1854. Slave. Owner, Charlotte Pullen.

PARKER,Plunkett,July,1854. Slave. Owner, Caleb D.Parker

PHELPS,William R.,May 20,1854. Parents, Thomas J. and Malinda P.Phelps. Father was a farmer.

PHELPS,John Booker,March 30,1854. Slave. Owner, Thomas J.Phelps.

PULLEN,Caroline,Feb.15,1854. Parents, William F. and Jane Pullen. Father was a farmer.

PAYNE,John R.,May,1854. Parents, Thomas Q. and Mary A. Payne. Father was a farmer.

PULLEN,Granville,F.,Oct.20,1854. Parents, Jesse and Frances Pullen, father was a farmer.

POINDEXTER,Dabney,Jan.4,1854. Parents, James W. and Sophia Poindexter. Father was a farmer.

PEARCY,Ann E.,Nov.1854. Parents, William and Frances O. Pearcy. Father was a farmer.

PEARCY,Henry,April,1854. Slave. Owner, William Pearcy

PETERS,Mosa, Nov.5,1854.Parents, James H. and Paulina S. Peters. father was a farmer.

PRESTON,Mary, May,1854. Slave. Owner, William Preston.

PREAS,Alex, Aug.12,1854. Slave. Owner, Thomas Preas

PERDUE,Emanuel,Nov.27,1854. Parents, JohnWW.and Lucy J. Perdue.

PATTERSON,Elizabeth,Oct.4,1854. parents, Moultry and Susan Patterson.

BIRTH RECORDS

PRESTON,Clay,Oct.9, Slave. Owner, Christopher Preston

PRESTON,Fletcher,Feb.22,1854. Slave. Owner, Christopher Preston.

PARKER,Banks,Aug.3,1854. Slave. Owner, martha D.Parker

PRESTON,Jesse A.,April 29,1854. Parents, John F. and Mary Ann Preston.

QUARLES,Edward B.,Dec.17,1854. Parents, John W. and Cornelia Quarles.

QUARLES,Caswell, April,1854. Slave. Owner, John W. Quarles.

QUARLES,Flora, 1854. Slave. Owner, Susan Quarles.

QUARLES,__?__, Nov.20,1854. Male. Slave. Owner,John Quarles.

Page # 46,

ROBERTSON,Celia Ann,May 1,1854. Parents, Nichoolas W. and Sally Robertson. Father was a farmer.

ROBERTSON,James,1854, Slave. Owner, Nicholas Robertson

ROBERTSON,Dennis,1854. Slave. Owner, Nicholas Robertson

RAMSEY,__?__, March 13,1854. (Died). Mother,Margarett Ramsey.

ROBERTSON,__?__, 1854.(Twins).(Died). Slaves. Owner, Francis W.Robertson.

ROBERTSON,__?__, 1854. Male. Slave.(Died). Owner,Francis Robertson.

ROBERTSON,__?__, 1854. Male.Slave. (Died).Owner,Francis Robertson.

ROBERTSON,__?__, 1854. Female. Slave. Owner, Francis Robertson.

ROBERTSON,1854. Male. Slave. Owner, Francis Robertson.

ROBERTSON,__?__, 1854. Female. Slave. Owner, Francis Robertson.

ROBERTS,Victoria,Sept.10,1854. Parents, Josiah B. and Ann A. Roberts.

ROBERTS,George F.,1854. Parents, John G. and Sally Roberts

SWAIN,__?__, June,1854. Male. Slave. Owner, Elijah Swain

SWAIN,__?__, June,1854. Female,Slave. Owner, Elijah Swain

SPRADLIN,Martha E.,July,1854. Parents, Meador Jr. and Sarah Spradlin.

SAUNDERS,__?__, Oct.1854. Female. Parents, Phillip and Eleanor Saunders.

BIRTH RECORDS

STAILEY,__?__, July,1854. Female. Parents, David and Martha Ann Stailey.

SWAIN,nancy S.,1854. Parents, Pleasant and Emily Swain.

SWAIN,Patricia Ann, March,1854. Parents, Robert G. and Eliza Swain.

STUMP,Sarah B., Feb.28,1854. Parents, William B. and Martha Ann Stump.

SAUNDERS,Prudence, May 10,1854. Slave. Owner, Julius Saunders.

SKINNELL,Missouri H.,Jan.1854. Parents, George E. and Elizabeth A. Skinnell.

SKINNELL,Lucinda,Jan.1854. Slave. Owner, George E. Skinnell.

STILLER,John P.,Oct.17,1854. Parents, John and Mary Ann Stiller.

SIMS,William T.W.,July 9,1854. Parents, William B. and Judith Sims.

SMITH,Julia,Aug.1,1854. Slave. Owner, William C. Smith

STEPTOE,Mary E.,May 2,1854. Parents, John R. and Sarah P.Steptoe. Father was a Clerk and farmer.

STEPTOE,John, May,1854. Slave. Owner, John R.Steptoe.

SAUNDERS,Martha, Feb.1854. Slave. Owner, Thomas T. Saunders

SCOTT,__?__, Oct.21,1854. Female. Parents, Thomas W. and Sarah M.Scott.Father was a Laborer.

SUBLETT,John Irvine, Dec.1854. Parents, Edmund and Sarah Sublett. Father was an Overseer.

STIFF,George W.,Sept.1,1854. parents, james M. and Lucy Ann Stiff. Father was a Carpenter.

SUBLETT,William Henry, July,1854. Slave. Owner, Nancy Sublett.

Page # 47.

Stevens,Elizabeth J.,June 1,1854. parents, John M. and Susan Stevens.. Father was a farmer.

SAUNDERS,__?__, Feb.1854. Female. Parents, Henry and Eliza Ann Saunders. Father was a farmer.

SAUNDERS,__?__, June 20,1854.Female. Parents, William and Florentine Saunders. Father was a farmer.

SAUNDERS,Waddy,march,1854. Slave. Owner, William Saunders.

BIRTH RECORDS

SMITH,_?_, Dec.1854.Male. Slave. Owner, Stephen Smith

SKINNELL,Daniel P.,Jan.1854. Parents, James and Rebecca
G. Skinnell.Father was a farmer.

STONE,_?_, May,1854. Parents, Thomas and Jane Stone.

SMELSOR,Charles W.,Dec. 1854. Parents,Paschal and
Frances Smelsor. Father was a farmer.

STCLAIR,Ruhanna A.,June 25,1854. Parents,Robert and
Rhoda STClair. Father was a Tanner.

SCRUGGS,Theophilus M.,Oct.8,1854. Parents, William B.
and Nancy M. Scruggs.

SCRUGGS,Henry,May 16,1854. Slave. Owner, William B.
Scruggs.

SMITH,John A.,July 7,1854. Parents, Alex B. and Mahala
Smith. Father was a farmer.

SWAIN,Jeffrey C.,March 2,1854. Parents, Callahill M.
and Ellen Swain. Farmer was a farmer.

SMITH,Lucy J.,June 16,1854. Parents, Alex A. and Ursula
Smith. Father was a farmer.

SMITH,Stephen,1854. Male. Slave. Owner, Alex A. Smith

SHOAN,Ann,March,1854. Slave. Owner,James K.Shoan

SETTLE,_?_, March 31,1854. Male. Parents, John S.and
Barberry Settle. Father was a farmer.

STIFF,_?_, June 5,1854. Male. Parents, Burwell and
July Ann Stiff. Father was a farmer.

STINETT,Tandy,April 13,1854. Parents, Pleasant E. and
Elizabeth Stinett.

SMITH,_?_, Nov.28,1854. Male. Parents, George W. and
Priscilla Smith.

THURMAN,_?_, Jan.4,1854.Female. Parents, Austin and
Anna Maria Thurman. Father was a Merchant.

THOMAS, Saml H.& Laura V.,(Twins).Feb.1,1854. Parents,
Nikson and Mary Jane Thomas.Father was a farmer.

TAYLOR,Sarah B.,Feb.1854. Parents, Elisha B. and
Sarah Taylor.

THOMASON,_?_, Nov.29,1854. Male. Parents, Thomas J.
and Sarah Thomason.

THOMAS,Rosey,Sept.1854. Slave. Owner, Fleming S.
Thomas.

THOMAS,Sarah E.,Oct.1854. Parents, John and Susan
Thomas.

TOMPKINS,____,Female. 1854. Slave. Owner, Daniel
Tompkins.

BIRTH RECORDS

TINSLEY,Adaline, Sept.10,1854. Slave. Owner, Saml
G. Tinsley.

TERRY,Sam,may,1854. Slave. Owner, Henry Terry.

TERRY,Lucy Ann, Dec.,1854. Slave. Owner, henry Terry.

THOMAS,Laura,Jan. 1854. Parents,Elderidge and Luvina
Thomas.

Page # 48,

UPDIKE,___?__ , Oct.1854. Male. Slave. Owner, Saml Updike

WINGFIELD,Milis,April 25,1854. Slave. Owner, Nelson
D. Wingfield.

WRIGHT,Nicholas,1854. Slave. Owner, james Wright

WRIGHT,Lettitia,1854. Slave. Owner,james Wright

WILLS,Robert,Sept.1854. Parents, Edward M. and Mary
Wills. Father was a farmer.

WILLS,America,May 25,1854. Slave. Owner, John B.Wills

WALKER,Jesse,April 12,1854. Slave. Owner, Thomas
Walker.

WILKS,Henry S.,Jan.26,1854. parents, William G. and
Elizabeth Wilks. Father was a farmer.

WRIGHT,Jubal,June,1854. Parents, Jubal J. and Martha
E. Wright

WHEELER,Mary A.,Feb.1854. parents, Wilson and Nancy
Wheeler.

WHORLEY,Virginia M.,Jan.1854. Parents, Francis W. and
Eliza Whorley.

WHORLEY,Louisa, Nov.1854. Slave. Owner, Francis Whorley.

WHITE,___?__, Dec.14,1854. Male.Parents, Samuel G. and
Catherine White.

WOOD,Martha Ann,Dec.15,1854. Parents, jeremiah and
Terrissa Wood.

WOOD,Laura E.,1854. parents, Charles W. and Mary Ann
Wood.

WITT,Albert R.,May 20,1854. Parents, John E.and Alis
Witt.

WILSON,___?__ , Nov.23,1854. Female. Parents, James R.
and Evalina Wilson.

WALKER,John W.,Dec.20,1854. parents, Saml P. and
Dosha Walker.

BIRTH RECORDS

WALKER,Joe, April 1854. Slave. Owner, Saml P. Walker

WITT,Susan,Feb.1854. Slave. Owner, William Witt

WOOD,Sally D.,Sept.9,1854. Parents, William H. and Patra Wood.

WILKERSON,Sam,1854. Slave. Owner, Joseph Wilkerson

WADE,Martha,June,1854. Slave. Owner, William Wade

WADE,___?__, Oct.1854. Male.(Died) Slave.Owner, Mary Wade.

WADE,Squin,Sept.15,1854.Slave. Owner, Mary E. Wade

WITT,Charles,Aug.1,1854. parents, William W. and Nancy A. Witt.

WAYNE,__?__, March 14,1854. Parents, John Q.A. and Margaret Ann Wayne.

WELLS,Christopher C.,Aug.21,1854. Parents, Richard M. and Harriet Wells

WELLS,Martha,June,1854.

WOOD,___?__, Aug.25,1854.Male. Parents, Tilghman A. and Jennetta Wood.

WOOD,___?__, Sept. 1854. Female. Parents, John B. and Julia Ann Wood.

WHITE,Julia, Aug.1854. Slave. Owner, Jesse White.

WHITE,William Henry, Sept.1854. Parents, Alex and Jane White.

WHITTEN,John P.,Feb.1854,Parents, Joseph and Jane P. Whitten.

WHITTEN,___?__, Nov.1854. Female.Slave. Owner,Joseph Whitten.

WOOD,Wesley C.,Sept.18,1854. Parents, William O. and Almara Wood.

WALROND,James,may 25,1854. Parents, Moses and Nancy Walrond.

WILLIAMS,Josafine,Oct.2,1854. Parents, Charles M. and Susan Williams.

WILKS,___?__, Oct.1854. Male (Died). Parents, Henry and Harry Wilks.

PAGE # 49,

WILLIAMS,Martha J.,Nov.1,1854. Parents, John J. and Selina Williams.

WHEELER,Littitia, June 6,1854.Slave. Owner, George Wheeler.

BIRTH RECORDS

WRIGHT,William H.,Sept.1854. Slave. Owner, Joseph Wright.

WHEELER,Gabriel T.,Sept.2,1854. Parents, Solomon and Elizabeth Wheeler.

WHEELER,Saml T.,June,1854. Parents, Thomas and Sarah E. Wheeler.

WADE,___?__, Dec.1,1854. Female. Slave. Owner,Isaac Wade

WADE,James T.,Nov.1854. Parents, Alex and Lucinda Wade

Page # 50 1855

AGEE,Peter Emmet,Nov.16,1855. Parents, Arkless E. and Barbara Ann Agee. Father was a farmer.

ARRINGTON,James,march 5,1855.parents, David and Nancy S.Arrington.Father was a farmer.

APPERSON,John Washington,July 24,1855.Parents, John G. and Sarah S. Apperson. Father was a farmer.

ADAMS,___?__, April 10,1855. parents, Stephen and Mary V.Adams.Father was a farmer.

ARTHUR,___?__, MARCH,1855.Male. Slave. Mother, Mary. Owner, Lewis C.Arthur.

ARTHUR,Jesse,April,1855, Slave. Mother, Parthena. Owner, Lewis C.Arthur.

ARTHUR,___?__, March,1855,(Died).Slave.Mother, Betsey. Owner, Lewis C.Arthur
ARTHUR,___?__, March 2,1855. Slave. Mother, Harriett. Owner, Lewis C. Arthur.

BONDURANT,William C.,May 10,1855. Parents, Silas F. and Elizabeth J.Bondurant. Father was a farmer.

BLACK,Mary Elizabeth, May,1855. Parents, Benjamin and Matilda Black

BOYLE,Mary Elizabeth, April 19,1855. Parents, James A. and Elnora G. Boyle.

BURKHOLDER,John,Oct.1855. Parents, James and Martha Burkholder. Father was a farmer.

BROWN,James Walker,Sept. 7,1855. Parents, John W. and Susan Brown. Father was a farmer.

BLAKE,Sarah Allis, FN. Aug.31,1855.Parents,Reubin and Mary Blake.

BOLEY,Agness McDaniel,March 26,1855.Parents,John and Martha Ann Boley.

BURNETT,Mary Nealy,July 16,1855.Parents,Charles T.and Catherine Burnett. Father was a farmer.

BIRTH RECORDS

BELL,John. June,1855, Slave. Mother, Malinda. Owner, Francis H. Bell.

BELL,___?___, July 28,1855. Female. Slave. Mother,Musidora. Owner, Francis H. Bell.

BROOKS,___?___, Dec.,1855. Male. Parents, John and Laniza Brooks, Father was a farmer.

BARNETT,Anna Wilmer, Oct.21,1855. Parents, David and Fannie R. Barnett.

BAKAN,___?___, Oct.8,1855.Male. Parents, Patrick and Elizabeth Bakan.

BRYANT,Gillmore,June 18,1855. Parents, Jesse S. and Phebe A. Bryant.

BRYANT,Hubbard Harrison, July 25,1855. Parents, Andrew and Mary Bryant.

BELLEMY,Sarah, Sept 15,1855.Slave. Mother, Margaret. Owner, Miss Patsey Bellemy.

BOWER,Mary Emily,Jan.14,1855. Parents, George H.Jr.and June Q.Bower. Father was a farmer.

BRUCE,___?___, June,1855. Female. Mother, Nancy Bruce

BROWN,Gerry,Oct. 1855.Slave. Mother, Dicy. Owner, Spottswood Brown.

BROWN,Sam,June,1855. Slave. Mother, Sarah. Owner, Spottswood Brown.

BOLEY,John Henry,July 10,1855. Slave. Owner, Doc Boley.

Page # 51.

CARNEFIX,Charles,May 14,1855. Slave. Mother, Mary. Owner, Edward Carnefix.

CARTER,Albert. Oct.15,1855.Parents,James A. and Lucy Carter. Father was a farmer.

COLEMAN,Bob,Aug.1855. Slave. Mother, Fillis. Owner, Leroy Coleman.

COLEMAN,Sarah Elizabeth, Aug.1855. Parents, Nicholas and Amanda Coleman.

COLEMAN,Nancy. may, 1855. Slave. Mother, Tina. Owner, Jesse Coleman.

COFER,Paulus Good, Sept.21,1855. Parents, John and Sophia Ann Cofer.

COFER,Edward, Oct.1855. Slave. Mother, Mary. Owner, James M.Cofer.

CLAYTOR,Harriett, Nov.1855. Slave. Mother, Milly. Owner, William Claytor.

BIRTH RECORDS

CLAY,Willie Shelton, March 28,1855. Parents,Paul A. and mary L. CLay. Father was a farmer.

CLAY,Washington, Dec.8,1855. Slave. Mother, Selia. Owner, paul Clay.

CLAY,Ann Eliza,Dec.22,1855. Slave. Mother, Mariah. Owner, Paul Clay.

CLAY,Cary, Oct.1855. Slave. Mother, mary. Owner, John A. Clay.

CHRISTIAN,Richard Bozwell, Feb.11,1855.Parents, Robert A. and Anna Christian. father was a Physician.

CHRISTIAN,George, Jen. 1855.Slave. Mother, Mariah. Owner, Francis Christian.

CHRISTIAN,Guy, June,1855. Slave. Mother, Sarah. Owner, Francis Christian.

CAMPBELL,Sallie, Jan. 13,1855. Parents, Thomas and Martha S. Campbell. Father was a farmer.

COBBS,Mahala,Jan.14,1855. Slave. Mother, Martha. Owner, John C. Cobbs.

CAMPBELL,John Monroe,April 25,1855. Parents, James W. and Elizabeth Campbell. Father was a carpenter.

CALLAWAY,John,Jan.15,1855.Slave. Mother, Rachel.Owner, John Callaway.

CALLAWAY,Quince,Feb.14,1855.Slave. Mother, Permelia. Owner, John Callaway.

CALLAWAY,Henry,Aug.6,1855.Slave. Mother, Ann. Owner, John Callaway.

CHEATWOOD,Carter, Dec.1855. Slave. Mother, Milly. Owner, Daniel B.Cheatwood.

CABLER,Alice,July,1855. Slave. Mother, Lucy. Owner, Mrs Catherine Cabler.

CABLER, Margaret, July,1855. Slave. Mother, Ann.Owner, Mrs Catherine Cabler.

COPPAGE,Alfred Brown, June 20,1855. parents, L.J. and Martha Ann Coppage. Father was a factory worker.

CARUTHERS,Azela, Oct.21,1855. Parents, William H. and Ann H. Caruthers. father was a farmer.

CARTER,Victoria,July 6,1855. Parents, Jefferson P. and Mary Ann Carter. Father was a farmer.

DAVENPORT,Ellen Victoria, Nov.1855. Parents, William and Minerva Davenport. Father was a farmer.

DONALD,John, July,1855. Slave. Mother, Caroline.Owner, Benjamin A. Donald.

BIRTH RECORDS

DAVIDSON,John,March,1855. Slave. Mother, Fanny. Owner,
Mayo Davidson.

DAMERON,MARY Emily. Feb.21,1855. Parents, Malachi and
Angeline H. Dameron.Father was a farmer.

DAMERON,Mary, Jan.1855. Slave. Mother, Frances. Owner,
Malachi Dameron.

DAVIS,William Henry. May 5,Parents, William A.S. and
Frances Davis. Father was a Carpenter.

DAMERON,Samuel Malachi, Jan.29,1855. Parents, Zachariah and Margaret W. Dameron.

Page # 52.

EWING,__?__, Nov.2,1855. Slave. Mother, Ann. Owner, Mrs
Nancy Ewing.

EWING,__?__, Dec.7,1855. Male. Parents, William and
Lydia Ewing. Father was a farmer.

EDGAR,Edward Emerson,June 14,1855. parents, John H.
and Catherine Edgar. Father was a Wheelright.

EUBANK,Elizabeth,May 20,1855. parents, Ambrose and
Frances Eubank. Father was a farmer.

ELLIOTT,Sally, Oct.20,1855. Slave. Mother, Catherine.
owner, James Elliott Jr.

EVERETT,__?__, Sept.1855.Male. Slave. Mother, martha.
Owner, Joseph H.Everett.

EVERETT,Morton,Oct.1855. Slave. Mother, Eliza. Owner,
John F. Everett..

EVERETT,Luella, Aug.8,1855. Parents, A.N. and Mildred
Ann Everett. Father was a farmer.

EVERETT,Rebechah,April,1855. Slave. Mother, Leannah.
Owner, A.N.Everett.

EVERETT,Emerline, Dec.,1855. Slave. Mother,Sophia.
Owner, Mrs Elizabeth Everett.

EWING,James Alexander. Sept. 19,1855. Parents, James
D. and Elenor Ewing.

FRANKLIN,Joseph Tosh,Oct.1855. Slave. Mother, Owner,
Benjamin H. Franklin.

FERREL,__?__, Aug.1855. Slave. Female. Mother, Temp.
Owner, Henry C.Ferrel.

FALLS,Charles Henry, June 27,1855. Parents, George W.
and Emily M. Falls. Father was a Miller.

FOSTER,John, July 3,1855. Parents, Alfred P. and Mary
M. Foster. Father was a farmer.

BIRTH RECORDS

FREEMAN,Marinda, April 9,1855. Parents, garland H. and Thermuthis Freeman. Father was a farmer.

FALLS,Garland, May 21,1855. Slave. Mother, Peggy. Owner, Benjamin Falls.

FALLS, Cornelius,Oct.26,1855. Slave. Mother, Winney. Owner, Benjamin Falls.

FALLS,Jane, Nov.30,1855. Slave. Mother, Emily. Owner, Benjamin Falls.

FORGIE,Araminter, June,1855. Slave. Mother, Rhoda. Owner, Daniel K. Forgie.

GILLS,___?___, Aug.1855, Slave. Mother, Abba. Owner, William Gills.

GOODE, mary Virginia, Feb.5,1855. Parents, Edmund and Ann M.Goode. Father was a farmer.

GOODE,Lucinda,Feb.2,1855.Slave. Mother, Mariah. Owner, Edmund Goode.

GLASS,Martha Mildred,May 25,1855.Parents, Thomas W. and Sarah Ann Glass. Father was a farmer.

GARRETT,John Bunyon, Aug.23,1855. Parents, Edward G. and Fanny F. Garrett. Father was a Merchant.

GWATKINS,Mildred & Frank, (Twins). July 15,1855.Slave. Mother, Caroline, Owner, mary J.Gwatkins.

GARRETT,Henry Daniel,Jan.15,1855. Parents, Henry M. and Elizabeth F. Garrett.

HURT,Ginny,Aug.1855. Slave. Mother, Nancy. Owner, Fountain G. Hurt.

Page # 53,

HOPKINS,Edward, March,1855. Slave. Mother, Malinda. Owner, John C.Hopkins.

HODGES,William Eldrid,Nov.16,1855. Parents, Thomas C. and Harriett S.Hodges.Father was a farmer.

HAWKINS,Eva, Feb.19,1855.Slave. Mother, Charlott. Owner, George W. Hawkins.

HAWKINS,Ann Eliza,Aug.3,1855.Slave. Mother, Sylvia. Owner, Fountain Hawkins.

HOMES,George Walter,Nov.31,1855. FN.Parents, Robert J. and Betsey Homes. Father was a factory worker.

HOLLER,Reubin,June,1855. Parents, james and Minerva Holler. Father was a farmer.

HICK,___?___, Nov.29,1855. Male. (Died). Parents, Daniel and Elizabeth C.Hick. Father was a farmer.

BIRTH RECORDS

HOPKINS,__?__, &__?__,(Twins).Slaves. Mother, Matilda. Owner, Price W.Hopkins.

HARDY,Adah,Jan.1855.Slave. Mother, Vina. Owner, William A.Hardy.

HARDY,William Dabney,Nov.23,1855.Parents, A.M. and Sarah E.Hardy.Father was a farmer.

HATCHER,Malinda,Aug.10,1855. Slave. Mother, Fanny. Owner, Uriah Hatcher.

HARDY,Henry,July 9,1855.Slave. Mother, Mariah. Owner, Joseph S.hardy.

HARDY,Lissa Christian,Nov.1,1855.Slave. Mother,Lucinda Owner, Joseph S.hardy.

HATCHER,james,April 5,1855. Slave. Mother, Nelly. Owner, Julius H.Hatcher Jr.

HOWARD,__?__, June,1855.Female. Parents, John A. and Cleopatra Howard. Father was a farmer.

HOWARD,Joseph William,Oct.8,1855. Parents, Samuel and Martha E. Howard. Father was a farmer.

HATCHER,Judy, April,1855. Slave. Mother, Ginny. Owner, Julius Hatcher Jr.

HAWKINS,Eller, Jan.1855. Slave. Owner, John F.Hawkins

HAWKINS,Isaac,Nov.3,1855. Slave. Owner, John F. Hawkins.

HARRIS,__?__, July,1855.Slave. Mother, Queen. Owner, Rev. William Harris.

HUDSON,Charles, April 5, Parents, William and Martha R.Hudson. Father was a farmer.

HARRISON,John,Feb.1855. Slave. Mother, Emily. Owner, James Harrison.

HATCHER,Roberta, March &,1855. Parents, Albert M. and Elizabeth Hatcher,

HOFFMAN,Charles Evans,Nov.1855. Parents. John and Angeline.A.Hoffman.

HOBSON,Luiza, Aug.1855.Slave. Mother, Martha. Owner, Samuel Hobson.

HOBSON,Clara & Edla,(Twins),Jan.1,1855.Slaves. Mother, Sarah. Owner, Samuel Hobson.

HOBSON,Isabella, Nov.1855. Slave. Mother, Emily. Owner, Samuel Hobson.

HOBSON.Ethalinda,Nov.1855. Slave. Mother, Mary. Owner, Samuel Hobson.

BIRTH RECORDS

HATCHER,Pleasant,Dec.1855, Slave. Mother, Mary.
Owner, Henry Hatcher.

HAWKINS,__?__, Oct.10,1855. Parents, Edward E. and
Adaline W. Hawkins. Father was a farmer.

HAWKINS,Willie Chapman. May 12,1855. Parents, Robert C.
and Mary F. Hawkins. Father was a farmer.

HUTTER,Emma Cobbs,March 16,1855. parents, Edward S.
and Emma W. Hutter. Father was a farmer.

HUTTER,Hunter,March 24,1855. Slave. Mother, Harriett.
Owner, Edward Hutter.

HUTTER,Frank, May 10, Slave. Mother, Susan. Owner,
Edward Hutter.

HAYNES,Mary Ellen, June 30,1855. Slave. Mother, Susan
Haynes.

JETER,Wilbert Thisco, Aug.28,1855. Parents, William
and Mary Jeter. Father was a farmer.

JONES,__?__, Oct.25,1855. Female. Parents, Benjamin
and Sarah Ann Jones. father was a farmer.

JONES,Pleasant Green, March 15,1855. Parents, William
and Elizabeth Jenes. Father was a farmer.

JENNINGS,Elizabeth,Aug.1855. Parents, Zachariah E. and
Lucy M. Jennings.

JENNINGS,William James, Aug.21,1855. Parents, James W.
and Rachel J.M. Jennings.

JONES,Amstead, April,16,1855. Slave. Mother, Sylvia,
Owner, George Jones.

JETER,Winston,Jan.27,1855. Slave. Mother, Emily.Owner,
jesse Jeter.

JETER, Smith,Nov.7,1855. Slave. Mother, Louiza. Owner,
Jesse Jeter.

JENKINS,John Thomas,Sept.21,1855. Parents, Thomas S.
and Louizat Jenkins. Father was a Shoemaker.

JOPLING,Peter, Aug.21,1855. Slave. Mother, Fanny.
Owner, Thomas B. Jopling.

PAGE # 54.

KENT,__?__, Dec.22,1855. Parents, Charles H. and Lucy
W. Kent. Father was a Merchant.

KEYS,Davis Leonidus, Oct.20,1855. Parents, Thomas H.
and Cissola A. Keys. Father was a farmer.

KEYS,Missouri Catherine, Jan.6,1855.Parents, Charles
and Mildred F.Keys. Father was a farmer.

BIRTH RECORDS

KENEDA,___?__, Aug.19,1855. Female. Parents, William and Mary Keneda. Father was a farmer.

KENEDA,James Pleasant,June 22,1855. Parents, John L. and Elizabeth Keneda.

KEITH,Selest Hadee,Aug.1855. Parents, Colin B. and Eliza Jane Keith. Father was a Farmer.

KELSO,Emily, Feb.1855. Slave. Mother, Nancy. Owner, Robert N.Kelso.

KNIGHT,George Herbert,July 28,1855. Slave, Mother, Fanny. Owner, John Q. Knight.

LINDSAY,Sarah,Nov.1855. Parents, Robert and Jenette Lindsay. Father was a Wheelright.

LUCK,Hillery, March,1855. Slave. Mother, Mary. Owner, George P. Luck.

LUCK,Laura, April,1855. Slave. Mother, Flora. Owner, George P.Luck.

LOWRY,___?__, June 10,1855. Female.(Died). Slave. Mother, Lucy. Owner, John H. Lowry.

ROSE,Ann Rebechah. Jan.1855. Mother, Mary Jane Rose.

LOGWOOD,Eliza. July,1855. Slave. Mother, Anna. Owner, Alexander Logwood.

LOGWOOD,___?__, July 17,1855.(Died). Parents, Robert R. and mary E. Logwood. Father was a farmer.

LOWRY,Moses,June,1855. Slave. Mother, Fanny. Owner, Lunsford Lowry.

LAWLESS,Sarah Martha,Jan.11,1855. Parents, James R. and Elizabeth A. Lawless. Father was a farmer.

LOWRY,Lucy,June,1855. Slave. Mother, Emerline. Owner, Nelson Lowry.

LOWRY,Willie & Bettie,(Twins),Parents, Richard W. and Cicely M.Lowry. Father was a farmer.

LEFTWICH,Alexander,Nov.25,1855. Slave. Mother, Nancy. Owner, John S.Leftwich.

LEFTWICH,___?__, Dec.1855. Parents, Ellener J. and Thomas W.Leftwich. father was a farmer.

LEFTWICH,_____,Dec.1855. Slave. Mother, Charlott. Owner, Thomas W. Leftwich.

LOWRY,Junisus Daniel, Dec.12,1855. Parents,Lucy A.M. and Charles B.Lowry.

LEFTWICH,Nelson,Sept.1855. Slave. Mother, Mary. Owner, William Leftwich.

BIRTH RECORDS

LEFTWICH,Ida,Sept.1855. Slave. Mother,Caroline. Owner, William Leftwich.

LEFTWICH,__?__ , July,1855. Slave. Mother, Everline. Owner, William Leftwich.

LEE,Tom,Dec.1855. Slave. Mother, Dinah. Owner, William H. Lee.

Page # 55

MOOSELEY,Edward Winston,Feb.2,1855. Parents, George C. and Mary D. Mooseley. Father was a farmer.

MARSHALL,Ossa Ann,June,1855. Parents, Robert W. and Ann M. Marshall.

MOORE,Elizabeth Price,June 3,1855. Parents, Goodrich and Susan Catherine Moore. Father was a farmer.

MCCARTY,Mary Elizabeth,Sept.8,1855. Parents, James M. and Mary McCarty.Father was a farmer.

MILES,Fanny,Oct.1855. Slave. Mother,Malinda. Owner, Henry W. Miles.

MARSH,Leona, Oct.16,1855. Parents, Robert B. and Martha Marsh. Father was a farmer.

MILLNER,William Jasper, July,1855. Parents, Jeremiah D. and Catherine Millner.

McDANIEL,Rose,July,8,1855. Slave. Mother,Genetta. Owner, Albert McDaniel.

MASON,Thomas Henry,Dec.1855. Parents, John J. and Mahala Mason.

MCCLINTOCK,__?__, Dec.1,1855. Slave. Mother, Amanda. Owner, Lee McClintock.

MITCHEL,Mary Susan,Sept.26,1855. Parents, Stephen A. and Sarah A. Mitchel. Father was a farmer.

MOORMAN,Gilbert,Aug.1855. Slave. Mother, Permela. Owner, Lodowick A. Moorman.

MOORMAN,Beverly,Nov.1855. Slave. Mother, Judy. Owner, Lodowick A. Moorman.

MARSH,James Robert, Dec.28,1855. Parents, Robert A. and Ann Jane Marsh. Father was a Painter.

MOSBY,Mary Allis, Nov.22,1855.Parents, Thomas Y. and Bettie M. Mosby. Father was a farmer.

McDANIEL,Moses, Dec.20,1855. Slave. Mother, Betsey. Owner, Mrs N.McDaniel.

MCDANIEL,Eller, Sept.16,1855. Parents, Samuel and Eliza S.McDaniel. Father was a farmer.

BIRTH RECORDS

McDANIEL, Molley,Feb.11,1855. Slave. Mother, Martha. Owner, Samuel MCDaniel.

McDANIEL,Nancy,March 15,1855. Slave. Mother, Nella. Owner, Samuel McDaniel.

MOSBY,Sally,Oct.1855. Slave. Mother, Sinor. Owner, Thomas Y.Mosby.

MERIWEATHER,Barinda, June 6,1855. Slave. Mother, Betsey Ann.Owner, James A. Meriweather.

MERIWEATHER, Jane, Oct.1855. Slave. Mother, Dilsey. Owner, James A. Meriweather.

MERIWEATHER,Margaret Douglas, Oct.1855. Parents, James A.Meriweather. Father was a farmer.

MERRIWETHER,James Addison, Aug.7,1855. Parents,Charles J. and Ellen Merriwether.

MERRIWETHER,Rachel, July,1855. Slave. Mother, Lucille Owner, Charles J. Merriwether.

METCALFE,Thorton,Jan.21,1855. Slave. Mother, Martha, Owner, James Metcalfe.

METCALFE,Stephen. may 6,1855. Slave. Mother, Easter. Owner, James Metcalfe.

MELTON,Susan Agness,Nov.16. Parents, Josiah and Susan Melton. Father was a farmer.

MORRIS,__?__, & __?__, (Twins).Oct.8,1855. Males. Parents, William and Mary Morris. Father was a farmer.

MENNIS,Emer,May,1855. Slave. Mother, Martha. Owner, William C.Mennis.

NOEL,Caleb Cornelius,Dec.30,1855. Parents, Caleb R. and Catherine J. Noel. Father was a farmer.

NELSON,Edwin Matthews,Oct.12,1855. Parents, T.H. And Mary Ann Nelson. Father was a Physician.

NELSON,Lewis,April,1855. Slave. Mother, Caroline. Owner, T.H.Nelson.

NELSON,Edward,Oct.1855. Slave. Mother, Nanny. Owner, T.H.Nelson.

NOEL,Margaret,July,1855. Slave. Mother, Landona.Owner, Robertine W.Noel.

NOEL,__?__, March,1855.(Died). Male. Slave. Mother, Amanda. Owner, Alex.J.Noel.

Page # 56,

OTEY,__?__, March 1,1855. Female. Slave. Mother,Malinda Owner, Mary C.Otey.

BIRTH RECORDS

OTEY,Austin,April 9,1855. Slave. Mother, Ann. Owner, Mary C.Otey.

OTEY,___?___, Feb.17,1855. Male. Parents, C.C. and Sarah P. Otey. Father was a farmer.

OGLESBY,William,Nov.9,1855. Slave. Mother,Malinda. Owner, Joshua B. Oglesby.

OGDEN,Margaret,April,1855. Slave. Mother, Malinda. Owner, Henry M.Ogden.

OGDEN,Mary,June,1855. Slave. Amanda. Owner, John Ogden.

OGDEN,Charlott,July,1855. Slave. Mother, Martha. Owner, John Ogden.

OGDEN,Rhody,Dec.1855. Slave. Mother, Mary. Owner, John Ogden.

OLLIVER,Mitton Derret,Feb.1855. Parents, John K. and Frances Olliver. Father was a farmer.

OVERSTREET,Charles Henry,Oct.25,1855. Parents,William H. and Viletta Overstreet. Father was a farmer.

ONEY,Susan Catherine, June 25,1855. Parents, J.W. and Mary F. Oney. Father was a farmer.

POWELL,April 15,1855. Slave. Mother, Charlott. Owner, William Powell.

POINDEXTER,Morris,Nov.9,1855. Slave. Mother, Lucinda. Owner, Anderson Poindexter.

POINDEXTER,Morris,Nov.9,1855. Slave. Mother, Jane. Owner, Anderson Poindexter.

POINDEXTER,Sophia, Nov.1855. Slave. Mother, Eliza. Owner, Anderson Poindexter.

POINDEXTER,Lucy,Dec.1855. Slave. Mother, Angeline. Owner, Anderson Poindexter.

PAGITT,Mary Frances,Sept.1855. Parents, John R. and Sarah F.Pagitt. Father was a farmer.

POINDEXTER,___?___, Oct.1855. Female,(Died). Parents, Willis G. and Emily Poindexter.Father was a farmer.

POINDEXTER,___?___, June,1855.Female. Slave. Mother, Aylsey. Owner, Willis Poindexteer.

POINDEXTER,___?___, June,1855. (Died).Slave. Mother, Frances. Owner, Elizabeth M.Poindexter.

PERROW,Henry Jackson,Sept.25,1855. Parents, Andrew J. and Martha A.Perrow. Father was a farmer.

PERROW,Henryetta,March 25,1855. Slave. Mother, Cornelia Owner, Andrew Perrow.

BIRTH RECORDS

POINDEXTER,Agness,Sept.9,1855.Slave. Mother, Agness. Owner, Eliza M.Poindexter.

POINDEXTER,Elijah Dabney Thomas,March 6,1855. Parents, Richard W. and mary Poindexter.Father was a farmer.

PERROW,Vina,May,1855. Slave. Owner, james S.Perrow.

PERROW,Urania Virginia,Sept.18,1855. Parents, James S. and Elizabeth Perrow.

PENN,Jefferson,July 31,1855.Slave. Mother, Adaline. Owner, Paul S.Penn.

PAGE,William Jasper,Jan.24,1855. Parents, Erastus and Frances Ann Page. father was a farmer.

PARKER,Sarah Clabourn,July 22,1855. Parents, George C. and Hester Ann Parker. Father was a farmer.

Page # 57.

ROSEBROUGH,Tom,Jan,1855. Slave. Mother, ,artha. Owner, Robert Rosebrough.

ROESBROUGH,Mariah,April,1855.Slave. Mother, Ann.Owner, Robert Rosebrough.

ROSEBROUGH,Henry,Sept.1855. Slave. Mother, Sally. Owner, Robert Rosebrough.

RUCKER,Cary, may,1855. Slave. Mother, Mary. Owner, James M.Rucker.

RUCKER,Lucinda, April,1855. Slave. Mother, Louiza. Owner, James M.Rucker.

RUCKER, Emily,May,1855. Slave. Mother, Mary. Owner, Burnard Rucker.

ROBINSON,Missouri,April 4,1855. Parents, James W. and Ann E. Robinson.

ROBINSON,Roderick,Sept.20,1855. Slave. Mother, Jane. Owner, Mrs Angeline H.Robinson.

RYAN,James Henry,March 30,1855. Parents, Phillip H. and Sarah E. Ryan. Father was a Stone Mason

RYAN,Sarah,Nov.5,1855. Slave. Mother, Julia.Owner, Phillip H. Ryan.

REYNOLDS,George Winfrey,Nov.5,1855. Parents, Charles D. and Martha Reynolds. Father was a Taylor.

RADFORD,Matilda,March 20,1855. Slave. Mother, Rozetta. Owner, Winston Radford.

REYNOLDS,Don Henry, June,1855. Parents, Theodore E. and Jane M. Reynolds. Father was a Depo Agent.

BIRTH RECORDS

RADFORD,Henry,Feb.10,1855. Slave. Mother, Luvina. Mother, R.C.W. Radford.

ROUTON,James Henry,April 9,1855. Parents, Samuel B. and Lucy A. Routon. Father was a farmer.

REYNOLDS,Hubbard Spinner,April,1855. Parents, Joel P. and Catherine Reynolds. father was a farmer.

REYNOLDS,Robert,April 30,1855. Slave. Mother, Martha. Owner, Charles B. Reynolds.

REYNOLDS,Emmet Baxter,Dec.1855. Parents, Luallen J. and Sarah Ann Reynolds. father was a farmer.

REYNOLDS,John,Oct.1855. Slave. Mother,Gene. Owner, Luallen Reynolds.

REYNOLDS,___?___, Female.(Died). Parents, Edward J. and Ann Elizabeth reynolds. Father was a farmer.

REECE,Richard Lewis, Oct.1855. Slave. Mother, Lucy. Owner, Joseph T. Reece.

SLUSSER,Edward JOnas, Aug.15,1855. Parents, Henry and Jane Slusser. father was a farmer.

SPENCE,William Andrews,Feb.3,1855. Parents, Andrew F. and Lucy Spence. Father was a farmer.

SALE,___?___, Dec.1855. Slave. Mother, Nancy. Owner, Richard A.Sale.

SAUNDERS,Elizabeth Morris,Jan.7,1855. Parents, John E. and Catherine Saunders. Father was a Merchant.

STEPTOE,Matilda,Oct.1855. Slave. Mother, Mary. Owner, Doc William Steptoe.

SAUNDERS,Eliza,Dec.1855. Slave. Mother, Martha. Owner, Mrs A.M.Saunders

STEPTOE,Eller,July 31,1855.Slave. Mother, Louiza, Owner, Robert C.Steptoe.

STEPTOE, Emmer, July,1855, Slave. Mother, Nancy. Owner, Robert Steptoe.

STEPTOE,Malinda, Oct.1855. Slave. Mother, Violet. Owner, Robert Steptoe.

STEPTOE,Isabel,Oct.1855. Slave. Mother, Rhoda. Owner, Robert C. Steptoe.

SEAY,Harriot,March 24,1855. Parents, David P. and Amanda S. Seay.

SPINNER,William Sherman,Aug.30,1855. Parents, Doc Jesse F. and martha Ann Spinner. Father was a Physician.

SPINNER,Ailsey,Aug.26,1855. Slave. Mother, Amanda. Owner, Doc Jesse Spinner.

BIRTH RECORDS

SLEDD,___?__, July 31,1855. Male. Parents, William E. and Arabella Sledd.

SLEDD,Wesley,July,1855. Slave. MOther, Betsey. Owner, William E.Sledd.

SLEDD,Moses,June,1855. Slave. Mother, Mary. Owner, William E.Sledd

SCOTT,Eller, March,1855. Slave. Mother, Eliza. Owner, Samuel Scott.

SCOTT,George, May,1855. Slave. MOther, Lucy. Owner, Samuel Scott.

Page # 58.

TAYLOR,Emily, Dec.14,1855. Slave. Mother, Eliza. Owner, John R.Taylor

THOMAS,Robert,Oct.17,1855. Parents, S.M. and Amanda P. Thomas. Father was a farmer.

THOMAS,John Stele,July 8,1855. Parents, John C. and Eliza B. Thomas. Father was a farmer.

THOMPSON,Chester,Feb.6,1855. Slave. Mother, Nancy. Owner, Mrs Rhoda M. Thompson.

THOMPSON,Amanda,July 15,1855.Slave. Mother, Milly. Owner, Jesse S.Thompson Est.

TOLLEY,Catherine & Dabney,March 21,1855. (Twins) Parents,Owen and Jermine Tolley.Father was a MIller.

TAYLOR,Thomas Henry,July 15,1855. Parents, Albert H. and Mary Jane Taylor. Father was a farmer.

THOMPSON,Lewis & Charlott,May,1855.(Twins).Slaves., Mother, Jenny. Owner, Nelson A.Thompson.

TINSLEY,___?__, May,1855. Female. Slave. Mother, Mourning, Owner, Mrs Lucy Tinsley.

THOMAS,___?__, Nov.1855. Male. Parents, Prosser P. and Susan P. Thomas. Father was a farmer.

TERPIN,Pocahontas,Jan.1855. Slave. Mother, Emerline. Owner, Roland G. Turpin.

TERPIN,Ned,Feb.1855. Slave. Mother,Julia. Owner, Roland G. Terpin.

THOMAS,Nepoleon Bonapart,April 7,1855. Parents,Anderson and Mary F.Thomas. Father was a farmer.

Turpin,Eliza Susan,Feb.28,1855.Parents, Spottswood H. and Lucitta Turpin. Father was a farmer.

TANNER,Almeda,FN. Jan.17,1855. Parents, Joseph and Rhoda Jane Tanner. Father was a farmer.

BIRTH RECORDS

TURPIN,Natt,Feb.28,2855. Slave. Mother, Louiza. Owner, Phillip Turpin.

TURPIN,Nancy,Nov.27,1855. Slave. Mother, Elmira.Owner, Phillip Turpin.

TURPIN,Jesse,Jan.1855. Slave. Mother, Margaret.Owner, Phillip Turpin.

Thaxton,Emily Susan,Dec.17,1855. Slave. Mother, Mariah Owner,David T.Thaxton.

Page # 59.

WATSON,Henry Mitchell,June 4,1855.Slave.Mother, Permelia. Owner, John Watson.

WOOD,Sarah Margaret,Jan.13,1855. parents, John T. and mary Elizabeth Wood.Father was a farmer.

WOOD,Harriott,June 20,1855. Parents, John and Jenette Wood. Father was a farmer.

WILLIAMS,Frances,June 15,1855. Slave, Mother, Marvella. Owner, Mrs Matilda Williams.

WILKERSON,Sarah,June,1855. Slave. Mother, Lucy. Owner, Holcomb Wilkerson.

WATSON,William Mitchel. March 13,1855. Parents, William D.Watson. Father was a farmer.

WHEAT,Sarah,Jan.4,1855. Parents, Hazel and Eliza Wheat Father was a farmer.

WHEAT,Emerline, June,1855. Slave. Mother, Phillis. Owner, Zach J.Wheat.

WATSON,William, Aug.2,1855. Slave. Mother, Tenah. Owner, barnett A. Watson.

WATSON,Mary Ann, Feb.14,1855. Parents, Joesph D. and Mary E. Watson. Father was a farmer.

WHITE,Charles Henry, May 29,1855. Slave. Mother, Elizabeth.Owner, Henry M. White.

WHITE,James Becknett, July 25,1855.Slave. Mother, Emily. Owner, Henry M.White.

WHITE,Sarah Martha,Sept.11,1855. Slave. Mother,Sarah. Owner, Henry M. White.

WHITE,Daniel Edgar, Dec.2,1855. Slave. Mother, Clara. Owner, Henry M. White.

WORLEY,Sarah Virginia, Aug.18,1855. Parents, William and Susan Worley. Father was a farmer.

WILSON,Nelson,Rosser,June 7,1855. Parents, James W. and Mary Wilson. Father was a Carpenter.

BIRTH RECORDS

WHITE,John,Jan.1855. Slave. Mother, Maysa. Owner, Mrs Nancy White.

WHITE,Alfred,Feb.14,1855. Slave. Mother, Frances. Owner, Mrs Nancy White.

WHITE,Ethelbert,June 17,1855. Slave. Mother, Sarah Ann. Owner, Mrs Nancy White.

WEBBER,Oliver Perry, Feb.1855. Parents, James B. and Nancy E. Webber. Father was a farmer.

WILKS,__?__, Feb.1855. Male. Slave. Mother, Sophiah. Owner, Benjamin Wilks.

WILKS,__?__, March,1855. Female. Slave. Mother, Elizabeth. Owner, benjamin Wilks.

WILKS,__?__, May,1855. Male. Slave. Mother, Ann Eliza. Owner, Henry Wilks.

WILKERSON,Jacob,July,1855. Slave. Mother, Rachel. Owner, Owen Wilkerson.

WHITE,Mary Catherine,Dec.6,1855. Parents, Henry A. and Elizabeth P. White. father was a farmer.

WIGGENTON,Alfred,May,1855. Slave. Mother, Polina. Owner, Benjamin Wigginton.

WIGGINTON,Orrange,June,1855. Slave. Mother, Sylvia. Owner, Benjamin Wigginton.

WIGGINTON,__?__, July,1855. Female. Slave. Mother, Martha,Owner, Benjamin Wigginton.

WIGGINTON,Leanna,Sept.,1855. Slave. Mother, Ginny. Owner, Benjamin Wigginton.

WATTS,Sallie Lee, Sept.2,1855. Parents, William P.and Elvira F. Watts. father was a farmer.

WRIGHT,Nanny Edgar,Nov.19,1855. Parents, John D. and Jane E. Wright. Father was a farmer.

WORLEY,Lewis Calvin.June,1855. parents, Richard A.and Mary Worley. Father was a farmer.

WHITE,Sarah Frances,Nov.7,1855. Parents, James and Mary A. White. Father was a farmer.

WILSON,Roderick,Nov.26,1855. Parents, Jesse P. and Amanda Wilson. Father was a farmer.

WHITE,Henry Edward, Sept.18,1855. Parents, John M.and Mary V. White.

WHITE,Major,Nov.1855. Slave. Mother, Eliza. Owner, Jacib S. White.

WATTS,Eliza Jane,1855. Parents, James D. and Mary Watts. Father was a farmer.

WIGGINTON,Cornelia Scott,Nov.2,1855. Parents, F.M.and Clara Wigginton. Father was a farmer.

BIRTH RECORDS

Page # 60,

ARTHUR, ? , Feb.1,1855. Female. Parents, William J. and Emily J. Arthur. Father was a farmer.

ANTHONY,Mary, May,1855. Slave. Owner, Emilia Anthony.

ALIFF, ? , March 15,1855. Male. Parents, Alex B.T. and Frances Ann Aliff. Father was a farmer.

AYERS, ? , Dec.1,1855. Male. Parent, Ishmael Ayers.

ANDREWS,Matilda,Sept.1855. Slave. Owner, William M. Andrews.

ANDREWS,Sally,Sept.1855. Slave. Owner, William Andrews.

ANDREWS,Kit,Dec.24,1855. Slave. Owner,William Andrews.

ADAMS, ? , Dec.24,1855. Male. Parents, Abram and Frances Adams.

ADAMS, ? , Oct.10,1855. Male. Parents, James and Elizabeth Adams.

AUSTIN, ? , Nov.1855. Female. Parents, Abram and Anunica Austin.

AYERS,Richard P.,Sept.19,1855. parents, John M. and Merinda Ayers.

AUSTIN,Clyerles,Oct.1855. Slave. Owner, Thomas Austin.

AUSTIN,Abnum,Feb.1855. Slave. Owner, Thomas Austin.

ANDREWS,Violet,1855. Slave. Owner, Mark Andrews.

AYERS,Fanny H.,Oct.14,1855. Parents, James W. and Elizabeth Ayers.

ADKINSON,William B.,march,1855. parents, Bunuele and Nancy Adkinson.

ADKINSON,Charles E.,Feb. 1855. Parents, Wilson and martha Adkinson.

ALLEN,Charles S.,Feb.11,1855. parents, Robert E. and Nancy Allen.

ATKINS,Eliza A.,April,1855. Parents, Joseph and Elizabeth Atkins.

ANDERSON,Jonus,July 10,1855. Parents, James M. and Virginia Anderson.

AUSTIN,Bo March,1855. Slave. Owner, William Austin.

ADAMS,Alonzo J.,Dec.11,1855. Parents, William S. and Nancy A. Adams.

BIRD,Martha S.,Aug.1855. Parents, Vincent M. and Sarah Bird. Father was a farmer.

BOARD, ? , 1855, Male, Slave. Owner, John Board.

BIRTH RECORDS

BOARD,martha,1855. Slave. Owner, John Board.

BOARD, __?__ , May,1855. Female. Slave. Owner, John Board.

BOND,Read, may,1855. Slave. Owner, Pleasant Bond.

BOND,Mildred,May,1855. Slave. Owner, Pleasant Bond.

BOND,Molly,Feb.,1855. Slave. Owner, Pleasant Bond.

BOWLING, __?__ , March,1855.(Died). Parent,William Bowling. Father was a farmer.

BELL,Heelow,Aug.14,1855. Parents, O.P. and Nancy Bell. Father was a Merchant.

BURROUGHS,Patsey,July,1855. Slave. Owner, John Burroughs.

BURROUGHS,Amanda,may 16,1855. Parents,Joseph N. and Sarah Ann Burroughs. Father was a farmer.

BURROUGHS, __?__ , Oct.1855. Male. Slave. Owner, Joseph N. Burroughs.

BURROUGHS,Julina,Sept. 1855. Owner, Catherine Burroughs

BROWN,martha E.,Aug.1855. Parents, Doctor L. and Landona Brown. Father was a farmer.

BURNETT,John W.,Oct.19,1855. Parents, William and Nancy Burnett. father was a farmer.

BOWLS,Elnora E.,June 16,1855. Parents, S. and Mary M. Bowls. Father was a farmer.

Page # 61,

BEARD,William S.,June 27,1855. Parents, Ro B. and Lovey Beard. Father was a farmer.

BOND,John W.,May 15,1855. Parents, Andrew J. and Mary Bond.

BURFORD,Frances E.,April 12,1855. Parents, John W.and Sarah Burford.

BANDY,Mary A.,Jan.8,1855. Parents, Compton G. and Susan E. Bandy.

BEARD,Rob J. Dec.4,1855. Parents, Rob M. and Elizabeth Beard.

BOARD,Misouri,July,1855.Slave. Owner, Thomas Board.

BOWLS,James S.,Nov.26,1855.Parents, james T. and Martha Bowls.

BUTTERWORTH,Lettitia,March 25,1855. Parents, James and Sarah E. Butterworth.

BOARD, __?__ , March,1855. Male. Slave. Owner,Maria Board.

BOARD,Nancy,June,1855. Owner, Maria Board.

BIRTH RECORDS

BOARD,Betsey Ann,Aug.1,1855.Slave. Owner, Saml H. Board.

BURNETT, ? , Female.Feb.14,1855. Parents, William L. and Elizabeth Burnett.

BURNETT,Charles W.,May 6,1855. Parents, William W.and Margarett L. Burnett.

BURNETT,America,April 30,1855. Parent, Elisha C.Burnett.

BROWN, ? , April,1855.Male. Slave. Owner, Saml Brown.

BROWN,James C.,June 13,1855. Parents, Thomas J. and Adaline Brown.

CRENSHAW,Stephen, March 3,1855. Slave. Owner, Priscilla Crenshaw.

CRENSHAW,George, March 3,1855. Slave. Owner, Priscilla Crenshaw.

CUNDIFF,Samuel H.,Aug.1855. parents, George W. and Sarah E.Cundiff.

CREASEY,Margaret,V.,Oct.27,1855. Parents, William A. and Harriett Creasy.

CLAYTOR, ? , Aug.1855,Female. Slave. Owner, William G. Claytor.

CLAYTOR, ? , May,1855. Female. Slave. Owner, Robert M. Claytor.

COCKMAN,Thomas,Dec.15,1855. Parents, Thomas and Elizabeth Cockman.

CLAYTOR, ? , Dec.1855. Feamle.Slave. Owner, Thomas R. Claytor.

COBBS,Emma, 1855. Slave. Owner, Tilghman A. Cobbs

COBBS,Eveline,1855. Slave. Owner, Tilghman A.Cobbs.

COBBS,Lindarill, Jan.1,1855. Slave. Owner, Tilghman A. Cobbs Jr.

CADWALLENDER,Prudence O.,Jan.2,1855. parents, James and Frances C. Cadwallender.

CREASY,Fanny,Feb.,1855. Slave. Owner, Thomas Creasy.

CREASY,Booker P. Dec.31,1855. Parents, John P. and Milissa Ann Creasy.

CREASY, ? , Nov.10,1855. Male. Parents, David H. and Charlotte Creasy.

CREASY,Charles Henry, March,1855. Slave. Owner, David H. Creasy.

BIRTH RECORDS

CARROL,Henry W.,Sept.1855, Parents, Henry and Catherine Carrol.

CHAFFIN,Martha C.,1855. Parents, Joseph and Lauvinia Chaffin.

CHEWNING,___?__, Dec.25,1855. Female. Slave. Owner, Calahill D.Chewning.

CRADDOCK,Ellen V, Nov.2,1855. Parents, H.N. and Emerline Craddock.

Page # 62.

CARTER,Silas B. May 14,1855. parents, Saml A. and Mary J. Carter.

CREASY,Saml T.,July 23,1855. parents, Leonard S. and Paulina J. Creasy.

CUNNINGHAM,Nancy A.,June,1855. Parents, James C. and Rebecca Cunningham.

CAMPBELL,___?__, 1855. Male. Slave. Owner, Nancy Campbell.

CAMPBELL,___?__, 1855. Female. Slave. Owner, Nancy Campbell.

CLAYTOR,___?__, 1855. Male. Slave. Owner, Saml Claytor.

CRENSHAW,Malinda, April 18,1855. Slave. Owner, Richard Crenshaw.

CRUMP,Lewis Green, Nov.20,1855. Slave. Owner, Beverly Crump.

CROUCH,John W.,Jan.15,1855. Parents, Achillis and Millisa Crouch.

CARNER,Nancy E.,July 4,1855. parents, William H. and Mary J. Carner.

CLAYTOR,Cora M.,June 16,1855. Parents, Saml H. and Eliza J. Claytor.

COX,Thomas H.,Dec.15,1855. Parents, William B. and Frances Cox.

CARNEY,William A.,Nov.1855. Parents, Abram and Nancy Carney.

CRAFT,___?__, Sept.1855. Female. Parents, George W. and Susan Craft.

CARNER,Wisley, Nov.1855. Slave. Owner, Elijah Carner.

CROUCH,___?__, April,1855. Female. Parents, Lewis O. and Mary Ann Crouch.

CREASY,Saml,March 27,1855. Parents, Saml H. and and Catherine Creasy.

CREASY,J.B.J.,may 11,1855. Parents, Charles and Sarah Creasy.

BIRTH RECORDS

COMPTON,Essex,Aug.15,1855. Slave. Owner, Isiah Compton's Heirs.

CHRISTIAN,Rufus, Oct.1,1855. Slave. Owner, Ann Christian.

DOWDY,Mary J.,Aug.8,1855. Parents, Jesse and Susan Dowdy. Father was a farmer.

DAVIS,Emily. June 28,1855. Slave. Owner, Lucy Davis

DOOLEY,Nancy B.,May 20,1855. parents, Charles H. and Catherine B.Dooley.

DEARDORFF,Robert H.,Feb.4,1855. Parents, Charles H. and Mary E. Deardorff.

DEBO,__?__, Nov.5,1855. Parents, Micheal and Wilmoth Debo.

DEARING,George W.,July 4,1855. parents, Richard and Celia Ann P. Dearing.

DOWDY,__?__, 1855. Male. Parent, Wyatt Dowdy.

DOWDY,Abbey,April 14,1855. Parents, Walter B. and Mildred T. Dowdy.

DOWDY,Saml M.,July 10,1855. Parents, William and Martha Ann Dowdy.

DLONG,A.C.,Oct.10,1855. Parents, Henry and Nancy Dlong

DREWRY,William T.,May 2,1855. Parents, James C. and Julia Ann Drewry.

DREW,Tom. 1855. FN. Mother, Catherine Drew.

DEARING,Sarah. Sept.6,1855. Parents, Edward W. and Fanny Dearing.

DOWILL,__?__, Oct.1855. Female. Parents, Thomas and Ruth Ann Dowill.

DOOLEY,Ann H.,Aug.9,1855. Parents, Henry W. and Sarah S. Dooley.

DENT,Charlotte, March,1855. Slave. Owner, M.H.Dent.

DOOLEY,Mary E.,Sept. 1855. Parents, H.A. and Levina F. Dooley.

Page # 63,

ELLIS,James T.,Jan.13,1855. Parents, William C. and Ann Elizabeth Ellis.

ENGLISH,Rhoda, March,1855. Slave. Owner, Stephen English.

ECHOLS,John T.,Jan.24,1855. parents, Jacob and Elizabeth Echols.

BIRTH RECORDS

ELLIS,Sarah F.,March 16,1855. Parents, Pleasant E. and Sarah Ellis.

FUQUA,Caleb,Aug.10,1855. Granville S. and Martha Ann Fuqua.

FERGUSON,Guy,June,1855. Slave. Owner, Julia Ferguson.

FUQUA,Mary, Oct.15,1855. Slave. Owner, Joshua Fuqua.

FIZER,John R.,Sept. 1855. parents, Richard and Sarah Fizer.

FARIS,___?___, Aug.1855. Male. Slave. Owner, Rebecca Faris.

FARISS,mary Jane,June 1,1855. Slave. Owner, John J. Fariss.

FIELDS,Saml G.,May 10,1855. parents, Saml and Mildred Fields.

FIZER,Charles O., Aug.10,1855. parents, William H. and mary Fizer.

MOORE,___?___, March,1855. Male. Slave. owner, Moore Est.

FRANKLIN,Sarah L.,July,1855. Parents, Jesse H. and Lockey Franklin.

FEATHER,Mary A.M.,April,1855. Parents, Joseph D. and Abigal feather.

FOUTZ,Mary A.,Sept. 1855. Parents, green B. and martha Foutz.

FRANKLIN,Milton W.,April 9,1855. Parents, Elias J. and Sarah J. Franklin.

FEATHERS,Harvey E.,July 12,1855.Parents, Joseph and Julia Ann Feathers.

FEATHERS,Selona,Feb.14,1855. parents, William R. and Mary A. feathers.

FLESHMAN,Thomas W.,Aug.10,1855.Parents, William H.and Mary Ann Fleshman.

FOSTER,Saml T.,July,1855. Parents, Joel E. and Martha Ann Foster.

GILL,Lucinda, Feb.8,1855. Slave. Owner, Charles Gill.

GILL,Monroe, April 3,1855. Slave. Owner, Charles Gill.

GIBBS,Andrew, Feb.15,1855. Slave. Owner, John Gibbs.

GIBBS,William H.,Aug.2,1855.Parents, Henry and Mary Gibbs.

GARRETT,William A.&___?___,(Twins).May,1855. Parents, Elijah and Margaret Garrett.

GARRETT,Henry,Jan.1855.Slave. Owner, Elijah Garrett.

GIBBS,___?___, 1855. Male. Slave. Owner, George Gibbs.

91

BIRTH RECORDS

GOGGIN,Martha, May,1855. Slave. Owner, Stephen Goggin

GOGGIN,Henretta, June,1855. Slave. Owner,Stephen Goggin.

Page # 64.

GARNER,Martha E.,Oct.7,1855. Parents,James W. and Sarah E. Garner.Father was a Tailor.

GOOLEY,Milton H.,April 7,1855. Parents,Alfred and Mary Gooley.

GWALTNEY,__?__, Aug.10,1855. Parents, John P. and Elizabeth Gwaltney.

GILWATER,George W.,Nov.12,1855. Parents, Preston and Sarah J.E. Gilwater.

GRIGSBY,Cary,Jan.27,1855. Slave. Owner, James T. Grigsby.

GILES,John S.,April 11,1855. Parents,John W. and Catherine Giles.

HUDSON,John S.,May 1,1855. Parents, John and Birchy M. Hudson.

HURT,Matilda,April,1855. Slave. Owner, Joel Hurt.

HOLT,__?__, 1855. Slave. Owner, John Holt.

HAGEN,Mary F.,Jan.1855, Parents, Thomas and Mildred Hagen.

HOLLAND,Greenberry,Nov.9,1855. Slave. Owner, Charles Holland.

HICKS,Bill, Jan.20,1855. Slave. Owner, William Hicks.

HEADEN,Flora, July,1855. Slave. Owner, Elizabeth Headen.

HACKWORTH,Columbus, Oct,1855. Parents,Wesley and Martha Hackworth.

HEPENSTALL,Celia, 1855. Slave. Owner,Caleb Hepenstall

HANCOCK,Victoria, March,1855. Slave. Owner, Saml Hancock.

HAUP,Saml M.,May 29,1855. Parents,George A. and Susanna Haup.

HOWELL,George W.,Nov.11,1855. parents, Washington and Martha J. Howell.

HOLDREN,George S.,Jan.28,1855. Parents, Abram and Frances Holdren.

HUNDLEY,James W.,March 7,1855. Parents, Peter M. and Sarah Hundley.

BIRTH RECORDS

HEARDY,Henry C.,Oct.28,1855. PArents,Joseph and Eaney J. Heardy.

HARRIS,Mack,April,1855. SLAve. Owner, Saml Harris.

HUDDLESTON,___?___, Bethena, Jan.1855. Slave. Owner,John Huddleston.

HATCHER,Mary, May 20,1855. Parents, Spencer and Joann Hatcher.

HANCOCK,___?___, ,April 18,1855. Parents, Simon and Betsey Ann Hancock.

HOWSER,Daniel,Dec.25,1855. Parents, William B. and Elizabeth Howser.

HAGEN,Eliza, July 1,1855. Parents, James and Nancy Hagen.

HASTEN,Mary M.,Jan.8,1855. Parents, William and Margaret Hasten.

HUDSON,___?___, April 20,1855. Parents, William and Sarah Hudson.

HUDNALL,Asa D.,June,1855. Parents, Jabey S. and Elizabeth Hudnall.

JOHNSON,___?___, May 29,1855. Parents, Robert and Rebbeca Johnson.

JORDAN,___?___, 1855. Male. Slave. Owner, Jubal Jordan

JORDAN,___?___, 1855. Female. Slave. Owner, Jubal Jordan

JOHNSON,___?___, 1855. Female. Slave. Owner, Robert Johnson.

Page # 65.

IRVIN, Tissy,June,1855. Slave. Owner, Alex Irvin.

IRVIN,Willis, 1855. Slave. Owner, Alex Irvin.

IRVIN, Dick, 1855, Slave. Owner, Alex Irvin.

IRVIN,Henry, 1855. Slave. Owner, Alex Irvin.

JACOBS,___?___, Aug.4,1855. Male. Parents, Elisha C. and Kiziah Jacobs.

JARROTT,Mary, Jan.1855. Parents, John and Polly Jarrott.

JENKINS,Joseph,Dec.8,1855. Parents, Obediah and Tabitha Jenkins.

JETER,Jane, Dec.1,1855. Slave. Owner, Henry J.Jeter.

JAMES,Joel P.,Nov.6,1855. Parents, Elias and Sally James.

JOHNSON,Maria E.,Nov.1855. Slave. owner, William Johnson.

BIRTH RECORDS

JOHNSON,Nancy Jane, Nov.1855. Slave. Owner, William Johnson.

JORDAN,Ann, Jan.1855. Slave. Owner, John Jordan.

JORDAN,Tansey, Aug.1855. Slave. Owner, John Jordan

JETER, __?__ , May 26,1855. Male. Parents, Fielden H. and Ann B. Jeter.

KOONTZ,Eliza,&.Margaret Ann,(Twins). March 6,1855. Parents, George and Ann Koontz.

KASEY,__?__ , Oct.12,1855. Slave. Owner, Newlon Kasey.

KASEY,Eliza Ann, 1855. Slave. Owner, Deborah Kasey.

KASEY,Lelia,March 8,1855. Parents, Thomas A. and Virginia M. kasey.

KASEY,Adaline,Sept. 1855. Slave. Owner, James C.Kasey.

KASEY,Scott, Nov.12,1855. Parents, James C. and Mary S. Kasey.

KIRBY,Elizabeth, Dec.16,1855. Parents, Thomas and Mary Jane Kirby.

KASEY,Elizabeth,Nov.1855. Slave. Owner, Thomas Kasey.

KELLY,Sarah M.,June 18,1855. Parents, David W. and Lydia C. Kelly.

KIDWELL,Mary J.,July 30,1855. Parents, Richard and Jane Ann Kidwell.

KISLER, William H.,Dec.2,1855. Parents, David C. and jane Kisler.

KASEY,William W.,April 1,1855. Parents, Alex and Mary N. Kasey.

KERNS,Mary, Sept.4,1855. Parents, jacob and Frances Ann Kerns.

KIDD,Pamela, April,4,1855. parents, John A. and Elizabeth Kidd.

LAUGHON,Misouri,Dec.24,1855. Parents, Isham and Mary Jane Laughon. Father was a farmer.

LOCKARD,James, Oct.1855. parents, Rufus and Martha Lockard.

LOWRY,__?__ , Dec.1855. Female. Slave. Owner, Ellen Lowry.

LEE, Thomas, May,1855. Slave. Owner, Garnet Lee.

LEE,Margarett, 1855. Slave. Owner, Garnet Lee.

LEFTWICH,James W.,Aug.9,1855. Parents, V.and Evaline Leftwich.

BIRTH RECORDS

LEFTWICH,Priscilla, Sept.1855. Slave. Owner, Alex
Leftwich.

LEFTWICH,Mary Ann,1855. Slave. Owner, Alex Leftwich.

Page # 66,

LEFTWICH,Mahala,Nov.1855. Slave. Owner, Alex Leftwich.

LEFTWICH,James, Jan.1855, Parents, Granderson and
Lucy Ann Leftwich. Father was a Wheelwright.

LANDSDOWN,__?_, March,1855. Parents, Lucian and Mary
Landsdown. Father was a farmer.

LOYD,Saml G.,Aug.11,1855. Parents, John H. and Sarah
F. Loyd.

LAYNE,Martha V.,May,1855. Parents, Joseph B. and Paulina Layne.

LAYNE,__?_, Sept.1855, Female, Slave. owner, Thompson
H. layne.

LAYNE,__?_, Nov.1855. Female. Slave. Owner, Thompson
H.Layne.

LAYNE,__?_, Nov.1855(Twin to the above).Male.Slave.
Owner, Thompson Layne.

LANTZ,Peter, May 24,1855. Parents, Henry S.Lantz.

LOYD,William T.,Feb.9,1855. Parents, mason and Mary S.
Loyd.

LEFTWICH,margaret A.,Dec.3,1855. parents, Lynch A. and
Ellen Leftwich.

LAZENBY,Charles, Oct.1855. Slave. Owner, Edward Lazenby.

LAUGHON,Jarrott,Nov.1855. Parents, John and Lydia Lauh-
on.

LEFTWICH,Walter, E.,Sept.1855. Parents, Etchison and
Massa Ann Leftwich.

LAUGHON,Louvinia,March 1,1855. Parents, Joshua and Eli
zabeth Laughon.

LAUGHON,Elizabeth P.,Aug.21,1855. Parents, Lewis and
Ardena E. Laughon.

LEFTWICH,Ider,Aug.4,1855. Slave. Owner, Ann B.Leftwich

LAYNE,Patrick Henry,Aug.1,1855. Slave. Owner, Thompson
H.Layne.

LAYNE,Taswell,Dec.7,1855. Slave. Owner, Thompson Layne

LAYNE,Harriett Ann,Dec.1855. Slave. Owner, Thompson H.
Layne.

95

BIRTH RECORDS

MITCHELL,Frances, Oct.1,1855. Slave. Owner, Rob C. Mitchell.

MERRIMAN,Neoma Ann,July 4,1855. Slave. Owner, Edward Merriman's Est.

MCGHEE,James B.S.,June 18,1855. Parents, Jack and Louvinia McGhee.

MANSFIELD,Berry S.,Dec.27,1855. Slave. William S.Mansfield.

MARTIN, __?__ , jan.8,1855. Male. Slave, Owner, James F. Martin.

MITCHELL,Harrett, 1855. Slave. Owner, Dr Thomas P. Mitchell.

MCGHEE,Thomas,Feb.1855. Slave. Owner, Susan McGhee.

MCGHEE,Sillia,June 24,1855. Parents,David R. and Littitia McGhee.

MARSH,Marion, Dec.18,1855. Slave. Owner, Rob Marsh.

MARTIN,James A.,April 1,1855. Parents, William D.Mand Frances Martin.

MUSGROVE,Lucy A.,Jan.1855. Parents, Dematris and Margaret Musgrove.

MANUEL,Thornton E.,Dec.17,1855. Parents, Jeremiah E. and Martha A. Manuel.

MILES, Caleb,Feb.18,1855. Parents, Joseph R. and Susan J. Miles.

MCBRIDE,Frances R.,Nov.5,1855. Parents, William and Emily McBride.

MORGAN,Jesse Dell, Aug.7,1855. Parents, Wesley and Cat_ herine morgan.

MORGAN,Medora S.,May,1855. Parents, William B. and Nancy Morgan.

MATTOX,Henry D.,Oct.9,1855. Parents, Robert and Martha M. Mattox.

MORGAN,Bacum A.,Aug.16,1855. Parents, Alex and Adaline Morgan.

MORGAN,Pleasant, Oct.15,1855. Slave. Owner, Alex Morgan.

MEADOR,Hack,June,1855. Slave. Owner, J,Meador.

MEADOR,Reece, 1855. Slave. Owner, J. Meador,?

Page # 67,

MEAD,Oxanna,Jan.1855. Slave. Owner, John Mead.

BIRTH RECORDS

MARKHAM,Martha A.,Aug.25,1855. Parents, Jacob S. and Nancy Markham. Father was a SalesMan.

MCMANAWA,James M.,Dec.8,1855. Parents, Charles H. and Nancy A. McManawa.

MILLER,Mary E.,July 8,1855. Parents, William and Amanda M. Miller.

MORRIS,Mary R.,Jan.21,1855. Parents,Joshu S. and Lydia Morris.

MEADOR,Mary F.,Dec.1855. Parents, Meredith and Mary Meador.

MEADOR,Peyton, Dec.14,1855. Slave. Owner, Obediah Meador.

MITCHELL, ? , Nov.1855. Female. Parents, William C. Mitchell.

MURPHY,Jeremiah E.,March 6,1855. Parents, Elijah and Emily Murphy.

MITCHELL,Lucy F.,Oct.27,1855. Parents, Joel D. and Frances Mitchell.

MOORMAN,Otueanna,Nov.1855. Parents, Granville S. and Mary Jane Moorman.

MATTOX,Susan J., June,1855. parents, Micheal T. and mary J. Mattox.

NANCE,John W.,Aug.4,1855. Parents, Thorp H. and Sarah E. Nance. Father was a farmer.

NELMS,Henrietta, March 20,1855. Slave. Owner, Eben Nelms.

NENIMS,Madison, July 2,1855. Slave. Owner, John N. Nenims.

NEWSOM,Lelia O.,march 27,1855. Parents, David M. And Susan E. Newsom.

NEWSOM,Edward B.,Oct.1855. Parents, John W. and Mary F. Newsom.

NANCE,Henry, Oct.1855. Slave. Owner, Thaddeus C.Nance

NININGHER,Ellen, Feb.1855. Parents, David S. and Caroline Niningher.

NEWMAN,Elisha, July 1,1855. Parents, Callahill M. and Julia Ann Newman.

NOEL,Jeffrey, Dec.1855. Slave. Owner, William Noel.

OVERSTREET,Lillia Ann, Aug.23,1855. Parents, Hiram N. and Mary Overstreet.

BIRTH RECORDS

OVERSTREET,Jasper A.,Dec.12,1855. Parents, Joshua and Mary Jane Overstreet.

OTEY,James A.,Nov.17,1855. Parents, John A. and Frances W. Otey.Father was Physician.

OVERSTREET,Martha,Feb.6,1855. Parents, William B. and Nancy Overstreet.

OBRIAN,John, July,1855. Parents, M. and Minerva Obrian

ORE,Spicer P. , Feb.28,1855. Parents, William and Sarah Ore.

ORE,Sar Elinda, Dec.12,1855. Parents, J. and America Ore.

OVERSTREET,William H.,March 25,1855. Parents, Charles and Barsheba Overstreet.

Page # 68,

PLOTT,___?___, Dec.25,1855. Male. Parents, Andrew S. and Frances Plott. Father was a MIller.

PATE,___?___, May,1855. Slave. Owner, Cornelius C.Pate.

PATE, Edward, 1855. Slave. Owner, Alex P.Pate.

PATE,Betty, 1855. Slave. Owner, Alex Pate.

PRESTON,___?___, Aug.12,1855. Parents, John A. and Elizabeth Preston.

PAYNE,Lewis, Sept.1855. Parents, Jesse P. and Charltte payne.

PRESTON,Martha A.,Sept.30,1855. Parents, John F. and Polly Ann Preston.

PHELPS,Emeline, Sept.5,1855. Slave. Owner, Thomas J. Phelps.

PRESTON,Seanna,1855. Parents, James S. and Mariah Preston.

PULLEN,Jonah, 1855. Slave. Owner, Granville R. Pullen.

PARKER,Virginia, June 30,1855. Slave. Owner, Ammon H. Parker.

PHELPS,___?__, Dec.1855. Male. Slave. Owner,A.M.Phelps

PHELPS,Frances, march,1855. Slave. Owner, Joseph Phelps.

PRESTON,Henry, April 29,1855. Slave. Owner, William Preston.

PATTERSON,William T.,March 7,1855. Parents, John M. and Sophia Patterson.

BIRTH RECORDS

PATTERSON,Jon Nickson, July,1855. Slave. Owner,Thomas W. Patterson.

PENN,Jesse,Dec.1855. Slave. Owner, Lucinda Penn.

PREAS,___?___, Oct.12,1855. Parents, Joseph and Mahala Preas.

PENDLETON,William H.,April 5,1855. Parents, James and Rhoda J. Pendleton.

PREAS,John R.,July,1855. Parents, William H. and Mary Jane Preas.

POWELL,John H.,June,1855. Parents, James and Mary Powell.

PAYNE,Thomas R.,July 13,1855. Parents, Thomas M. and Frances Payne.

PENDLETON,William J.,May,1855. Parents, Thomas and Mildred Pendleton.

PENDLETON,Rufus,Oct.1,1855. Slave. Owner, Ann Pendleton.

POLLARD,Adaline,Feb.28,1855. Slave. Owner,Frances Pollard.

POWELL,Thomas, April,1855. Slave. Owner, Thomas Powell

ROACH,Harvey P.,July,1855. Parents, John A. and Martha Roach. Father was an Overseer.

RORER,John J.,Dec.14,1855. Parents, John Q. and Sally B.Rorer.

RUCKER,___?___, June,1855. Slave. Owner, Anthony Rucker.

ROBERTSON,Fanny, March,1855. Slave. Owner, Thomas W. Robertson.

ROBERTSON,George W.,Sept.1855. Parents, Nicholas N. and Sarah E. Robertson.

ROSE,James M.,May 7,1855. Parents, William H. and Martha E. Rose.

Page # 69,

SMITH,Mary E.,Aug.6,1855. Parents, William C. and Paulina Smith. Father was a farmer.

SMITH,Rob H.,May 17,1855. Parents, James A. and Martha Jane Smith.

SMITH,___?___, Dec.7,1855. Parents, Alex A. and Ursula Smith.

STEWART,Estill A.W.,July, 1855. Parents, Saml G. and Mary A.E.J. Stewart.

BIRTH RECORDS

STRATTON,Sarah,June 17,1855. Slave. Owner, Jack Stratton.

STINNETT,Tandy,April11,1855. Parents, Pleasant and Elizabeth Stinnett.

SAUNDERS,Preston W.,Aug.31,1855. Parents, Thomas T. and Eliza Saunders.

SAUNDERS,___?___, Jan.1855.Female. Slave. Owner,Thomas Saunders.

SAUNDERS,___?___, July,1855. Male. Slave. Owner, Thomas Saunders.

SAUNDERS,___?___, 1855.Male. Slave. Owner, Thomas T. Saunders.

STEVENS,___?___, June,1855. Female. Slave. Owner, William W. Stevens.

SKINNELL,Fannie,Oct.1855. Parents, George E. and Elizabeth A.E. Skinnell.

SCHIMED,Henry A.,Sept.2,1855. Parents, Gottlieb and Catherine Schimed.

SCHIMED,Charles A.,June 6,1855. Parents, Barnard and Elizabeth Schimed.

Stailey,Harriett E.,Aug.9,1855. Parents, David and Martha Ann Stailey.

SELDON,Mary E.,Oct.30,1855. FN. Parent, Sarah Seldon.

SCRUGGS,Toby, July,1855. Owner, William B. Scruggs

STINNETT,Sarah F.,Oct.5,1855. Parents, Lindsay and Judith Stinnett.

STEPTOE,___?___, Oct.3,1855. Parents, John R. and Sarah P. Steptoe.

STINNETT,James M., 1855. Parents, Parents, Alex and Catherine Stinnett.

STONE,___?___, Jan.1855. Male. Slave. Owner, Martha Stone

STEWART,Martha M.,Dec.25,1855. Parents, Littleberry and Parthena Stewart.

SMITH,___?___, Dec.1855. Female. Slave. Owner, Stephen Smith.

SAUNDERS,James A. Oct.1855. Parents, James D. and Ann Saunders.

Saunders,___?___, Harriett April 23,1855. Slave. Owner, Kenny Saunders.

SWAIN,Permelia,Aug.9,1855.Parents, Callahill M. and Charlotte E. Swain.

BIRTH RECORDS

SAUNDERS,__?__, Nov.11,1855. Parents,James C. and Mary Saunders.

SHEPHERD,__?__, July,1855. Parents, John A. and Elizabeth Ann Shepherd.

SHEPHERD,Julina, May 8,1855. Slave. Owner, John A. Shepherd.

SWAIN,__?__, 1855. Male. Slave. Owner, Elijah Swain.

SAUNDERSON,Emmett J.,1855. Parents, Thomas N. and Mary Jane Saunderson.

SAUNDERS,__?__, June 10,1855. Female. Parents, George G. and Martha J. Saunders.

SAUNDERS,America, June 25,1855. Slave.Owner, George G. Saunders.

SAUNDERS,Eliza, Feb.1855. Slave. Owner, Thomas Saunders

SCRUGGS,__?__, 1855. Female. Slave. Owner, Elizabeth Scruggs.

STONE,Richard C.,July 8,1855. Parents,Thomas A. and Jane Stone.

SETTLE,__?__, Sept.26,1855. Parents, William S. and S. Settle.

SETTLE,__?__, Nov.1855, Female. Slave. Owner, Littleberry Settle.

SETTLE,Joseph S.,March 31,1855. Parents, John and Barbery Settle.

STIFF,William H.,June,1855. Parents, B.and Julia Ann Stiff.

STIFF,__?__, Dec.1855. Male. Slave. Owner, Bur. Stiff.

STIFF,__?__, Nov.1855, Male. Slave. Owner, H.Stiff.

STIFF,__?__, Dec.1855. Female. Slave. Owner, H.Stiff.

SAUNDERS,Emma D., June 16,1855. Parents, J. and Angeline Saunders.

Page # 70,

SPRADLIN,Charles R.,Sept.4,1855.Parents, Charles H. and Emily E. Spradlin.Father was a farmer.

SMELSOR,William H.,May 11,1855. Parents, Henry K. and Rhoda E. Smelsor.

STEVENS,James F.,march,1855. Parents, Daniel B. and Agnes Stevens.

STEVENS,Lucy Ann E.,Parents, William H. and Mary E. Stevens.

BIRTH RECORDS

STEVENS,__?__, July,1855. Female. Parents, John M. and Susan D. Stevens.

SAUNDERS,Saml R.,Feb.26,1855. Parents, Joseph and Elizabeth Saunders.

SAUNDERS, Mariah, July,1855. Slave. Owner, Joseph Saunders.

TURNER,Tabitha F.,June 27,1855. Parents, Elijah H. and Sarah A. Turner. Father was a farmer.

TURNER,__?__, July,1855. Parents, Thomas W.and Caroline Turner.

TURNER,__?__, Oct.20,1855. Female. Slave. Owner, Hardaway Turner.

TURNER,Comora O.,Aug.1855. Parents, Charles E. and Nancy Turner.

TOWLER,Mary Ann, Oct.1855. Parents, Absalom and Polly Towler.

THURMAN,Emma F.,Jan.4,1855. Parents, Aug S. and Ann Maria Thurman.

TOMPKINS,__?__, July,1855. Male. Slave. Owner, David Tompkins.

TUCK,George T.,July 26,1855. Parents, George and Mary Tuck.

THOMAS,,__?__, Aug.19,1855. Male. Slave. Fleming S.Thomas.

THOMAS,Charles F.,June 23,1855. Parents, William P. and Sarah Thomas.

TUCK,Sarah Ann, Sept.21,1855. Parents, Stephen H. and Sarah J. Tuck.

UPDIKE,Sarah C.,Oct.3,1855. Parents, Anon and Caroline F. Updike.

UPDIKE,__?__, Sept.10,1855. Male. Parents, Chris and Louisa Updike.

Page # 71,

WADE, Virginia, Sept.11,1855. Parents, Callahill M. and Virginia Wade. Father was a farmer.

WHITTEN,Ben, Nov.1855. Slave. Owner, Joseph Whitten.

WOOD,Saml T.,march,1855. Parents, Thomas and Rebecca Wood.

WITT,Lucy Ann, June 21,1855. Parents, Albert M. and Margarett Witt.

WALKER,William Gillmon, June 2,1855. Slave. Owner, Edward T. Walker.

BIRTH RECORDS

WALES,___?___, 1855. Male. Slave. Owner, Richard M Wales.

WAGGONER, William O.,Aug.3,1855. Parents, J.R. and Martha O. Waggoner. Father was Minister of Gospel.

WILKS,Nancy C.,Oct.22,1855. Parents, William C. and Elizabeth Wilks.

WRIGHT, Sarah A.,July 1,1855. Parents, Bartley and Hannah A.V. Wright.

WITT,___?___, Nov.27,1855. Parents, William W. and Nancy Witt.

WITT, _____,&_____,(Twins).March 15,1855. Males. Parents Roland and Eliza Jane Witt.

WALKER, Eletha H.,July 12,1855. parents, David H. and Caroline Walker.

WITT, Louisa, May 1,1855. Slave. Owner, William Witt.

WITT,___?___, May 25,1855. Female. Slave. Owner, William Witt.

WITT, Engeline,May 28,1855. Slave. Owner, William Witt

WILDMAN,Gideon,Oct.10,1855. Parents, Elisha S. and Mary Wildman.

WILSON,Nancy E, April 6,1855. Parents, Elijah C. and Martha S. Wilson.

WITT,Queen, Nov.16,1855. Parents, Reubin and Mary M. Witt.

WRIGHT,Sarah E.,Dec.8,1855. Parents, George W. and Fanny Wright.

WELLS, Rob A.,April 15,1855. Parents, David G. and Florentine W. Wells.

WALKER, Henry Clay,Oct.11,1855. Slave. Owner, James A. Walker.

WALKER, Rufus,April 7,1855. Slave. Owner, James Walker

WALKER, Frederick,Sept.6,1855. Slave. Owner, James Walker.

WADE,Mary M.,April,1855. Parents, William A. and Mary Wade.

WADE,___?___, July,1855, Slave. Owner, William Wade.

WRIGHT, Charles, Sept.1855. Slave. Owner, James Wright

WRIGHT, Walter C.,Aug.14,1855. Parents, James O. and Mariah S. Wright.

WRIGHT, Saml T.,Jan.2,1855. parents, Peter M. Jr. and Sarah J. Wright.

BIRTH RECORDS

WRIGHT, Major, Dec.1855. Slave. Owner, Peter Wright Sr

WINGFIELD,Ann E.,march 11,1855. Parents, Nelson D. and Harriett Wingfield.

WATSON,Jame P.,Jan.27,1855. Parents, Green and Mary Jane Watson.

WIGGENTON,James MUnroe, June,1855. Slave. Owner, Isaac Wiggenton.

WIGGENTON,Calidonia,June,1855. Slave. Owner, Isaac Wiggenton.

WIGGINTON,Phoebe M.,Dec.11,1855. parents, William and Elizabeth Wigginton.

WIGGINTON,Charles A.,Nov.9,1855. Parents, Robert and Caroline Wigginton

WALROND,Saml T.,June 10,1855. Parents, Moses and Nancy Walrond.

WILLIAMS,Edward, Nov.15,1855. Parents, Sep. S.and Sarah F. Williams.

WADE,Saml, Aug.1,1855. Slave. Owner, Alex Wade.

ADAMS, Victoria, Aug.7,1855. Slave. Owner, N.Adams

WITT, Ann BOoker, Nov.24,1855. Slave. Owner, M.A.Witt

WHITE, Gilla, Nov.2,1855. Parents, John E.and Alis White.

WILSON,Maria S.,Jan.23,1855. Parents, James R.and Eveline Wilson.

Page # 72,

WRIGHT,William P.,July 8,1855. Parents, James M. and Mary F. Wright.

WHEELER, Saml T.,Jan.15,1855. Parents, Thomas and Sarah Wheeler.

ZIMMERMAN,Rob.B.,may 17,1855. Parents, William and Adaline Zimmerman.

Page # 73,   1856.

ANDERSON,James Alexander, Sept.,1856. Parents, William A. and Penelope E. Anderson.Father was a farmer.

ARRINGTON,Alex,March 9,1856. Parents, William and Elizabeth Ann Arrington. FATHER WAS A FARMER.

ARRINGTON,James R.Edward,June 10,1856. Parents, Hampton Jr. and Delilia Ann Arrington.

ARRINGTON,Eliza, April,1856, Slave, Mother, Charlott. Owner, Edmond Arrington.

BIRTH RECORDS

ABBOTT,Nancy Ann,June 14,1856.Parents, Robert M. and Frances Abbott. father was a farmer.

ANDERSON,Beverly, Jan 9,1856. Slave. Mother, Leannah. Owner, John N. Anderson.

ANDERSON,John, June 4,1856. Slave. Mother, Martha. Owner, John N. Anderson.

ACREE,Edward Hopkins, Dec.4,1856. Parents, Alban J. and Ann Eliza Acree.Father was a farmer.

ALLEN,Laura,Oct.1856. Slave. Mother, Ellen. Owner, Robert Allen.

ARRINGTON,Mary Ann, March 7,1856. Parents, John and Martha R. Arrington.

ALMUND,Sarah Elizabeth,March 30,1856. Parents,John and Sarah E. Almund. Father was a farmer.

BURNETT,William Edwin,Oct.11,1856. Parents, James C. and Eliza E.Burnett.Father was a Carpenter.

BILBRO,Edward, May,1856. Slave. Mother, Lucy. Owner, William Bilbro.

BALLARD,James Winston, May 27,1856. Parents, C.J. and Mary Ann Ballard. Father was a farmer.

BELL,__?__, July,1856. Slave. Mother, Ann. Owner, F.H. Bell.

BRYANT,Samuel, July 28,1856. Parents, Peter H. and Elizabeth Bryant. Father was a farmer.

BROWN,Charles Alva & Emer Swanthis,Sept.14,1856.(Twins) Parents, Alfred A. and Ann brown. Father was Shoemaker.

BURKS,Betsey, July,1856. Slave. Mother, Nancy. Owner, Jesse S.Burks.

BURKS,William Sherman, Sept.24,1856. Parents,John D. and Dolly Burks. Father was a farmer.

BURFORD,Daniel, May,1856. Slave. Mother, Judy.Owner, Lucy F.Burford.

BELL,Thomas, April 14,1856. Slave. Mother, Patsy. Owner, William S.Bell.

BURKS,Julia Ann, Aug.1856. Slave. Mother, Betsey. Owner, Martin Burks.

BURKS, Margarett,Oct.1856. Slave. Mother, Mary Ann. Owner, Martin Burks.

BURWELL,__?__, Dec.1856. Female. Slave. Mother, Eliza. Owner, William M.Burwell.

BIRTH RECORDS

Page # 74

CARTER,,Elzira Virginia,July 4,1856. Parents, Little berry and Eliza Carter.Father was a farmer.

COBBS, ? , Oct.26,1856.Female. Parents, James G. and Sarah J.CObbs. Father was a farmer.

CARTER, Wellington,April,1856. Parents, James M. and Frances Ann Carter. Father was a farmer.

CARTER,Willie Jane,June 28,1856. Parents, Pleasant and Frances H. Carter. Father was a farmer.

COTTRIAL,Liddie Allice,April 28,1856. Parents, James and Margaret Cottrial.

COLEMAN,Adam,Aug.,1856. Slave. Mother, Margaret. Owner Leroy Coleman.

CLARK,Robt Bennett, April 1,1856. Parents, Isham and Mariah Clark.Father was a farmer.

CARNEFIX, Sam,May 9,1856. Slave. Mother, Eliza. Owner, E.M.Carnefix.

COFER, ? , Aug.,1856. Female. Slave. Mother, Matilda. Owner, Mrs Lucinda Cofer.

COFER, ? , Sept.19,1856. Female. Parents, John C.and Sarah B.Cofer.

CAMPBELL,Thomas,Aug.1856. Slave. Mother, ANgeline. Owner, Thomas Campbell.

CAMPBELL,Lafayett,Jan.28,1856. Slave. Mother, Ellen. Owner, Thomas Campbell.

CRANK,Henry, May 29,1856. Parents, William J. and Segus Crank. Father was a farmer.

CHEATWOOD,Samuel McDaniel,July,1856.Parents, Hiram and Julia Cheatwood. Father was a farmer.

CHEATWOOD,George, Sept.1856.Slave. Mother, Lucinda. Owner, Hiram S.Cheatwood.

CHEATWOOD,Sarah. Aug.1956.Salve. Mother, Mary. Owner, Hirem Cheatwood.

CHILDRESS,Sarah Jane, 1856. Parents, William T. and Elizabeth Childress.Father was a farmer.

CRANK,Anna Constance,March 29,1856. Parents, James L. and Susan L. Crank.Father was a farmer.

CREASY,George Christopher,Sept.8,1856. Parents, Benjamin F. and Mary Creasy.Father was a farmer.

COTTRIAL, ? , Dec.8,1856. Parents, Thomas J. and Martha Jane Cottrial.Father was a farmer.

CARDER,Cornelia Eubank,Jan.1856. Parents, James M.and Sarah Carder. Father was a Cabinet Maker.

BIRTH RECORDS

CARR,__?__, Nov.10,1856. Parents, A.S.and Elizabeth C. Carr. Father was a Stone Cutter.

CHILDRESS,William, Dec.1856. Parents, William H. and Sally Ann Childress. father was a Miller.

CRANK,Bettie Alberta,March 2,1856. Parents, Albert G. And Elizabeth C. Crank. Father was a Carpenter.

CHAFFIN,William Leonard, April 12,1856. Parents, Edwin and Mary Chaffin. Father was a farmer.

CALE,William Robert, Jan.27,1856. Parents, Samuel O. and Catherine E. Cale.father was a farmer.

CAMPBELL,Thomas, March 6,1856. Slave. Mother, Frances. Owner, Henry Campbell.

CAMPBELL, Sarah Allice, Dec.3,1856. Parents, Alex S. and Mary Ann Campbell. father was a farmer.

DOOLEY,Virginia, Dec.1856. Parents, John and Ann Dooley. Father was a farmer

DEARDORFF,Talula Nina,Sept.8,1856.Parents, John H. and Emily J. Deardorff. Father was a Miller.

DAY,Alice Ann,Jan.26,1856. parents, John J. and Sarah C. Day. Father was a Wheelright.

Daugherty,Martha Nelson,Aug.1,1856. Parents, A.C. and Nancy S. Daugherty.Father was a farmer.

DONALD,Mary E.,July,1856. Slave. Mother, Fanny. Owner, Benjamin Donald.

DONALD,Jesse,Sept.31,1856. Slave. Mother, Margarett. Owner, Benjamin Donald.

DEWITT,James Mitton,May 18,1856. Parents, William H. and Louiza Ann Dewitt. Father was a farmer.

DOUGLASS,Lewis,Aug.4,1856. Slave. Mother, Patria, Owner, Sarah Douglass.

DICKERSON,Amy Ann,March,1856. Slave. Mother, Marcella. Owner, William Dickerson.

Page # 75,

EARLY,Mary Elizabeth, Jan.1,1856. Parents, John W. and Sarah Agness. Father was a farmer.

EUBANK,Frank, July,1856. Slave. Mother, Matilda. Owner Joseph Eubank.

EUBANK,Sarah, July,1856. Slave. Mother, Harriett.Owner Joseph Eubank.

EUBANK,Susan Isabella,May,1856. Parents,Ambrose and Frances Eubank.Father was a farmer.

BIRTH RECORDS

FERGUSON, Wilmoth Ann,Dec.17,1856. Parents, Alfred A. and Susan S. Ferguson.Father was a Shoemaker.

FARMER,Fannie Susan,July 4,1856. Parents, James A.and Eddy Ann Farmer. Father was a Blacksmith.

FERRELL,Edward Royal,Feb.24,1856. Parents, Mitton P. and Lucy H.ferrell. Father was a farmer.

FORGIE,__?__, Sept.18,1856. parents, Daniel K. and Nancy A. Forgie. Father was a farmer.

FERRELL,Mary, Aug.15,1856. Slave. Mother, Temp.Owner, Henry C.Ferrell.

FERRELL,Samuel Huff, Nov.30,1856. Parents,James M. and Mary Jane Ferrell.Father was a farmer.

FOSTER,John Edward, June 30,1856. Parents, Faris and Mary S.Foster. Father was a Carpenter.

FIFER,Sarah Fanny,Jan.28,1856. Parents, Isaac and Mary Fifer. father was a farmer.

FISHER,__?__, Nov.23,1856.Parents, Thomas and Fanny Fisher. Father was a Carpenter.

FOWLER,John Henry. April,1856. Slave. Mother, Emily. Owner, William D. Fowler.

FOWLER, Nelly,may, 1856. Slave. Mother, Matilda.Owner, William D. Fowler.

GOODWIN,George Osearr,July 22,1856. Parents, Jesse B. and Jane A.E.goodwin. Father was a farmer.

GOODE,__?__, Oct.26,1856. Male. Parents, Edmond and Mary Ann Goode. Father was a farmer.

GOODMAN,Frances. Nov.1856. Slave. Mother, Matilda. Owner, Nancy Goodman.

GOODMAN,William Edward, Jan.8,1856. Parents, John and Martha S. Goodman.Father was a farmer.

GOODMAN,Henry,April 2,1856. Slave. Mother, Mary. Owner, Lucy Goodman.

GOFF,__?__, April 19,1856. FN. Male. Parent, Jane E.Goff

GRAVES,Ellen, Sept.26,1856. Slave. Mother, Lucy. Owner John P.Graves.

GILLS, Lee, Oct.1856. SLave. Mother, Abbey. Owner, William H.Gills.

GILBERT,Charlott Annah,June 15,1856. Parents, Clifton and Mary Ann Gilbert.Father was a farmer.

GILLS,Eller Jane,Oct.23,1856. Parents, William W.and Angeline Gills. Father was a farmer.

GILLASPIE,__?__, July 15,1856. Female. Parents, E.B. and Mary F. Gillaspie.Father was a farmer.

BIRTH RECORDS

Page # 76

HODGES,Missouri Allis,Feb.23,1856. Parents, Benjamin W. and Judy Angeline.Father was a farmer.

HODGES, Samuel Thomas, Jan.1856. Parents, Samuel J. and Sarah Hodges. Father was a farmer.

HALLEY,___?___, Nov.16,1856.Female. Parents, Richard B. and Sarah E. Halley.Father was a Merchant.

HUNTER, Robert,April,1856. Slave. Mother, Mariah. Owner, Aenias Hunter.

HATCHER, Stephen. Aug.1856. Slave. Mother, Sophiah. Owner, Uriah Hatcher.

HURT,Eller, Feb.1856. Slave. Mother, Betsey. Owner, John P. Hurt.

HATCHER,Sue Fannie. Oct.2,1856. Parents, Hanibal W. and Mary C. Hatcher. Father was a farmer.

HUTTER,Peggy,Oct.29,1856. SLAVE. Mother, Lydia. Owner, E.S.Hutter.

HARDY,Mary Fletcher,Jan.,1856. Parents, James A. and Lucinda D. Hardy.Father was a farmer.

HATCHER,Albon,June 9,1856. Parents, Thomas A. and Mary E. Hatcher. Father was a farmer.

HARRIS,Harriett. March 1,1856. Slave. Mother, Mariah. Owner, Hanibal Harris.

HORSLEY,Benjamin Wilks. Sept.15,1856. Parents,Nicholas and Elizabeth L.Horsley.Father was a farmer.

HATCHER,Betty, April 24,1856. Slave. Mother, Martha. Owner, Allen D.Hatcher.

HARRIS,Sarah Lewis,May 21,1856. Parents, C.J. and C.H. Harris. Father was a farmer.

HATCHER,James Harvey,July 13,1856. Parents,Caleb H. and Florentine McD Hatcher.Father was a farmer.

HATCHER, Eller Jane, Oct.1856. Slave. MOther, Mary. Owner, Caleb H.Harris.

HARRIS,Mary Ann,Aug.1,1856.Slave. Mother, Polina. Owner, James M.Harris.

HEWITT,James, Aug.27,1856. Slave. Mother, Lucy. Owner, H.H.Hewitt.

HAWKINS,Ellen Boles,Oct.1856. Parents, Alfred and Elizabeth Hawkins. Father was a farmer.

HOWELL,James William,Nov.2,1856. Parents,A.M. and Ann B. Howell. Father was a farmer.

BIRTH RECORDS

HAWKINS,Peachy Frances,Aug.1,1856. Parents, James and Elvira Hawkins.

HENSLEY, _?_, Oct.1856. Parents, Joel and Luvenia E. Hensley. Father was a farmer.

HARRISON,Robert, June,1856. Slave. Mother, Emily.Owner James Harrison.

HOLT,Frank, Feb.10,1856. Slave. Mother, Fillis. Owner, John W. Holt.

HOLT, Sally,Oct.24,1856. Slave. Mother, Jane. Owner, John Holt.

HOBSON,Isabella, 1856. Slave. Mother, Emily. Owner, Samuel Hobson.

HOBSON,Rier, 1856. Slave. Mother, Mary. Owner,Samuel Hobson.

HOBSON,Ethalina, 1856. Slave. Mother, Mary. Owner, Samuel Hobson.

HOBSON,Rosser, 1856. Slave. Mother, Betsey. Owner, Samuel Hobson.

HOBSON, Susan, 1856. Slave. Mother, Eady. Owner, Samuel Hobson.

HOBSON, Caleb, 1856. Slave. Mother, Julia. Owner,Samuel Hobson

HOBSON,Allice, 1856. Slave. Mother, Fanny. Owner, Samuel Hobson.

HATCHER, Selene, May 30,1856. Parents, Granvill and Calista hatcher. father was a farmer.

HATCHER, James Henry, Sept. 1856. parents, Jeremiah G. and Angeline W. Hatcher.

HOWARD, John Walker, Aug.2,1856. Parents, John A. and Cleopatra Howard. Father was a farmer.

Page # 77

JOPLING,Jesse Spottswood,Feb.10,1856. Parents, Thomas B. and Sarah E. Jopling.Father was a farmer.

JONES,_?_, Aug.1,1856. Parents, John W. and Elizabeth J.Jones. Father was a Merchant.

JONES,Minerva, Feb.,1856. Slave. Mother, Lucinda.Owner, Mrs Sally P. Jones.

JONES,Martha. July,1856. Slave. Mother, Harreitt.Owner Mrs Sally P. Jones.

JENNINGS,James Edward, Oct.11,1856. Parents, Zachariah E. and Lucy A. Jennings. Father was a farmer.

BIRTH RECORDS

JENNINGS,Marcella, Jan.1856. Slave. Mother, Vina. Owner, James C. Jennings.

JENNINGS,Dilcey,March,1856. Slave. Mother, Judy. Owner James C.Jennings.

JONES, Allice. April 5,1856. Parents, Samuel P. and Mary Va Jones. Father was a farmer.

JENNINGS,Zachariah Benjamin. Sept.8,1856. Parents, James W. and Rachel J.N. Jennings.

JETER, Moses, Dec.13,1856. Slave. Mother, Emily. Owner, Jesse Jeter.

JETER, William, May,1856. Slave. Julia. Owner, Julia. Owner, Jesse Jeter.

JOPLING,Samuel Emmet, June 25,1856. Parents, William W. and Julia Ann Jopling. Father was a farmer.

KARNES,Julian Owen, may 28,1856. Parents, Abraham and Ann Karnes. Father was a farmer.

KARNES, William Hudnall, July 5,1856. Parents, William R. and Nancy Karnes. father was a farmer.

KARNES, Alexander Hamilton. Oct.9,1856. Parents, John J. and Salinda Ann Karnes. Father was a farmer.

KEY, Charles Marion,Sept.1856. Parents, Charles H. and Mildred F. Key. Father was a farmer.

KENT,Frank Russell,May 15,1856. Parents, John D. and Mary O. Kent. Father was a Physician.

KARNES, Eliza Turner, Feb. 2,1856. Parents, William A. and Sarah F. Karnes.Father was a farmer.

KNIGHT,Nanny Leigh,Nov.9,1856. Parents, John J. and Susan C. Knight. Father was a farmer.

KELSO,Benjamin, April,1856. Slave. Mother, Mary.Owner, Robert N. Kelso.

KELSO, Mariah, May,1856. Slave. Mother, Nancy. Owner, Robert N. Kelso.

KELSO,__?__, July. 1856. Slave. Mother, Lucy.

LUCK,James Paschal,Aug.4,1856. Parents, George P. and Nancy Luck. Father was a farmer.

LEE, Robert, Aug.30,1856. Slave. Mother, Ellen. Owner, Thomas N. Lee.

LOWRY,Martha, may 25,1856. Slave. Mother, Lucy. Owner, John Lowry.

LOWRY, William Austin, May 27,1856. Slave. Mother, Betsy. Owner, John Lowry.

LOWRY, Price, Nov.16,1856. Slave. Mother, Mary. Owner, John Lowry.

BIRTH RECORDS

LEFTWICH,__?__, Sept.,1856. Slave. Mother, Hannah.
Owner, Thomas W. Leftwich.

LOWRY,Allice. June,1856. Slave. Mother, Eldy. Owner,
John W.Lowry.

LOWRY,Cephas, Oct.9,1856. Slave. Mother, Ann. Owner,
Lilburn Lowry.

LOWRY,Ellen, Nov.20,1856. Slave. Mother, Mary.Owner,
Henry Lowry.

LOWRY, __?__, Dec.1856. Slave. Mother, Sarah. Owner,
Milton Lowry.

LAWLESS,Elizabeth Virginia,Oct.1856. Parents, James
and Betsy Ann lawless. Father was a Carpenter.

LOWRY,Flora, Dec.1856. Slave. Mother, Clary. Owner,
Nelson Lowry.

LOCKIE,Alfred, Nov.9,1856. Slave. Mother, Harriett.
Owner, Mrs Emily Lockie.

LOGWOOD,Ferdinand,March 25,1856. Slave. Mother, Mary.
Owner, Alexander H. Logwood.

LOGWOOD, James Edward, Nov.30,1856. Parents, Robert R.
and Mary E. Logwood. Father was a farmer.

Page # 78,

MOOR,Susa Martha Rebeckah,June 10,1856. Parents, Good-
ridge and Catherine Moor.

MARSHALL,Sarah Samantha,March 1,1856. Parents, John A.
and Elzira Marshall.Father was a farmer.

MARSH,Mary Permelia,Dec.30,1856.Parents, Robert B. and
Martha Marsh. Father was a farmer.

MARSH,Mary Lawra,Oct.1856. Parents, Thomas E. and Lyd-
da C. Marsh. Father was a farmer.

MARKHAM,Roland, Jan.28,1856. Slave Mother, Lucy.Owner,
matha Markham.

MEADOR, __?__, June,1856. Male. Parents, John W. and
Eliza Meador. Father was a farmer.

MILLNER, __?__, March 1,1856. male. Parents, Madison F.
and Elizabeth Millner. Father was a farmer.

MILLNER,George, nov.1856. Slave. Mother, Martha,Owner,
Albert G. Millner.

MCDANIEL,Tazewell,July 19,1856,Slave. Mother, Lydia.
Owner, Albert McDaniel.

MELTON,Joseph Morton Thomas,July 9,1856. Parents, Samuel and Mariah W. Melton.

MCDANIEL, __?__, April 1,1856.Parents, Jesse W. and Mary
F. McDaniel. Father was a farmer.

BIRTH RECORDS

MORMAN,William Dabney,May,1856. Slave. Mother, Ann.
Owner, Lodowick Morman.

MORMAN,Henry Clay, Aug.1856. Slave. Mother, Betsy.
Owner, Lodowick Morman.

MOORMAN,Martha Ann, Feb.20,1856. Slave. Mother, Eliza
Owner, G.S.Moorman.

MOORMAN,Ann, April 28,1856. Slave. Mother, Mary.Owner,
G.S.Moorman.

MERRIWEATHER,James. March,1856. Slave. Mother, Polly.
Owner, C.J. Merriweather.

MASON,Lucy Eldridge,April 3,1856. Parents, George E.
and Elizabeth F. Mason. Father was a Miller.

METCALFE,__?__, 1856. Slave. Mother, Caroline.Owner,
James Metcalf.

METCALFE,__?__, 1856, Female. Slave. Mother, Ginny.
Owner, James Metcalf.

MINNICK,Elvira Emily,Oct.1856. Parents, George W. and
Catherine M. Minnick.Father was a Cabinet Maker.

MORRIS,Mary Elizabeth,Sept.3,1856.Parents, William H.
and Mary Ann Morris.Father was a farmer.

MAJOR,Edna, Oct.1856. Parents, S.A. and Kitty Major.
Father was a farmer.

MEEKS,Mary Wiatt,march 23,1856. parents, Eldridge and
Martha Virginia Meeks. Father was a Carpenter.

NEWMAN,Rosea William, June,1856. Parents, Jesse and
Mary Newman. Father was a Carpenter.

NEWMAN, Mildred Key, Sept.,1856. Parents, Robert and
Sarah P. Newman. Father was a farmer.

NOEL, Charles, April,1856. Slave. Mother, Catherine.
Owner, John C.Noel.

NOEL,Abner, Nov.1856. Slave. Mother, Marge. Owner,John
C.Noel.

NOEL,Margaret, Nov.,1856. Slave. Mother, Martha. Owner
John C. Noel.

NOEL, Robert Hall,may 19,1856. Parents, Palestine and
Ann Eliza Noel. father was a farmer.

NOEL,Frances, Oct.15,1856. Slave. Mother, Angeline.
Owner, Palestine Noel.

NOEL,Eliza, March 20,1856. Slave. MOther, Amanda. Owner
Alexander J.Noel.

NOEL,__?__, Nov.8,1856. Female. Parents, Erasmus D. and
Catherine Noel.Father was a farmer.

BIRTH RECORDS

NORCROSS,Frances,Nov.1856. Parents, Samuel and Frances Norcross. Father was a Wheelright.

Page # 79,

OVERACRE,Emily, May 10,1856. Parents, George W. and Emily Overacre. Father was a farmer.

OWNBY,___?___, April 14,1856. Female. Parents, Charles P. and Catherine J. Ownby. Father was a farmer.

OTEY,Julia Ann, June,1856. Slave. Mother, Kitty. Owner, Mrs Mary C. Otey.

OVERSTREET,Charles Lewis, July 12,1856. Parents, Charles A. and Phebe Ann Overstreet.father was farmer.

ORRANGE,James William, July 31,1856. Parents, Edward N. and Eliza Jane Orrange. Father was a farmer.

ORRANGE,Tilman Smith,Sept. 28,1856. Parents, Burwell S. and Ann Elizabeth Orrange.Father was a farmer.

OGLESBY,Albert, Dec.31,1856. Parents, Joshua B. and Sarah F. Oglesby.Father was a farmer.

OGLESBY, David, Aug.,1856. slave. Mother, Mariah. Owner, Joshua Oglesby.

OGDEN,Cornelia, April, 1856. Slave. Mother, Jane. Owner, Henry M. Ogden.

OGDEN,Annah, May,1856. Slave. Mother, Harriett. Owner, Henry M.Ogden.

OGDEN,Lniza,March,1856. Slave. Mother, Polina. Owner, William Ogden.

OLLIVER, ___?___, Sept.23,1856. Male. Parents, John K. and Tabitha A. Olliver. Father was a farmer.

OLLIVER, Lueresey,Oct.1856. Parents, Derrett N. and Margaret Olliver.Father was a farmer.

OLLIVER,___?___, Oct.,1856. Female. Parents, James W. and Lumbia Ann Olliver. Father was a farmer.

POWELL,Cisaley, June 17,1856. Slave. Mother, Sarah. Owner, Miss Polly Powell.

PIERCE,Robert Lee, April 13,1856. Parents, Moses and Elizabeth Pierce. Father was a farmer.

PALMER, Charles, April 4,1856. Parents, Robert J. and Caroline Palmer. Father was a farmer.

PAGITT,___?___, Oct.10,1856. Male. Parents, James A. and Lucy Pagitt. Father was a farmer.

PAGITT, Rebeckah Jane, Oct.,1856. Slave. Mother, Jane. Owner, Beverly Pagitt.

BIRTH RECORDS

PERKINS,Pleasant, Feb.,1856. Slave. Mother, Mary.
Owner, Mrs D.A.Perkins.

POINDEXTER, Frances Susan, April 7,1856. Parents,
Davis D. and Ann Elizabeth Poindexter.Father was a
farmer.

POINDEXTER, Alla, May,1856. Slave. Mother, Mary. Owner
Davis D. Poindexter.

PHELPS, Phill, April 13,1856. Slave. Mother, Matilda.
Owner, Peter W.Phelps.

PLOTT,Frances Rebeckah Dillard, March 10,1856. Parents
Lewis E. and Martha E. Plott.Father was a Miller.

PONTON,John James,Nov.28,1856. Parents, John F. and
Emily Ponton. Father was a Carpenter.

PERROW, Sarah, june 15,1856. Slave. Mother, Nancy.
Owner, James S. Perrow.

POINDEXTER, ? , Sept.1,1856. Slave. Mother, Aylsey.
Owner, Willis G. Poindexter.

POINDEXTER,James,July 1,1856. Slave. Mother, Susan.
Owner, Martha G. Poindexter.

PENN, William Cornelius, Feb.29,1856. Parents, P.S.and
Mary C.Penn. Father was a farmer.

PATTERSON,Mary Elizabeth, March,1856. Parents, William
and Elizabeth Patterson,Father was a Carpenter.

PETTICREW,Rufus, Sept.7,1856. Parents, Matthew and Ann
Petticrew. Father was a Lock Keeper.

PATTERSON,Lizzie Letton, 1856. Parents, Thomas and
Phebe Jane Patterson. father was a farmer.

Page # 80,

ROY,James Hersey, June 1,1856. Parents,William W. and
Elizabeth Roy. Father was a farmer.

ROY,Fill, Sept. 1856. Slave. Mother, Sally. Owner, John
Roy's Estate.

ROSE, Sarah Frances, June 22,1856. Parents, Thomas E.
and Catherine Rose. Father was a farmer.

READ, Lelia Jane, Oct.14,1856. Parents, E.T.and Eliza
A. Read. Father was a farmer.

RILEY, ? , Feb.28,1856. Female. Parents, George and
Elizabeth Riley. Father was a farmer.

RUSHER, Geles, April 13,1856. Slave. Mother, Ann.Owner,
James Rusher.

BIRTH RECORDS

ANDERSON,Lucy, Aug.1856. Parents, John H. and Mary Anderson. Father was a farmer.

ROSE, John T.Alexander, May 19,1856. Parent,Keziah Rose.

ROBINSON,Ellen Grace,March 15,1856. Parents, Edward N. and Martha M. Robinson. Father was a farmer.

ROBINSON,Mariah, Oct.,1856. Slave. Mother, Malinda. Owner, Edwaed N. Robinson.

RUCKER, Hanibal, Feb.13,1856. Slave. Mother, Amanda. Owner, James M. Rucker.

RUCKER, Natt, April 15,1856. Slave. Mother, Julia Ann. Owner, James Rucker.

RADFORD,Marshall, Aug.,1856. Slave. Mother, Mahala. Owner, William Radford.

RADFORD, David, Sept.,Slave. Mother, Octavus, Owner, William Radford.

RADFORD, Martha, Sept.,1856. Slave. Mother, Susan. Owner, William Radford.

RADFORD, Nathan, June, 1856. Slave. Mother, Lydia. Owner, William Radford.

REECE, Daniel, Sept.4,1856. Slave. Mother, Mariah. Owner, Joseph T. Reece.

RADFORD,Mina Jordan, April,1856. Parents, Winston and Ann M. Radford. Father was a farmer.

READ, ___?___ , April, 1856. Slave. Mother, Sylvia. Owner, William A. Read.

RICE, Ann Elizabeth, Aug.,1856. Parents, William C. and Amanda Virginia Rice. Father was a farmer.

SMITH, William Thomas, March 15,1856. Parents, James and Martha F. Smith. Father was a farmer.

SHELTON,Charles, Oct.,1856. Slave. Mother, Nancy. Owner, Wesley Shelton.

STANLEY,Virginia Stanley,Oct.22,1856. Parents, John N. and Martha Stanley. Father was a farmer.

STEPTOE, Noah, March 22,1856. Slave. Mother, Molly. Owner, Robert C. Steptoe.

SNEAD, Virginia Ann, Sept.5,1856. Parents, George W. and Caroline Snead. Father was a farmer.

SMITH, Emmer Lewis, Feb.29,1856. Parents, William Jr. and Catherine Smith. Father was a farmer.

SLAUGHTER, Archer, Aug.,1856. Slave. Mother, Mariah. Owner, James C. Slaughter

BIRTH RECORDS

SCOTT,Florah, May,1856. Slave. Mother, Caroline.
Owner, Samuel M.Scott.

SCOTT, Spencer, Feb.1856. Slave. Mother, Harriett,
owner, Elizabeth M.Scott.

SLEDD, __?__ , Dec.,1856. Slave. Mother, Betsey. Owner,
William E. Sledd.

SMOOT,James Thomas, May 10,1856. parents, William H.
and Mary F. Smoot. Father was a Marchant.

STCLAIR,Elizabeth Frances, Oct.7,1856. Parents, Samuel
and Martha Ann StClair, Father was a Miller.

SEAY,Mary Elizabeth, Sept.,23,1856. Parents, David P.
and Amanda M. Seay.Father was a Wheelright.

Page # 81,

THOMPSON,__?__ , Dec.2,1856. Female. Parents, Alexander
S. and Margaret R. Thompson. Father was a Merchant.

THOMPSON,Amanda, Feb.,1856. Slave. Mother, Sally.
Owner, Nelson A. Thompson.

THOMPSON, Betsey, March 4,1856. Slave. Mother, Dosha.
Owner, Nelson A. Thompson.

THOMPSON,Caroline, Sept.,1856. Slave. Mother, Jane.
Owner, Nelson A. Thompson.

TANKISLEY,Anderson, Oct.17,1856. Parents, Richard A.
and Mary Jane Tankisley. Father was a farmer.

TURPIN,Henry Ann, Dec.,1856. parents, Elisha G. and
Amanda Turpin. Father was a farmer.

TOMS,George Washington, Oct.30,1856. Parents, G.W. and
Henrietta A. Toms. Father was a Blacksmith.

THOMAS, Frances Julia, Dec.6,1856. Parents, Rufus N.
and Sarah L. Thomas.

TURPIN,Laura Riverta, July,1856. Parents, Robert H.and
Sally Ann E. Turpin. Father was a farmer.

TURPIN,Madison, Dec.1856. Slave. Mother, Julia. Owner,
R.G.Turpin.

TURNER, Jesse, June 22,1856. Parents, Rev. Jesse H.
and Sallie F. Turner. FAther was a farmer.

THOMASON,Joseph Green, May 21,1856. Parents, John N.
and Mary D. Thomason. Father was a Factory Worker.

THAXTON,Wiatt, 1856. Slave. Mother, Harriett. Owner,
N.F.Thaxton.

THOMPSON, __?__ , Sept.1856. Female. Parents, David E.
and Mildred Thompson. Father was a farmer.

BIRTH RECORDS

VARNER, Fanny Bell, Nov.,1856. Parents, John W. and Mary F. Varner. Father was a farmer.

WATSON, Hubert Florain, Jan.4,1856. Parents, Jordan and Nancy Watson. Father was a farmer.

WILLIAMS, Susan, March 9,1856. Slave. Mother, Caroline Owner, J.M.Williams.

WILLIAMSON,George, March,1856. Slave. Mother, Nancy. Owner, Solomon Williamson.

WILKERSON,Hugh Brown, Feb.16,1856. Parents, William L. and Keziah Wilkerson. Father was a farmer.

WILKERSON,Isaac, Sept.26,1856. Slave. Mother, Susan. Owner, William L. Wilkerson.

WILKERSON,George Washington, Aug.,15,1856. Parents, Joseph B. and Juliett B. Wilkerson.Father was a farmer

WILKERSON, Magdalen, Jan.,1856. Slave. Mother, Agness. Owner, William O. Wilkerson.

WATSON,Martha, April, 1856. Slave. Mother, Catherine. Owner, Mrs Nancy Watson.

WILLIAMSON,Moses, March,1856. Slave. Mother, Polly. Owner, Caleb Williamson.

WILLIAMS, Cary, July 3,1856. Slave. Mother, Sarah. Owner, Mrs Matilda Williams.

WOOLFOLK,George, Feb.15,1856. Slave. Mother, Julia. Owner, William H. Woolfolk

WILSON,__?__, Dec.9,1856. Male. Parents, William and Mary E. Wilson. Father was a farmer.

WHITE,Walter, Feb.,1856. Parents, Jacob S. and Catherine S. White. Father was a farmer.

WILSON,Mariah Jane, April 4,1856. Parents, Thomas J. and Elizabeth S. Wilson.Father was a farmer.

WILKS, Malinda & Lucinda, May 12,1856. (Twins).Slaves Mother, Eliza. Owner, Benjamin Wilks.

WILKS, Burwell, Jan.,1856. Slave. Mother, Sophiah. Owner, Benjamin Wilks.

WILSON,Georgianna,March,1856. Parents, George W. and Eliza Ann Wilson. Father was a Millright.

WHITTEN,Mary, Nov.,1856. Slave. Mother, Milly. Owner, J.H.Whitten.

WOODY,Martha Jane,Oct.4,1856. Parents, Richard R. and Mary Ann Woody. Father was a Lockkeeper.

WATSON,Rozetta Jane, Feb.16,1856. Parents, Uriah and Mary Ann R. Watson.father was a farmer.

BIRTH RECORDS

WHITE, Allice Mason, Sept.15,1856. Slave. Mother,Elizabeth. Owner, Henry M. WHite.

WHITE, Henrietta Leek, May 20,1856. parents, Jeremiah C. and Elvira W. White. Father was a farmer.

WILKERSON,Othur Rush, Oct.8,1856.Parents, James D.and Louiza F. Wilkerson. Father was a farmer.

WILKERSON, Sally, Nov.2,1856. Slave. Mother, Nancy. Owner, N. Wilkerson.

WORLEY,Mariah Elizabeth, Sept.2,1856. Parents, Henry A. and Catherine M. Worley. Father was a farmer.

WATSON,Rebeckah Jane, 1856. Parents, Joseph D. and Mary E. Watson.Father was a farmer.

Page # 82,

WATSON,Armonia Sale, Dec.8,1856. Parents, Benjamin R. and Nancy J. Watson.Father was a farmer.

YOUNG,Catherine, June 9,1856. Parents, John H. and Lucy Young. Father was a father.

Page # 83,   1856

ARTHUR, Malinda,March, 1856. Parents, Elias and Martha Arthur. Father was a farmer.

AGNEW, Alex,June,1856, Slave. Mother, Susan. Owner, Martha Agnew.

ANDERSON,Vangeline, Oct.1856 Parents, joel C. and Betsy Anderson. Father was a farmer.

ARTHUR, Ardina, June, 1856. Parents, Admire and Phoebe Arthur.

ALLEN, James Thomas, Oct.,1856. Parents, Charles W. and Elizabeth Allen. Father was a farmer.

AYERS, William D.,July,1856. Parents, John J. and Eliza A. Ayers.

ANTHONY,Daniel, June,1856. Slave. Mother, Sally. Owner, Emslen Anthony.

ASHWELL,__?__, Dec.,1856. Male. (Died). Parents, William B. and Elvira J. Ashwell.Father was a farmer.

ANDERSON, __?__, Feb.,1856. Male. Slave. Mother, Nancy. Owner, Mark Anderson.

ANDREWS, Billy, March,1856. Slave. Mother, Celia. Owner, William W. Andrews.

ANDREWS,Sally, Sept.,1856. Slave. Mother, Ginny. Owner, William W. Andrews.

ANDREWS,Chris, 1856. Slave. Mother, Martha. Owner, William W. Andrews

BIRTH RECORDS

ANDREWS, William P.,Nov.,1856. Parents, William M. and Sarah E. Andrews. Father was a farmer.

ADAMS, Oscar V.,May,1856. Parents, Joshua C. and Tabitha C. Adams. Father was a Merchant.

AYERS, Lewis M. April,1856. Parents, Tolbert and Jincy Ayers. Father was a farmer.

SAUNDERS, Charles R.,Oct.,1856. Parents, Jubal S.B. and Agnes Saunders. Father was a farmer.

ANDERSON, Jacob C.,Jan.,1856. Parents, William H.S.and Frances A. Anderson. Father was a farmer.

ANTHONY,Caleb, Jan.,1856. Slave. Mother, Lucy. Owner, Abner Athony.

ANTHONY, Carrutta, May,1856. Slave. Mother, Martha. Owner, Abner Anthony.

ANTHONY, Jane, April,1856. Slave. Mother, Emma. Owner, Abner Anthony.

ANTHONY,Morga, June,1856. Slave. Mother, Lizzie.Owner, Abner Anthony.

ALLEN, John William, Aug.,1856. Parents, Robert E.and Nancy Allen. Father was a farmer.

BANDY, John A.,Nov.,1856. Parents, Samuel W. and Harriett E. Bandy. Father was a farmer.

BANDY, Lew Allen,July. 1856. Parents, Cornelius and Sarah Bandy. Father was a farmer.

BOARD, ___?___, AUg.,1856. Male. Slave. Mother, Martha. Owner, Saml Board.

BEARD, John S.,April,1856. Parents, John and Martha A. Beard. Father was a farmer.

BARTON, William, Feb.,1856. Parents, William and Frances J. Barton.Father was a farmer.

BLANKENSHIP,__?__, Dec.,1856. Parents, Michael J. and Sarah Blankenship. Father was a farmer.

BOND,Delen J.,Sept.,1856. Slave. Mother, Laura. Owner, PleaSANT Bond.

BRADLEY,John R.,Nov.,1856. Parents, James H. and Parnetta A. Bradley. Father was a farmer.

BRAMBLETT,Ann E.,Jan.,1856. Parents, John S. and Mary C. Bramblett. Father was a farmer.

BURNETT, William S.,Feb.,1856. Slave. Mother, Eliza. Owner, William S. Burnett.

BURNETT,Fountain, 1856. Parents, Chris A. and Orphy Burnett. Father was a farmer.

BIRTH RECORDS

BURROUGHS, Phoebe, April,1856. Slave. Mother, Mari. Owner, John Burroughs.

BURNETT, Rebecca F.,June,1856. Parents, John and Mary A. Burnett.

BLANKENSHIP,James C.,Sept.,1856. Parents, John J. and Christina Blankenship.

BONDURANT, Ausnetto E.,Aug.,1856. Parents, William W. and Sarah M. Bondurant. Father was a Miller.

BANDY, Alvanine, Feb.,1856. Parents, Thomas S. and Frances J. Bandy. Father was a Carpenter.

BOARD, Olive May, Oct.,1856. Parents, Charles A. and Elizabeth A. Board. Father was a Physician.

BURNETT, John William, July,1856. Parents, Elisha C. and Jane Burnett. Father was a farmer.

BROWN, Ann B.,June,1856. Parents, James C. and Lucy Brown./Father was a farmer.

Page # 84,

BURNETT, James A.,June,1856. Parents, William W. and Margaret S. Burnett. Father was a farmer.

BURNETT, Mary C.,Aug.29,1856. Parents, Williamson and Celia Burnett. Father was a farmer.

CUNDIFF, Mary Malinda, June,1856. Parents, Uriah H. and Elizabeth Cundiff. Father was a farmer.

CORLEY,Thomas, Feb.,1856. Parents, Thomas and Eliza-beth Corley. Father was a farmer.

CROWDER, Martha M.,May,1856. Parents, John H. and Elizabeth F.Crowder. Father was a faremr.

CHEWNING,Marcella, May,1856. Parents, C.D. and Elizabeth Chewning. Father was a farmer.

CREASY,Eldridge,Aug.,1856. Slave. MOther, Paulinn. Owner, William Creasy.

CARNER, Chales C.,Nov.,1856. Parents, Elias and Janetta Carner.

CADWALLENDER,Martha Ann, Oct.,1856. Parents, James and Frances Cadwallender. Father was a Carpenter.

CADWALLENDER,Mary E.,May,1856, Parents, Thomas and Mariah Cadwallender. Father was a farmer.

CREASY, John Lear, Nov.,1856. Parents, Charles H. and Lucy Ann Creasy.

CARTER, Edward S.,Feb.,1856. Parents, James M. and Sarah Carter.

BIRTH RECORDS

Page # 85,

CARROLL, _--?_ , May,1856. Male. Parents, Major A. and Martha C. Carroll.

CARNER, Edward E.,June, 1856. Parents, John H. and Marenda Carner. Father was a farmer.

GRAGHEAD, William R.,Dec.,1856. Parents, Robert A. and Elizabeth F. Craghead. Father was a farmer.

CADWALLENDER,James C.,Feb.,1856. Parents, Daniel and Milissa Ann Cadwallender. Father was a farmer.

CARTER, William W.,July,1856. Parents, James W. and Julia A. Carter.

CAMPBELL,_ ? _, & _ ? _, July,1856. Females. (Twins). Mother, Julia A. Campbell.

CREASY,Amanda, APril,1856. Slave. Mother, Cheritta. Owner, Thomas Creasy.

DICKERSON,Mossouri E.,March 12,1856. Parents, Clemons and Mary Ann Dickerson. Father was a farmer.

DICKERSON,Sarah, Oct.,1856. Parents, David and Rhoda Dickerson. Father was a farmer.

DICKERSON, Polly, Dec. 1856. Parents, James and Eve-line Dickerson.

DOBBINS, Missouri J.,Feb.,1856. Parents, Griffin A. and Eliza S. Dobbins.

DREWRY, marinda, May,1856. Parents, Andrew P. and Eli-zabeth F. Drewry.

DENT, Morgan,June,1856. Parents, Morgan G. and Martha Dent.

DICKERSON, Fanny, July,1856. Slave. Mother, Sallie. Owner, William Dickerson.

DREWRY,Sarah C.,Feb.1856. Parents, Joseph C. and Mary F. Drewry.

DEARING, Silas G.,May,1856. Parents, Green and Rhoda J. Dearing.

DAVENPORT, John N.,Nov.,1856. Parents, Chris and Lydia Davenport. father was a farmer.

ELLIS,Zachariah, Aug.,1856. Parents, Thomas D. and Mary Ellis. Father was a farmer.

ENGLISH, Eliza Ann, Aug.,1856. Parents, John W. and Sarah E. English.

ENGLISH, Joe, July. 1856. Slave. Mother, Amelia.Owner, P. English.

EARLY, Robert A.,Jan.,1856. parents, James A. and Sarah J. Early.

BIRTH RECORDS

CREASY,___?___, May,1856. Parents, Jefferson and Louisa
J.Creasy. Father was a farmer.

CHEEK,Stephen W., Aug.,1856. Parents, William B. and
Susan F. Cheek. Father was a farmer.

CUNDIFF, Susan C.,June,1856. Parents, John and Sarah
Cundiff. Father was a farmer

CRAIGHEAD, Sarah F.,Jan.1856. Parents, William B. and
Martha Ann Craighead.

COON,Burwell S.,Oct.,1856. Parents, Jacob and Elizabeth Coon.

PENDLETON,Edward N.& Dora V.,(Twins),May,1856. Parents
Henry and Nancy Pendleton. Father was a farmer.

CREASY, Jesse T.,Nov.,1856. Parents, Samuel H. and
Cathandra Creasy. Father was a farmer.

CREASY, Saunders, Sept.,1856. Slave. Mother, Amelia.
Owner, Meredith S. Creasy.

CLAYTOR, Maria, Nov., 1856. Slave. Mother, Amarilla.
Owner, Samuel G. Claytor.

CLAYTOR, Duke, March,1856. Slave. Mother, Betsy.Owner,
Samuel G. Claytor.

CLINGHAMPEEL,Benjamin, Jan.,1856. Parents, Jack and
Nancy Clinghampeel. Father was a farmer.

CALLOWAY,___?___, 1856. Male. Slave. Mother, Dafury.
Owner, William B. Calloway.

CRAWFORD, Saml S.,Jan.,1856. Slave. Mother, Sylva.
Owner, Saml Crawford.

HICKS,___?___, 1856. Female. Slave. Mother, Charlotte.
Owner, William Hicks Sr.

CROUCH,Saml D.,Feb.,1856. Parents, Benjamin D. and
Adline Crouch. Father was a farmer.

CLAYTOR, Oscar, July. 1856. Slave. Mother, Jane.Owner,
Robert M. Claytor.

CULLOHAN,___?___, 1856. Female. Parents, Abner and Julia
Ann Cullohan. Father was a Miller.

CROWDER,___?___, 1856. Female. Parents, Henry and Elizabeth Crowder. Father was a farmer.

COBB,___?___, 1856. Male. Slave. Mother, Jane. Owner, Til
man A. Cobbs Sr.

COBB,___?___, 1856. Male. Slave. Mother, Sarah. Owner,
Tilghman A. Cobb Sr.

COBB,___?___, 1856. Female. Slave. Mother, Matilda.Owner,
Tilghman A. Cobb Sr.

BIRTH RECORDS

Page # 86,

FEATHER, John T.,Sept.,1856,Parents, William R. and Mary A. Feather. Father was a farmer.

FRAILING,George , July,1856. Slave. Mother, Priscilla Owner, Daniel Frailing.

FRANKLIN,Molenzo, Oct.19,1856. Parents, James T. and Elizabeth Franklin.

FRANKLIN,John W.,Aug.10,1856.Parents, Arch'd H. and Martha Franklin. Father was a farmer.

FRANKLIN,James H.,Jan.,1856. Parents, Eleas J. and Jane Franklin. Father was a farmer.

FRANKLIN, Gilly A.F.,Dec.8,1856. Parents, Jesse H.and Locky Ann Franklin. Father was a Miller.

FUQUA, Eliza J.,April,1856. Slave. MOther, Fanner, Owner, Martin S. Fuqua.

FIZER, George S.,May,1856. Parents, Charles B. and Frances J. Fizer. Father was a farmer.

FALLS,William D.,March,1856. Parents, Danl and Cynthia Falls. Father was a farmer.

FRANKLIN,Sarah J.,March,1856. Parents, James C. and Louiza A. Franklin. Father was a Carpenter.

FOSTER, Saml H.,Aug.,1856. Parents, Richard A. and Nancy Foster, Father was a farmer.

FUQUA, Euretta, April,1856. Parents, Benjamin B. and Jane Fuqua. Father was a farmer.

FISHER, Ellmore S.,June,1856, Parents, Matthew and Mary M. Fisher. Father was a Mechanic.

FUQUA, ___?___ , June,1856. Female. Slave. Mother, Eliza. Owner, Joshua Fisher.

FISHER, ___?___ , May,1856. Female. Slave. Mother, Charlott. Owner, Abner Fisher.

FARRISS,Anderson, Sept.,1856. Slave. Mother, Eliza. Owner, Anderson C. Farriss.

FARRESS, Minta M.,Nov.,1856. Slave. Mother, Frances. Owner, John J. Farress.

FUQUA,Julia A.,June,1856. Parents, Thomas and Mary S. Fuqua. Father was a farmer.

FRAILING,Nancy O.E.,June,1856. Parents, Robert A. and Sarah F. Frailing.

FIELDS, Fannie F.C.,Sept.,1856. Parents, William M. and Louisa W. Fields.

BIRTH RECORDS.

GARRETT,John R.,April,1856. Parents, John J. and Mildred J. Garrett. Father was a farmer.

GILWATER, Preston G.,Nov.12,1856. Parents, Preston and Sarah J.E. Gilwater.

GILLS, ? , April,1856. Male. Parents, Asa and Caroline E. Gills. Father was a farmer.

GIBBS, Martha, Sept.,1856. Slave. MOther, Betsy Ann. Owner, George S. Gibbs.

GROSS, Mary, march,1856. Parents, Abram and Lydia Gross. Father was a farmer.

GRAY,Sarah S.,April,1856. Parents, William and Sarah E. gray. Father was a farmer.

GOAD, Robert William, March,1856.Parents, Uriah and Lucinda J. Goad. Father was a Mechanic

GOAD, ? , Aug.,1856. Female. Parents, Davis A. and Julia Ann Goad. Father was a farmer.

GOAD, ? , Female. March,1856. Parents, William R. and Frances Goad. Father was a Wheelright.

GIBBS, George W. & John W.,(Twins). Nov.,1856. Parents, Paschal N. and Elizabeth Gibbs.Father was a farmer.

GIBBS, Ginny, March,1856. Slave. Mother, Mary. Owner, Paschal Gibbs.

GRAHAM, George H.,Dec.,1856. Parents, Lawson and Elizabeth Graham. Father was a farmer.

GRAY, ? , Female, July,1856. Parents, James W. and Judia Gray. Father was a farmer.

GWALTNEY, Lydia Ann., Aug. 1856. Parents, John and Elizabeth Gwaltney. Father was a farmer.

GRAY, ? , Male. April,1856. Slave. Mother, Ginny. Owner, James Gray Sr.

GIBBS, Marinda, May,1856. Parents, Paschal B. and Mary Gibbs. Father was a farmer.

GWALTNEY, ? , Aug.6,1856. Parents, Albert and Mary Gwaltney. father was a farmer.

Page # 87,

HANNABAS, Ambrose, May,1856. Parents, David M. and Marcella Hannabas. Father was a farmer.

HANNABAS, Thomas A.,Sept.,1856. Parents, Thomas G. and Nancy E. Hannabas. Father was a farmer.

HARDY, Mary E.,March,1856. Parents, Robert and Nancy Hardy. Father was a farmer.

BIRTH RECORDS

HAWLEY, Julia F., Feb.1856. Parents, James B. and Elawizer Hawley. Father was a farmer.

HAWLEY, Eugenia, June, 1856. Parents, Joseph C. and Elizabeth Hawley. Father was farmer.

HORN, James B.,June,1856. Parents, Cornelius and Hudley Horn. Father was a Mechanic.

HUBBARD, Stephen S.,Jan.,1856. Parents, Stephen and Lydia A. Hubbard.

HANCOCK,Samuel E.,May,1856. Parents, John H. and Martha Hancock. Father was a farmer.

HURT, Sophia, Jan.,1856. Slave. Mother, Narcissa. Owner, Joel Hurt.

HURT, Matilda, Jan.,1856. Slave. Mother, Sally. Owner, Joel Hurt.

HUBBARD, ___?___, Aug.,1856. Parents, Burr G. and Ann Hubbard.Father was a farmer.

HARRIS, William, July,1856. Parents, Saml M. and Eliza Harris. Father was a farmer.

HUDDLESTON, Charles R.,March,1856. Parents, Richard and Elizabeth Huddleston. Father was a farmer.

HUDDLESTON,Nancy, May,1856. Slave. Mother, Ann. Owner, Richard Huddleston.

HURT,Sarah M.,Sept.,1856. Parents, Elijah C. and Mary Hurt. Father was a farmer.

HACKWORTH,Saml F.,Nov.,1856. Parents, Washington and Malinda H. Hackworth. Father was a farmer.

HAMMER, Charles W.,April,1856. Parents, John D. and Edna J. Hammer. Father was a farmer.

HUNT,James C.,Oct.12,1856. Parents, Thomas H. and Sophia Hunt. Father was a farmer.

HOWELL,Milly, Oct.,1856. Parents, Pleasant A. and Salina Howell. Father was a farmer.

HODGES, ___?___, July,1856. Male. Parents, Milton E. and Sally Hodges. Father was a farmer.

HAMBRICK,Charmian,Jan.,1856. Parents, A.S. and Rebecca Hambrick. Father was a Mechanic.

HOLT,___?___, Jan.,1856. Female. Slave. Owner, William S. Holt.

HUDNALL, ___?___, Sept.1856.Male. Slave. Mother, Jane. Owner, Frances Hudnall.

HURT,William L.,June,1856. Parents, Josephus and Charlott Hurt. Father was a farmer.

BIRTH RECORDS

IRVINE, Andrew, Nov.,1856. Slave. MOther, Julia. Owner, Benjamin H. Irvine.

JETER, John H.,Aug.,1856. Slave. Mother, Elizabeth. Owner, Fielding H. Jeter.

JOHNSON,Martha, April,1856. Parents, Drury H. and Mildred W. Johnson. Father was a farmer.

JONES, Elizabeth F.,Aug.,1856. Parents, Ed W. and Ellen Jones. Father was a farmer.

JONES, __?__, April,1856. Male. Parents, Ed C. and Martha Jones. Father was a farmer.

JORDAN, Andrew, Jan.,1856,Slave. Mother, Maria. Owner, William V. Jordan.

JOHNSON, __?__, March,1856. Female. Parents, George W. and Sarah E. Johnson.

Page # 88,

JOHNSON,Mary E.,May,1856. Parents, William H. and emerline F. Johnson. Father was a farmer.

JOHNSON,William H. ,Sept.,1856. Mother, Sarah Johnson FN.

JOHNSON,William W.,May,1856.Parents, Martin S. and Nancy F. Johnson. Father was a farmer.

KASEY,JERRY, Jan.,1856, Slave. Mother, Jane. Owner, Thomas Kasey.

KASEY, Nancy J.V.,Oct.1856. Parents, Thomas A. and Virginia M. Kasey.Father was a farmer.

KASEY, __?__, Sept.,1856. Female. Slave. Mother, Rhoda. Owner, John G. Kasey.

KIDD, Paulina P. Aug.1,1856. Parents, Henry D. and Mary C. Kidd. Father was a farmer.

LOYD, Octavia, Sept.,1856. Slave. Mother, Jane. Owner, Henry Jr.

LAZENBY,Bettie, May,1856, Slave. Mother, Minerva. Owner, Edward Lazenby.

LESLIE, Latherat M.,Sept.,1856. Parents, James D.and Mary J. Leslie. Father was a Blacksmith.

LOYD,Elizabeth E.,Sept.,1856. Parents, Joseph G. and Margaret Loyd. Father was a Mechanic.

LAZENBY, __?__, July,1856. Slave. Male. Mother, Jane. Owner, Rizin Lazenby.

LIPSCOMB,Clara Ellen, Feb.,1856. Parents, George D. and Susan Lipscomb. Father was a Tanner.

BIRTH RECORDS

LUMPKIN,Harry, July,1856. Slave. Mother, Charetta. Owner, Robert W. Lumpkin.

LUMPKIN,Fox, June,1856. Slave. Mother, Racheal. Owner, Robert W. Lumpkin.

LAUGHLIN,Lockie L.,March,1856. Parents, James and Elizabeth Laughlin. Father was a farmer.

LAUGHON,Joseph, July 9,1856. Parents, Joshua and Elizabeth Laughon. Father was a farmer.

LEE,__?__, June,1856. Female. Parents, James G. and Susan Lee. Father was a farmer.

LACY,Anderson F.,Sept.,1856. Parents, Thomas J. and Susan M. Lacy. Father was a farmer.

LANCASTER, Frances, Aug.,1856. Slave. Mother, Esther. Owner, James Lancaster.

LOWRY, __?__, Nov.,1856. Slave. Mother, Ellen. Owner, Elliott Lowry.

LOWRY, __?__, May,1856. Female. Slave. Mother, Bettie. Owner, Elliott Lowry.

LAZENBY,__?__, Aug.,1856. Male. Parents, William R.and Annis B. Lazenby. Father was a Blacksmith.

LEFTWICH, __?__, Aug.,1856.Male. Slave. Mother, Sarah. Owner, George W. Leftwich.

MEADOR, James. Oct,1856. Slave. Mother, Susan. Owner, Wilson Meador.

MCLAIN,James D.,April,1856. Parents, McHenry and Jane Sarah McLain. Father was a farmer.

MCCABE, James, Jan.,1856. Slave. Mother, Salona,Owner, Malinda McCabe.

MCLAIN,Leroy,Sept.,1856. Parents, Jesse and Mary McLain. Father was a farmer.

MCLAIN,Henry C.,Dec.,1856. Parents, William and Letitia McLain. Father was a farmer.

MCMANAWAY,Ann, Dec.,1856. Slave. Mother, Lilla. Owner, Nancy McManaway.

METTS, Lucy L, June,1856. Parents, James R. and Matilda V. Metts. Father was a farmer.

Page # 89,

MARTIN,Lucy,March,1856. Slave. Mother, Jasmine. Owner, James F. Martin.

MARTIN,__?__, Nov.,1856. Male. Parents, Green B. and Neomi C. Martin. Father was a farmer.

BIRTH RECORDS

MORGAN,Marcella W.,1856. Parents, Jesse and Julennea
J. Morgan. Father was a farmer.

MARTIN,Thomas J.,Oct.,1856. Parents, Samuel and Elizabeth Martin. Father was a farmer.

MARTIN,___?___, June,1856. Parents, Job and Cynthia Martin. Father was a farmer.

MORRIS, Micajah, April,1856. Parents, Micajah G. and
Lively M. Morris. Father was a farmer.

MAYS, ___?___, May,1856. Slave. Mother, Adline. Owner,
Joseph M. Mays.

MAUPIN,Correnia, Nov.14,1856. Parents, Carr M. and
Frances Maupin.

MCGHEE, Henry F.,March,1856. Parents, Saml H. and
Martha McGhee. Father was a farmer.

MITCHELL,___?___, March 8,1856. Female. Parents, William C. and Lucy M. Mitchell. Father was a farmer.

MITCHELL,___?___, April 1,1856. Female, Slave. Mother,
Caroline. Owner, William C. Mitchell.

MARSHALL, ___?___, Dec.,1856. Female. Parents, Poindexter
C. and Mary J.E. Marshall. father was a farmer.

MUSGROVE, William W.,June,1856. Parents, Demetrius
and Martha Ann Musgrove. Father was a farmer.

MITCHELL,JOHN G.,May,1856. Parents, Danl and Juleanea
Mitchell. Father was a farmer.

MILES, Emma N., July,1856. Parents, Joseph R. and
Susan G. Miles. Father was a farmer.

METTS,___?___, June,1856. Parents, George F. and Elizabeth Metts. Father was a farmer.

MITCHELL, Elvira, Aug.,1856. Slave. Mother, Sarah.
Owner, Saml M. Mitchell

MCDANIEL, Matilda & Pattie,(Twins). Slaves. Mother,
Maria. Owner, Elizabeth McDaniel.

MCDANIEL,Agness Nov., 1856. Slave. Mother, Lucinda.
Owner, Elizabeth McDaniel.

MORGAN,___?___, Nov.,1856. Slave. Mother, Ann. Owner,
Chris Morgan

MURPHY,Jeremiah E.,March,1856. Parents, Elijah F. and
Emily Murphy. Father was a farmer.

MERRYMAN, Malinda, May,1856. Slave. Mother, Jane.
Owner, Elenor merryman.

MITCHELL,James W.,May,1856. Parents, John A. and Eliza
Mitchell. Father was a farmer.

BIRTH RECORDS

MATTHEWS,Thomas J.P.,June,1856.Parents, James M. and Elizabeth R. Matthews. Father was a Manufacter.

NELMS, Winston,July,1856. Slave, Mother, Idelia, Owner, Eben Nelms.

NANCE, ___?___, Oct.,1856. Parents, Thomas W. and Elizabeth J. Nance. Father was a farmer.

NEWSOM,William H.,Aug.,1856. Parents, David M. and Susan E. Newsom. Father was a farmer.

NICHOLS, Rhoda J.,Sept.,1856. Parents, Saml W. and Sarah J. Nichols.

NANCE, John A.,Jan.,1856. Parents, Edwin G. and Sarah Nance. Father was a farmer.

NEWMAN, Callohill M.,March,1856. Parents, Joseph W.and Mary Ann Newman. Father was a farmer.

NEWMAN, William C.,Jan.1856. Parents, Elias and Martha Newman. Father was a farmer.

NICHOLS, Betesy, June,1856. Slave. Mother, Caroline. Owner, Griffin Nichols.

NELMS, Leroy E.,Dec.,1856. Parents, Charles D. and Mary E. Nelms.

NIMMO,John W.,July,1856. Parents, Josiah H. and Mary Star Nimmo. father was a farmer.

NANCE, Sarah E.,June,1856. Parents, Albert F. and Jane G. Nance. Father was a farmer.

NICHOLS, J.L.,Aug.18,1856. Parents, Thomas F. and Bersheba. Father was a farmer.

Page # 90,

OVERSTREET,Ellen, July,1856. Parents, William B. and Catherine Overstreet. Father was a farmer.

OVERSTREET, ___?___, Sept.,1856. Female. Parents, Jeremiah and Catherine Overstreet. Father was a farme.

OVERSTREET, Addison, Sept.,1856. Parents, Jesse and Ann Overstreet. Father was a farmer.

OVERSTREET, ___?___, Dec.,1856. Female. Parents, Thomas and Frances Overstreet. Father was a farmer.

OVERSTREET, ___?___, March,1856. Female. Parents, Hiram W. and Mary J. Overstreet.Father was a farmer.

OVERSTREET,___?___, Oct.,1856. Female. Parents, Alexander and Tabitha Overstreet. Father was a farmer.

OVERSTREET, William, Nov.,1856. Parents, Stephen and Mary Overstreet. Father was a Mechanic.

BIRTH RECORDS

PEARCY, Maria E.,June,1856. Parents, William and Linia
Pearcy. Father was a farmer.

PHELPS,Sandy, Jan.,1856. Slave. Mother, Harriett.Owner,
Ammin M.Phelps.

PHELPS, __?__ , Nov.,1856. Male. Slave. Mother, Louisa.
Owner, James M. Phelps.

PARKER, Catherine E.,March,1856. Parents, Calvin F. and
Julia A. Parker. Father was a farmer.

PAYNE,Benjamin M.,May,1856. Parents, John F. and Emerline Payne. Father was a farmer.

POWELL,Thomas A.,Nov.,1856. Parents, John M. and Julia
Ann Powell. Father was a farmer.

PATE,Ed, Dec.,1856. Slave. Mother, Fanny. Owner, Corn-
nelius Pate.

PATE, Hannah, 1856. Slave. MOther, Martha. Owner,
Cornelius Pate.

PATE, __?__ , April,1856. Slave. Mother, Mary. Owner,
Cornelius pate.

PATE, William, March,1856. Slave. Mother, Amanda.Owner,
Cornelius Pate.

PRESTON, __?__ , May,1856. Female. Slave. Mother, Milly.
Owner, Thomas J. Preston

POINDEXTER, Marrianna, Jan.,1856. Parents, James W.and
Sophia A. Poindexter. Father was a farmer.

PULLEN, Robert A.,March,1856. Parents, Jesse and Fanny
Pullen. Father was a farmer.

PATTERSON, Robinetta F.,May,1856. Parents, John M. and
Sophia E. Patterson. Father was a farmer.

PAYNE, Wesley Thomas, Feb.,1856. Parents, Thomas Q. and
Mary Ann Payne. Father was a farmer.

PLYMALE, Perry L.,Feb.,1856. Parents, Samuel P. and
Mary C. Plymale. father was a farmer.

PETERS, Mary Bell, Feb.5,1856. Parents, Wesley and
Mahala J. Peters. Father was a farmer.

PRESTON, Jane, Jan.,1856. Slave. Mother, Sarah. Owner,
William Preston

PRESTON, Caroline, Dec.,1856. Slave. Mother, Harriett.
Owner, William Preston

PRESTON, Adline, Jan.,1856. Slave. Mother, Caroline.
Owner, William Preston

PARKER, John, July,1856. Slave. Mother, Racheal.Owner.
Martha D. Parker

BIRTH RECORDS

PRESTON, Martha A.,Sept.,1856. Parents, John F. and Mary Ann Preston. Father was a farmer.

PAYNE, Octavia, Oct.,1856. Parents, John B. and Elizabeth Payne. Father was a farmer.

PREAS, Celia F.,Sept.,1856. Parents, Henry and Elizabeth Preas. Father was a farmer.

PRESTON,Olivia L.,March,1856. Parents, John L. and Elizabeth Preston.

PRESTON, Ammin, May,1857. Slave. Mother, Mary. Owner, John L. Preston,

POLLARD, ___?___, Feb.,1856. Female. Parents, Saml C. and Sarah C. Pollard. Father was a farmer.

Page # 91,1856

QUARLES, James M.,Aug.,1856. Parents, Abram G. and Frances Quarles. Father was a farmer.

QUARLES, ___?___, Oct.,1856. Slave. Mother, Elizabeth. Owner, John Quarles.

QUARLES, Mary F.,May.1856. Parents, John F. and Elizabeth M. Quarles. Father was a farmer.

ROBERTSON, Pleasant, Nov.,1856. Slave , Mother, Cindarilla. Owner, Nicholas W. Robertson.

RAMSEY, Lily Lee, March,1856. Parents, James M. and Martha Ramsey. Father was a farmer.

RITCHERSON,Daniel, June,1856. Parents, Clinton and Nancy Ritcherson.Father was a farmer.

ROBERTS, Alex.,Feb.,1856. Slave. Mother, Rena. Owner, David Roberts.

ROBERTS, Albert, March,1856. Slave. Mother, Harriett, Owner, David Roberts.

ROBERTS, Mary F.,Aug.,1856. Parents, Josiah B. and Ann B. Roberts. Father was a Farmer.

REESE, Jim, April,1856. Slave, Mother, Jane. Owner, William W. Reese.

RAMSEY,Elizabeth M., Jan.,1856. Parents, Powhatan and Sarah C. Ramsey. Father was a farmer.

ROBERTS, John, Aug., 1856. Slave. Mother, Nancy. Owner, William H. Roberts.

RADFORD, ___?___, Jan.1856, Female. Slave. Mother, Jane. Owner, Munford W. Radford.

RADFORD, ___?___, May,1856. Male. Slave. Mother, Sally. Owner, Munford W. Radford.

BIRTH RECORDS

RADFORD, __?__ , June, 1856. Female. Slave. Mother,Mary.
Owner, Munford W. Radford.

RADFORD, __?__ , Sept.,1856. Male. Slave. Mother, Martha
Owner, Munford W. Radford

STIFF, Mary L,Aug.,1856. Parents, James M. and Lucy A.
Stiff. Father was a farmer.

SWAIN,Admire D.,Sept.,1856. Parents, Pleust P. and Emily
Swain. Father was a farmer.

SKINNELL, Nathaniel, April, 1856. Parents, James and
Rebecca G. Skinnell. Father was a farmer.

STUMP,John W.,Feb.23,1856. Parents, William B. and
Martha Ann Stump. Father was a Shoemaker.

SUTPHIN,Haner, June 22,1856. Parents, Powhatan C. and
Martha J. Sutphin. Father was a Physician.

STONE, Spencer, Feb.1856. Slave. Mother, Permelia.Owner
Micajah Stone.

STONE, Alice Lee, Feb.20,1856. Parents, Micajah and Catherine Stone. Father was a farmer.

SMITH, Giles. March,1856. Slave. Mother, Jane. Owner,
Alex A. Smith.

SMITH, __?__ , Nov.,1856. Male. Slave. Mother, Manerva.
Owner, Stephen P. Smith.

STCLAIR, Joseph D.,Sept.,1856. Parents, Harry F. and
Sarah J. StClair. Father was a farmer.

STCLAIR, Drucilla, May.1856. Parents, Bird L. and Emily
StClair. Father was a farmer.

STCLAIR,Thomas L.,Nov.,1856. Parents, John D. and Margaret StClair. Father was a farmer.

STCLAIR, Richard F.,Aug.,1856. Parents, Robert and Roda
StClair. Father was a farmer.

SMELSER, Mary, Dec.,1856. Slave. Mother, Margarett.
Owner, Puschal Smelser.

Page # 92,

SAUNDERS, __?__ , May,1856. Female. Slave. Mother, Martha
Owner, William Saunders

STCLAIR, William F.,March,1856. Parents, John F. and
Martha F. StClair.Father was a farmer.

STONE, Everett B.,March,1856.Parents, James F. and Paulina B. Stone. Father was a Merchant Taylor.

STEPTOE, Ida, Nov.,1856. Parents, Henry C. and Louis-
anna Steptoe. Father was a Physician.

BIRTH RECORDS

SAUNDERS, __?__ , Sept.,1856.Female. Slave. Mother, Susan, Owner, Thomas F. Saunders.

SCRUGGS, Mary, Jan.,1856. Slave. Mother, Jane. Owner, Reeves L. Scruggs.

SCRUGGS, Eliza, Feb.,1856. Slave. Mother, Mary. Owner, Reeves L. Scruggs.

SAUNDERS, Jane, Oct.,1856. Slave. Mother, Ailsey. Owner Julius Saunders.

SCRUGGS, __?__ , Dec.,1856. Male. Slave. Mother, Fanny. Owner, Throphilus Scruggs.

STEVENS, Genevery, Oct.,1856. Parents, John M. and Susan Stevens. Father was a farmer.

SHELTON, John, Oct.,1856. Slave. Mother, Adline. Owner, George W. Shelton

SAUNDERS, __?__ , Dec.,1856. Slave. Mother, Fanny. Owner, Danl Saunders.

TURNER, Orvilla, June,1856. Slave. Mother, Ann. Owner, Admire Turner.

TERRY, Amanda, Dec.,1856. Slave. Mother, Vina. Owner, henry Terry.

TERRY, Chaney, Oct.,1856. Slave. Mother, Sally. Owner, Henry Terry.

THURMAN, Adeline C.,July 7,1856. Parents, Alex.L. and Susan M Thurman. Father was a School Teacher.

TOMPKINS, __?__ , Nov.,1856. Male. Slave. Mother, Eliza. Owner, Danl Tompkins.

TATE, Julia P.,may, 1856. Parents, Hugh A. and Mary D. Tate.

THACKER, Melissa, July,1856. Parents, Samuel and Harriett Thacker. Father was a farmer.

THURMAN, Jim, Dec.,1856. Slave. Mother, Judea. Owner, Sophia S. Thurman.

THURMAN, Jerry, Nov.,1856. Slave. Mother, Mema. Owner, Sophia S. Thurman.

TURNER, Judy A.,April,1856. Parents, Obediah W. and Parthena Turner. Father was a farmer.

TURNER, Margarett D.,March,1856. Parents, John W. and Margarett F. Turner. Father was a farmer.

Page # 93,

WILLIAMSON,Richard A.P.,June 24,1856. Parents, Thomas J. and Mahala A. Williamson. Father was a Bootmaker.

BIRTH RECORDS

WHITE, Joseph F.,Oct.,1856. Parents, Samuel G. and Catherine White. Father was a farmer.

WORLEY,William Tell, jan.1856. Parents, Francis W. and Eliza Worley.Father was a farmer.

WILLIAMS, __?__, Nov.,1856. Male. Parents, Joseph A. and Mary Williams. Father was a farmer.

WRIGHT, Stephen, April, Slave. Mother, Ellen. Owner, Joseph P. Wright.

WRIGHT, Robt, Dec.,1856. Slave. Mother, Martha. Owner, Joseph P. Wright.

WOOD, Bennett L, Nov.,1856. Parents, William O. and Almary Wood. Father was a farmer.

WOOD, Milissa E.,May,1856. Parents,Charles W. and Mary A. Wood.   Father was a farmer.

WRIGHT, Martha P.,Oct.,1856. Parents, Jubal J. and Emma F. Wright. Father was a farmer.

WRIGHT, R.F.Ellen, Nov.,1856. Parents, James and Judith P. Wright. Father was a farmer.

WRIGHT, __?__, May 17,1856. Slave. Male. Mother, Amy. Owner, James Wright.

WRIGHT, __?__, May 17,1856.(Twin to the above).Slave. Female. Mother, Amy. Owner, James Wright.

WHITE, Henry D. Aug.,1856. Parents, Addison M. and Mary Ann White. Father was a Miller.

WHITTEN, Martha A.,Jan.27,1856. Parents, James and Jane Whitten. Father was a farmer.

WILLARD, Nicholas R.,July 17,1856. Parents, Winfrey and Margaret Willard. father was a farmer.

WITT, Maria, June,1856. Slave. Mother, Mary. Owner, William Witt.

WALKER, __?__, Nov.,1856. Slave. Female. Mother, Maria. Owner, James A. Walker.

WADKINS, Lelia L. March,1856. Parents, James A. and Martha J. Wadkins. Father was a Schoolteacher.

WIGGENTON, John J. Sept.,1856. Parents, John J. and Nancy P. Wiggenton. Father was a farmer.

WADE, Sarah, Oct.,1856. Salve. Mother, Nancy. Owner, Arch'd Wade JR.

WADE, James M.,July,1856. Parents, Silas G. and Nancy Wade. Father was a Farmer.

WILKS, Henry C.,March,1856. Parents.Saul H. and Sarah Wilks. Father was a farmer.

BIRTH RECORDS

WADE, ___?___, May,1856. Slave. Mother, Eliza. Owner, Isaac Wade.

WADE,___?___, June,1856. Slave. Mother, Judy. Owner, Alex. Wade.

WHITE, ___?___, Aug.1856. Female. Parents, George and Susan White. Father was a Blacksmith.

WEEKS, Mary L. May,1856. Parents, William D. and Ellen Weeks. Father was a farmer.

WILLIAMS, Henry O.,Jan.1856. Parents, Charles W. and Susan A. Williams. Father was a Mechanic.

WILLS, William, July 17,1856. Parents, Harvey A. and Fannie Wills. Father was a farmer.

WILSON, Mary J. April,1856. Parents, John N. and Julia A.F. Wilson. father was a farmer.

WHITE, James M., May,1856. Parents, Alex and Sophia J. White. Father was a farmer.

WILSON, John R.,Nov.21,1856. Parents, Elijah C. and Martha L. Wilson. Father was a farmer.

WRIGHT, Albert, April,1856. Slave. Mother, Winny.Owner, Joel Wright.

WHEELER, John A.,Jan.,1856. Parents, Gabrial Jr and Gilly E. Wheeler. Father was a farmer.

WHEELER, Solomon J.,Aug.1856. Parents, Thomas And Sarah Wheeler. Father was a farmer.

WALKER, Mary E.,Jan.,1856. Parents, Joel and Nancy C. Walker. Father was a Farmer.

WHERLEY,Maria L, Sept.,1856. Parents, John and Emily Wherley. Father was a farmer.

WADE, Irvine, Feb.1856. Slave. Mother, Adline. Owner, Mary E. Wade.

WELLS, Alice R.,May,1856. Parents, Richard M. and Harriett Wells. Father was a Farmer.

WELLS, Catherine R.,May,1856.(Twin to the above). Parents, Richard M. and Harriett Wells.

WELLS, William, Feb.1856. Slave. Mother, Ann. Owner, Richard Wells.

WELLS, Malinda, Dec.,1856. Slave. Mother, Ellen. Owner, Richard Wells.

WRIGHT, Gairy, Feb.1856. Parents. Robert W. and Leanor Wright. Father was a farmer.

INDEX

ABBOTT,Frances E.M.1,104;
   Nancy A.104;Robt.M.104.
ADAMS,Abram 14,85;Alonzo 85;
   Eliz.85;Frances M.14;
   Frances 85;Grief 51;Jim
   51;James 85;Mary V.69;
   Mary C.14;Joshua C.119;
   Nancy 85;Oscar V.119;Ruth
   51;Saml 51;Stephen 69;Wm.
   S.85. Victoria 103.
ADKINSON,Burwell 15;Bunuele
   85;Chas.85;Martha 85;Mil-
   dred Ann 15;Nancy 15,85;
   Wm.B.85;Wilson 85.
ACREE,Allan J.35;Ann E.35;
   Alban 104;Ann Eliza 104;
   Edw.104;Thos.Oliver 35.
AGEE,Arkless E.35,69;Barbara
   Ann 1,35,68;E.1;Mary Jane
   1;Matilda 15;Matthias 1;
   Peter Emmet 69;Reason G.
   15.
AGNEW,Alex.118;Martha 118;
   Susan 118.
ALIFF,Alex.B.T.15,85;Clemen-
   tine 15;Frances Ann 85.
ALLEN,Arena 1;Charlott 35;
   Chas.W.118;Ellen 35,104;
   Ester 1;Frances R.1;Geo.
   35;James Thos.103;Laura
   103;Mary 35;Nancy 118;
   Robt.1,35,103,118.
ALLEN,Chas.85;Jeremiah 15;
   Laura 104;Nancy 15,85;
   Robt.S.15;Robt.E.85.
ALMUND,John 104;Sarah Eliz.
   104.
ANDERSON,Agnes M.51;Betsey
   15,51,118;Beverly 104;
   Frances Ann 15,118;James
   A.103;James M.85;James T.
   15;Jacob C.118;Joel 118;
   John 104John H.114;John
   Harvey 35;John N. 35;
   Jubal L.B. 51;Judith E.L.
   51;Jonus 85;Joel C.15,51;
   Lewis G.15,51;Louisa 35;
   Leannah 104;Lucy 114;
   Mark 118;Mary 114;Martha
   35;Martha S.15;Martha
   Jane 15;Nancy 118;

ANDERSON,CONT.
   Penelope,35,103;Penelope E.
   1;Rich.15;Virginia 85;
   Vangeline 117;Wm.103;Wm.A.
   35;Wm.H.L. 15;Wm.H.S.118;
   W.N. 1.
ANTHONY,Ann 15;Abner 51;Almi
   ra 51;Caleb 118;Carrutta
   118;Daniel 118;Emma 118;
   Emelia 85;Emslen 118;Jane
   118;Lucy,118;Lizzie 118;
   Mary 85;Morga 118;Martha
   118;Sally 118; Wm.Thos.15.
ANDREWS,Billy 118;Celia 118;
   Chris 118;Ginny 118;Martha
   117;Sally 118;Sarah E.119;
   Wm.P.119;Wm.M.118;Wm.W.117
ANDREWS,Amanda 15;Celia 15;
   Chesley 1;Frances 15;Jinny
   15;Kit 85;Mark 15;Matilda
   85;Marilla 15;Margaret Ann
   1;Mark 51,85;Molly 15;Mari-
   a 15;Munford 51;Sally 85;
   Sarah E.51;Sandy 15;Thomas
   15;Violet 51,85;Wm.85;Wm.
   M.51;Wm.W. 15.
APPERSON,John G.69;John Wash-
   ington 69;Sarah S.69
ARRINGTON,Abner 51;Catherine
   51;Charlott 103;Alex 103;
   Delilia Ann 103;David 69;
   Edmon 1,103;Eliz 103;Eliza
   103;Eliza Ann 1;Frances 1;
   Hampton 35,103;James E.35,
   69;James R. 103;John 104;
   Lila Ann 35;Mary 35;Mary C.
   35;Mary Ann 104;Martha R.
   104;Martha Frances 35;Nancy
   Ann 35;Nancy S. 69;Nancy 1;
   Rich.1,35;Parham 35;Wm.35,1,
   103.
ARTHUR,Albon 51;Ardina 118;
   Admire 118;Betsey 15;Cath-
   erine 14;Elias 118;Emily
   J.85;Harriett 69;Henry 15,
   51;Jesse 69;Lewis C.15,69;
   Mary 69;Mariah M.14;Martha
   118;Malinda 118;Parthena 69;
   Phoebe 118;Wm.J.85;
ASHWELL,Beldire A.E.51;Elvira J.
   118;Emeline 51;Mary 14;

INDEX

ASHWELL,Cont.
    Pleasant 51; Wm.B.118.
ATKINS,Eliz.85;Eliza A.85;
    Jos.85.
ATKINSON,Eliz.51;Eliza Ann 51;
    Jos.51
AUSTIN,Abram 51,85;Abnum 85;
    Anunica 51,85;Bob 85;Clye-
    ries 85;Emma 15;Martha 15;
    Thos.51,85;Wm.85;Wm.N.15.
AYERS,Bishop 15;Eliz.J.51;
    Elijah Q. 51;Eliz.15,85;
    Eliza A. 118;Fanny 85;
    Henretta 15;Ismael 15,85;
    James W.14,85;John N.14;
    John M.14,85;John J.118;
    Jinny 119;Jane 15;Mary H.
    14;Lewis M.119;Mary J.51;
    Mary H.14;Masten J.15;
    Marinda 85;Missouri 15;
    Nancy 15;Saml J. 51;Sebert
    15;Sarah P.14;Tolbert 119;
    Wm.D.117.

BAKAN,Eliz.70;Patrick 70;
BAKER,Burwell 52;Margaret
    Jane 52;Wm.B.52;
BALLARD,C.J.103;Clarbourne L.
    36;James Winston 103;Mary
    Ann 36,103;Mary Eliz.36;
BANDY,Alvarine 120;Cornelius
    52,118;Celona 16;Compton
    G.86;Harriett E.118;Harri-
    et 16;Frances J. 120;John
    A.118;Mary A.86;Nancy Ann
    16;Lew Allan 118;Richard
    H.16;Mary Eliz. 16;Rich.
    52;Sally 52;Samuel 118;
    Sarah 118;Susan E.86;
    Thos.S.120
BARBER,Mary 2; Rev.F.M.2
BARNETT,Anna Wilmer 70;David
    70;Fannie R.70.
BARTON,Frances Jane 16;Jane
    E.15;Frances 119;Martha
    Ann 16;Reed 15; Wm.16,119;
    Wingfield 15
BATES,Betsey 16;Charlotte 17,
    51;California 16;Eliz.Ann
    17;Henry 17;Henry Mahlon
    16;Lewis 17;Mary M.17;
    Wm.17,51;

BEARD,Eliz.17,52,85;John 0.52;
    John S.118;Lovey 86;Martha
    A.52,118;Robt.M.85;Rob.J.85;
    Robt.M.17.Ro'b.86;Sarah V.52;
    Wm.S.86;
BECKNER,Elizabeth 16;John S.16;
    Mary E.16.
BEEL,Francis H.2;Misidora 2.
BELL,Ann 103,104;Bob 36,52;F.H.
    103,104;Francis H.70;Heelow
    85;Frances H.36.John 70;M.O.
    16;Malinda 70;Musidora 36,70;
    Nancy 85;Nancy B.16;Orville P.
    16,52;O.P.85;Patsey 104;Robt
    H.36;Thos.104;Wm.S.104
BELLEMY,Margaret 70;Patsey 70;
    Sarah 70.
BILBRO,Andrew 36;Benj.36;Chas.36;
    Edward 103;Julus 36;Lucy 36,
    103;Matilda 36;Mary L.36;Mary
    M.36;Wm.36,103;Wm.M.36
BIRD,Martha 85;Sarah 85;Vincent
    M.85
BETZ,Belinda 16;Wm.16;Wm.Henry 16;
BLACK,Benj.69;Mary Eliz.69;
    Matilda 69.
BLAKE,Isham 1;Mary 69;Mary Ann 1;
    Mildred Ann 36;Edward Step-
    toe 36;Reubin 69;Sarah Allis
    69;Wm.36;
BLAKENSHIP,Christina 119;Christ-
    enna 52;James C.119;Joel 17;
    John 52;John J.119;Sarah 118;
    Susan 1;Michael J.118;WM.P.52;
    Wm.R.1;
BOARD,Ann 16;Betsey Ann 86Bob 51;
    Chas.A.119;Eliz.A.119;Ester
    16;Frances 56;Geo.56;Jim 15;
    John 15,86;Maria 15,86;Mary 16,
    15;Martha 86,118;Maria 16;Mary
    Prescilla 16;Milly 15;Nancy 86;
    Olive May 119;Sam 16;Saml 118;
    Saml H.15,51,86;Thos.87;Thos.
    B.16;S.M.16;
BOBLITS,Mary 1;Wm.R. 1;
BOLEY,Agness McDaniel 69;Betsey
    103;Jesse E.103;Doc 70;John
    69;John H.70;John F.2;Martha
    Ann 2,68;Nancy 103;
BOND,Andrew J.17;David 51;Delen
    J. 118;Fanny 16;Laura 118;
    Mary 17;Nicholas 16;

INDEX

BOND, Cont.
Andrew J.86;John W.86;Mild
red 86;Mary 86;Molly 86;
Pleasant 16,51,86,118;
Read 86;Wm.G.17;
BONDURANT,Sandy R. 16;Sarah M.
16;Wm.W.16;
BOWER,Geo.H.70;June Q.70;Mary
Emily 70;
BOWLS,Elnora E.85;S.85;James
S.85;James T.85;Mary M.85;
Martha 85;
BOWLES,Frances 52;Mildred 52;
Wm.A.52;
BOWLING,Dr.A.2;Jane 2;Julia
H.17;Martha S.17;Wm.86;
Wm.H.17;
BOYLE,Elnora G.69;James A. 69;
Mary Eliz.69;
BONDURANT,Ausnetto 119,Eliz.
J.53,68;James Alex.36;John
P.36;Mary B.36;Sarah M.119;
Silas 53;Silas F.68;Wm.C.
68,119;Wm.53;
BRADLEY,Ann 52;James 52,119;
John R.119;Mary S.52;
Parnetta A.119;
BROOKS,John 70;Laniza 70;
BROWN,Adaline 17,86;Alfred
36,103;Ann 103;Ann B.120;
Ann L.36;Bates 52;Catheri-
ne 17;Chas.Alvin 103;Cinda
36;Dicy 2,69;Doctor L.86;
Doctor S.17;Emer Swanthis
103;Gerry 70;Granville 36;
James 17;James C.86,120;
James W.69;Job.W.36;Lando-
na 86;Lucinda 36;Lucy 120;
Mary 17;Mary James 36;
Martha E.86;Sam 70;Saml T.
52;Sandonna 17;Sarah 70;
Susan 69;Spottswood 2,8,
67;Thos.J.17,86;Violet 52;
Wm.M.17;
BRAMBLETT,Ann E.119;John S.
51,119;Mary C.51,119;Wm.I.
51;
BRUCE,Nancy 70;
BRYANT,Eliz.103;Gillmore 70;
Jesse S.70;Jesse L.2;Peter
H.103;Philby Ann 2;Phoebe
A.70;Samuel 103;

BUFORD,Alfred 16;Charlotte 52;
John W. 16;Paschal 52;
Sarah B.16;
BURKS,Betty B.52;Burton 52;
Betsey 104;Dolly 103,104;
Dolly Wallis 2;Eliz.52;
Eliza 2;Frances 2;Edw.C.52;
Isaac 36;Jesse 36;John D.2,
103,104;Julia Ann 104;Maha-
lia 36;Margarett 104;Mary
Ann 104;Martin 104;Martin
P.2,36;Nancy 36,104;Mitton
36;Wm.Sherman 103,104;
BURKHOLDER,Henrietta W.17;
James 69;John 69;Martha 1,
69;Mary Ann 17;
BURFORD,Daniel 104;Frances E.
86;John W.86;Judy 104;Lucy
F.104;Sarah 86;
BURNETT,America 86;Calvin 36;
Catherine 69;Chas.T.69;Cel-
ia 120;Chris.A.118;Elisha
C.86,119;Eliz.86;Eliza 118;
Eliza E.104;Fountain 118;
James A.120;James C.104;
James H.52;John 52,120;John
W.86;John Chris.36;John Wm.
119.Jane 119;Lavina 52;Mary
A.52,120;Mary B.36;Mary C.
120;Mary E.17;Mary Nealy 69;
Mary S.52;Margaret S.120;
Margarett L.86;Nancy 86;
O rphy 118;Rebecca F.120;
Wm.C.118;Wm.86;Wm.Edwin 104;
Wm.L.86;Wm.W.17,51,86,120;
Sarah E.17;Chas.W.86.
BURNETTE,Celia Ann 16;Christ A.
17;Elisha C.16;Lockey 17;
Margaret V.J.16;Mildred C.16;
Orphey 17;Sarah Ann 16;
Williamson 16;
BURROUGHS,Amanda 86;Amanda S.16;
Catherine 16,86;Eliza R.36;
Emily 16;James B.36;James L.
51;Jane 16;John 51,86,120;
Jos.51;Jos.N.80;Julina 86;
Patsey 86;Sarah 51;Sarah Ann
86;Sarah F.36;Thos.16,51;
BURWELL,Eliza 104;Wm.M.104
BUSSEY,J.2;Sarah Ann 2;
BUTLER,James R.16;Ruth 16;Wm.16;

INDEX

BUTTERWORTH,Frances 16;
    James 16,86;Lettitia 86;
    Sarah E.86;
CABLER,Alice 71;Ann 71;Cath-
    erine 71;Lucy 71;Marga-
    ret 71;
CADWALLENDER,Daniel 121;Fran
    ces C.87;James 87,120;
    James C. 121;Martha A.
    120;Mariah 120;Mary E.120;
    Milissa A.120;Prudence O.
    87;Thos.120;Frances C.120;
CALE,Catherine E.106;Samuel
    O.106;Wm.Robt.106;
CALLAHAN,Melvina F.54;Thos.
    54;Wm.54;
CALLAWAY,ADDA #&:Ann 71;Ari-
    anna Mariah 3;Dufary 122;
    Emerline 37;Fillis 37;
    Henry 71;John 37,71;John
    W.3;Louiza 37;Permelia 71;
    Queen 37;Quince 71;
    Rachel 71;Thos.Wm.3;Wm.B.
    122;
CAMPBELL,Alex S.106;Ann 38;
    Angeline 38,105;Chas.53;
    Charlott 38;Ellen 2,3,
    105;Eliz.3,71;Frances 3,
    106;Henry 106;James W.3,
    71;James Wm.3;John Monroe
    71;Julia A.121;Lafayett
    105;Martha S.71;Mary A.
    106;Nancy 53,88;Sallie
    71;Sarah Alice 106;Susan
    38,53;Thos.2,3,38,54,71,
    105;Wm.54;
CARDER,Cornelia Eubank 105;
    James M.18,53,105;Lucy
    Ann 53;Sarah 18,53,105;
    Thos.P.18;
CARNEFIX,Chas.70;Eliza 37,
    105;E.M.105;Edw.70;Edw.M.
    37;Geo.37;Mary 70;Mary
    Jane 37;Robt.Benj.37;Sam
    105;
CARNER,Amanda 18;Chales 120;
    Edw.E.121;Elias 18;Elijah
    18,88;Janetta 120;John H.
    120;Let.18;Lucy 18;Mary
    J.88;Nancy E.88;Osier 18;
    Wisley 88;Wm.H.88;

CAROLL,Catherine 17;Henry 17;
    Susan 17;
CARROL,Catherine 88;Hannah 54;
    Henry 88;Martha J.54;Thos.
    D.54;
CARROLL,Chas.C.3;Ida Washington
    3;M.A.36;Major A.121;Martha
    C.36,121;John Wm.36;Martha
    Jane 3;
CARR,Abeil S.3;A.S.106;Eliz.3;
    Eliz.C.106;Geo.Wm.3;
CARNEY,Abram 19;Nancy E.19;Rob.
    S.19;
CARTER,Albert 54;Alex 54;Ann H.
    7;Benj.F.54;Berry L.54;Berry
    S.17;Charlott 17,54;Edw.James
    38;Eliza 36,105;Elzira 105;
    Frances 4;Frances A.105;Fra-
    nces H.105;Fleming Moses 36;
    Frederick 2;James 54;James
    Alex 2;James C.38;James M.4,
    105;James Napoleon 4;James W.
    2,121;Jefferson 2;Jefferson
    P.71;Littleberry 36,104;Lucy
    54;Martha Ann 54;Mary Ann 2;
    Mary J.88;Saml A.88;Sarah
    Ann 38;Silas B. 88;Susanna 38;
    Susannah 2,Tabitha 2;Texanah
    2;Victoria 71;Wellington 105;
    Willie Jane 105;Wm.S.2;Wm.W.121;
CARUTHERS,Azela 71;Ann H.71;
    Annie Henry 3;Viola 3;Wm.H.3,
    71;
CHAFFIN,Edwin 106;Jos.88;Lauvi
    nia 88;Martha 88;Mary 106;Wm.
    Leonard 106;
CHEEK,Stephen W.122;Susan 122;
    Susan F.53;Wm.B.122;Wm.H.53;
CHEATWOOD,Ann 37;Charlott 37;
    Daniel B.37;Milly 37;Sally P.
    37;
CHEWNING,C.D. 120;Bob 54;Callo-
    hill 17,88;Callahill D.54;
    David 18;Dicey 18;Eliza Jane
    17;Eliz.120;Henry 18;James 18;
    James B.17;Marcella 120;Pau-
    liña 18,Susan 18;
CHILDRESS,Eliz.3,105;Eliza 3;
    Sally A.106;Spottewood 3;
    Sarah Jane 105;Thos.B.3;Wm.3,
    106,Wm.H.106;Wm.T.105;Wm.T.37;
    Wm.Newton 37;Eliz.37;

INDEX

CHILTON,Geo.2;Harvey 2;Henry
    Lee 38;James 38;Jane 2;
    John P.2;Martha Jane 2;
    Sarah E.38;
CHRISTIAN,Anna 71;Francis
    71;Ann 89;Geo.71;Guy 71;
    Mariah 71;Rich.Bozwell
    71;Robt.A.71;Rufus 89;
    Sarah 71;
CHEATWOOD,Daniel B.3,71;
    Carter 71;Eliza 3;
    Fanny 3;Geo.105;Hiram
    3,105;Julia 105;Luc-
    cinda 105;Mary 105;Mary
    Wilson 3;Milly 71;Sally
    P.3;Samuel McDaniel 105;
CHAPPELL,Adam 37;Prudence
    37;Richard 37;
CLARK,Sally 37;Samuel 37;
    Woodson 37;
CLAY,Ann Eliza 71;Cary 71;
    Emmer 38;Fanny 37;Fran-
    ces 38;J.A.38;John 71;
    Judy 37;Lucinda 3,38;
    Lucy Ann 37;Mariah 37,
    71;Martha 4;Mary 71;
    Mary L.71;O.G.37,38;
    Ogsen G.3,4;Pattrick 37;
    Paul A.37,71;Rich.4;
    Sarah 38;Selia 71;Theo-
    docia 37;Tolbert 3;Was-
    hington 71;Willie Shel-
    ton 71;
CLARK,Dorothea R.3;Geo.E.3;
    GEO.W.53;Isham 2,105;
    Josiah 53;Malinda 53;
    Mariah 105;Mariah Speed
    2;Mary Eliz.2;Robt.B.105;
    Woodson 3;Allen 3;Adal-
    line 3;Geo.W.52;John 3;
    Josiah 52;Malinda 52;
CLAYTOR,Adaline 54;Amar-
    rilla 122;Betsy 18,34,
    122;Bob 18;Cora M.88;
    Duke 122;Eliza 88;Eliza
    Jane 17;Edw.M.54;Harri-
    ett 70;James M.17;Jane
    122;Mary 17;Maria 122;
    Milly 70;Oscar 122;Rob.
    M.18;Robt.M.122;Rose 18;
    Samuel G.122;Saml H.17,
    88;Saml G.18;Sophia 18;

CLAYTOR, Cont.
    Thos.R.54,87;Wm.70;Wm.G.17;
CLAYTOR,Edw.M.18;Fanny 18;Geo.87;
    Maria 18;Mary P.53;McHenry 53;
    Robt.M.87;Sally 18;Saml 88;
    Susan 18;Thos.R.18;Wm.G.53,87;
CLEMENT,Eliza A.37;Emerline 38;
    James M.37;John 38;Margaret
    Jane 37;Robt.A.38;
CLINGHAMPEEL,Benj.122;Jack 122;
    Nancy 122;
COBBS,Benj.F.38;Betsy 18;Doctor
    54;Emma 87;Eveline 87;Frances
    Rebecca 36;James G.105;James
    V.36;James Walter 38;Jane 122;
    John C.37,71;Landonia E.38;
    Lindarell 87;Mahala 71;Maria
    17;Martha 71,Martha B.37;
    Matilda 122;minna 54;Nelly
    Ann 54;Nicholas Hamner 37;
    Oscar 18;Sarah 122;Sarah Ann
    54;Sarah J.105;Sarah Jane 36;
    Tilghman A.17,18,53,54,87,122;
COCHRAN,Louiza 38;Mary 38;Thos.38;
COCKE,Frances Atoway 3;Susan Lee
    3;Wm.B.3;
COFER,Ann Eliza 36;Edw.70;James M
    3,70;John 70;John C.36;Lucinda
    105;Mary 70;Mary Ella 3;Mary
    Jane 36;Matilda 105;Paulus
    Good 70;Pleasant D.36;Sallie
    N.3;Sarah B.36;Sophia Ann 70;
    Ursula 36;
COFEE,Bannister 4;Eliza Ann 37;
    Holcomb L.37;Oshallen 37;
COCKMAN,Eliz.87;Thos.87;
COLEMAN,Adam 105;Amanda 70;Bob
    70;Cyrus 38;Fillis 38,70;
    Harriet 37;Jesse 70;Leroy 37,
    70,105;Lucy 37;Margaret 105;
    Mariah 36;Mary Ann 36;Nancy
    70;Nicholas 70;Robt.38;Samu-
    el 36;Sarah Eliz.70;Tina 70;
COON,Burwell 122;Eliz.122;Jacob
    122;
COPPAGE,Alfred Brown 71;L.J.71;
    Martha Ann 71;
COPPEDGE,John Gilbert 3;Lievallen
    3;Martha Ann 3;
CORLEY,Eliz.120;James 19;James B.
    18;James Wm.19;Judith 18;Po-
    lly 19;Texanna 18,Thos.120;

INDEX

COTTREAL James 37;Mary Ann Margaret 37;Victoria Ellen 37;
COTTRAIL,James 105;Liddie Allice 105;Margaret 105; Martha Jane 105;Thos.J.105;
CRAFT,Geo.N.18;Geo.W.18,88; Susan 18,88;
CRAIGHEAD,Eliz.121;Frances 18; Julia A.53;Martha 52;Martha A.53,122;Rob.A.18;Robt A.121;Sarah F.122;Thos.B. 53;Virginia R.52,53;Wm.B. 52,53,122;Wm.R.121;
CRAIG,Archabald G.4;Henry-etta 4;Rich.Hopkins 4;
CRADDOCK,Ellen V.88;Emerline 88;Elvira Morton 4;David 4;H.N.88;Mary Tucker 4;
CRANK,Anna Constance 105; Albert G.106;Bettie Alberta 106;Eliz.C.106; Henry 105;James L.37,105; Nancy 37;Sallie Ann 37;Sejies 37;Sequs 105;Susan J. 37;Susan L.105;Wm.J.37,105;
CREASY,Ann 4;Amanda 19,121; Amelia 122;Benj.F.105; Booker P.107;Cathandra 122; Catherine 88;Cathcinda 19; Chas.A.19,88;Chas.H.120; Chas.Henry 87;Charlotte 53, 87;Cheritta 121;Clarbourn 4;DAvid H.53,87;Eldridge 120;Edw.S.120;Fanny 87; Frances Marion 4;Geo.Chris. 105;Harriett 87;Harriett L. 53,122;J.B.J.88;James M. 120;Jefferson 53;Jesse T. 122;John Lear 120;John P. 87;Leonard S.17,88;Louisa 122;Louiza Jane 53;Lucy A. 120;Margaret V.87;Mary 105; Meredith 122;Milissa Ann 87; Paulina 17;Paulina J.88; Pauling Jane 17;Paulinn 120; Roseley 17;Sarah 19,53,88, 120;SAml 19,88,122;Saunders 122;Thos.87,121;Wm.17,120; Wm.A.87;Wm.Robt.17;
CRENSHAW,Alex 53;Ellen 19;Elvira 19;Emily 53;Frank 19;

CRENSHAW, Cont.
Joanna 53;John 53;Malinda 88;Prescilla 19;Priscilla 87;Richard 53,88;Sam 19; Steven 87;
CRAWFORD,Saml 122;Saml S.122; Sylva 122;
CROUCH,Achilles 88;Adaline 122;Benj.122;Dennis 19; Jeremiah 19;Joel 54;John W. 88;Joicy 19;Levies 19;Mary 19;Mary A.88;Mary C.19; Martha Ann 54;Millisa 88; Molly 18;Rolley 18;Saml D. 88,122;Sarah 54;
CROWDER,Eliz.122;Eliz F.53,120; Henry 122;James T. 53;John H.53,120;Martha M.120;
CROUSE,Chas.3;Elmira 3;Margaret 3;
CRUMP,Ben 53;Beverly 18,88; Clarisa 18;Darcus 18;Frances M.53;Lewis Green 88; Lucy 18;Mary 18;Susan M.53;
CRUMPACKER,Edw.3,38;John E.18; Mary 38;Mildred 18;Rich.A. 18;Robt.38;
CUNDIFF,Amanda 18;Chris 18; Eliz.52,53,120;Geo.W.17,87; Hezekiah 18;Isaac 52,53; John M.17;John 122;Lelia B. 53;Mary S.52,53;Mary Malinda 120;Sarah E.17,87;Sarah Jane 53;Sarah 122;Samuel H. 87;Susan C.122;Uriah 120; Wm.B.53;
Cox,Ann 38;Frances 88;Jane 38; Thos.H.88;Wiatt 38;Wm.B.88;
CULLOHAN,Abner 122;Julia A.122;
CUNNINGHAM,James 18;James C.88; Lavina 18;Nancy 88;Rebecca 88;Susan B.18;

DAMERON,Angeline H.72;Frances 72;Malachi 72;Margaret W.72; Mary 72;Mary Emily 72;Samuel Malachi 72;Zachariah 72;
Daugherty,A.C.106;Martha Nelson 106;Nancy S.106;
DAVENPORT,Chris 121;Ellen Victoria 71;John N.121;Lydia 121;Minerva 121;Wm.121;

INDEX

DAVIS,Caroline 4,38;Charlott
    4,38;B.38;Ellen Eliz.4;
    Emily 19,89;Geo.4,19;
    Frances 72;Harriett 19;
    James 4;Lucy 19,89;Mary
    Susan 19;Mary Ann 38;Mati-
    lda 38;Micajah 4,38;Wm.A.
    S.72;Wm.Henry 72;
DAMERON,Angeline 4;Chas.Joshua
    4;Margaret Willis 4;Malac-
    hi 4;Texas 4;Zach.4;
DAVIDSON,Fanny 72;John 72;
    mayo 72;
DAWSON,Lucy 4;roderick D.4;
    Sarah Emily 4;
DAY,Alice Ann 106;John J.106;
    Sarah C.106;
DEARDORFF,Chas.19,89;Emily J.
    106;John H.106;Mary E.19,
    89;Robt.H.89;Susan E.19;
    Talula Nina 106;
DEARING,Cecelia 20;Celia Ann
    P.89;Eliza 54;Edw.54;Edw.
    W.89;Fanny 89;Florilla C.19
    Fran.19,54;Geo.W.89;Green
    19,121;Rachel Sarah 19;
    Rhoda J.121;Rhoda Jane 19;
    Rich.89;Sarah 89;Silas 20;
    Silas G.121;Wm.W.19;
DEBO,Jane 55;John 55;John F.P.
    20;Mary 55;Michael 55;Mich-
    ael 55;Wilmoth 55;Wilmouth
    20;
DENT,Ann Booker 55;Arbuter 55;
    Charlotte 89;Chas.55;Harri-
    ison 19;Joel 55;John J.55;
    Edmund 54;Marbel N.19;Marb-
    ell N.55;Martha 54,121;
    Mary 55;Morgan 121;Morgan-
    ly 54;M.H.89;Peter 19;Reb-
    ecca 19;Solomon 19;Susanna
    19;
DEWITT,Chas.Scott 4;Eliza
    Dennis 38;Eliz.4;James M.4;
    James Mitton 106;Louiza
    Ann 106;Wm.H.106;
DICKERSON,Amanda 19;Amy Ann
    106;Clemons 54,121;Daniel
    19;David 121;Eveline 121;
    Eviline 54;Fanny 121,Fran-
    ces Eliz.54;James 19;54;
    121;Jane 19;Kitty 19;

DICKERSON,Cont.
    Polly 121;Marcella 106;Mary
    Ann 54,121;Mossouri 121;
    Rhoda 121;Robin 55;Sallie
    121;Sarah 121;Sarah J.54;
    Stephen 55;Wm.19,54,55,106;
    121;
DICKEY,Catherine A.54;Harriet
    T.R. 54;Rufus L.54;
DOBBINS,Eliza S.121;Griffin A.
    121;Missouri J.121;
DONALD,Benj.1o6;Benj.A.4,71,
    Caroline 4,71;Fanny106;Jesse
    106;John 71;Lucy 4;Margaret
    106;Mary E.106;
DOOLEY,Alex 38;Andrew 38;Ann 38,
    89;Ann Eliza 38;Ann H.89;
    Catherine B.89;Chas.H.89,
    Frances 38;H.A.89;Harmony 55;
    Henry W.89;Jabez 55;James
    Alex 38;John 38,55,89;John C.
    38;Levina F.89;Martha Susan
    38;Mary E.89;Mary Nancy 19;
    Nancy B.89;Sarah A.E.19;Sarah
    S.89;Thos.E.19;Virginia 89;
DOUGLAS,Lewis 106;Patria 106;
    Sarah 106;
DOWDY,Abbey 89:James E.19;Jesse
    19,89Martha Ann 89;Mary J.89;
    Mildred L 19;Mildred T.89;
    Parry Franklin 19;Saml M.89;
    Susan 19,89;Walter B.19,89;
    Wyatt 89;
DOWILL,Ruth Ann 89;Thos.89;
DLONG,A.C.89;Henry 89;Nancy 89;
DREW,Jane 20;Mary 20;Catherine
    89;Tom 89;
DREWRY,Andrew P.12;Eliz F.121;
    James 54;James C.19;Elijah 19;
    James C.89;Jos.C.19,54,121;
    Julia Ann 19,89;Marinda 121;
    Mary,19;Mary F.19;121;Sarah C.
    121;Wm.19;Wm.T.89;
DUNCAN,Geo.W.4;John J. 4;Mary
    Eliz.14;

ECHOLS,Eliz.89;Jacob 89;John T.
    89;
EDGAR,Catherine 39,72;Edw.Emers-
    on 72;John H. 39,72;
EARLY,Chas.Edw.39;Eliza R.55;He-
    len B.55;John W.39,106;James

INDEX

EARLY,Cont,
121;Mary Eliz.106;Samuel 39;
Robt A.121;Sarah 39,106;
Sarah J.121;
ELLIOTT,Catherine 72;Chas.H.55;
Frances 55;James 72;Roth-
vell M.55;Sally 72;
ELLIS,Ann Eliz.89;James T.89;
Lelia Wella 39;Lucy C.39;
Mary 121;Pleasant 90;Sarah
90;Sarah F.90;Thos.D.121;Wm.
39;Wm.C.89;Zachariah 121;
ENGLISH,Amelia 121,Eliza Ann
121;John W.55,121;Joe 121;
Mary Jane 55;Rhoda 89;Sarah
E.55,121;Stephen 89; P.121
EUBANK,Ambrose4,72,106;Eliz.72
Frances 72,106;Frank 106;
Harriett 39,106;John 39;
John James 4;Jos.39,106;
Matilda 39,106;Rachel 39;
Sarah 106;Sarah Wright 4;
Susan Isabella 106;
EVERETT,Eliz.72;Eliza 72;A.N.
72;Emerline 72;John 39;John
H.72;John F.72;Jos.39;Jos.H.
72;Leannah 72;Luella 72;
MarthA 4,39,72;Mildred Ann
72;Morton 72;Rebechah 72;
Robt 4;Solomon 39;Vilett 39;
Zachariah 4;Sophia 72;Jos.H.
4;
EWING,Ann 72;Elenor 72;James
72;James Alex 72;Lewis Henry
39;Lydia 4,39;Wm.4,39;Wm.Edw
4;Nancy 72;

FALLS,Cynthia 123;Danl 123;
Wm.D.123;
FARISS,Anderson C.55;Mary 55;
Rebecca 90;
FARRIS,Clara 20;Edw.Bruce 20;
John J.20,90;Mary 20;Mary
Jane 90;
FARRISS,Anderson 123;Eliza 123;
FARRESS,Minta M.123;Frances
123;John J.123;
FALLS,Benj.5,73;Emily 73;Emmaly
5;Elmira 5;Fendal 5;Peggy 5;
73;Wm.B.5;
FARMER,Eddy Ann 107;Fannie
Susan 107;James A.107;

FEATHER,Ann Eliz.55;Alex 21;
Abiga190;Henry P.55;Harvey
90;John T.123;Jos.21,90;
Jos.D.90;Julia Ann 21,90;
Mary A.90,123;Mary A.M.90;
Mary Ann 20;Laura Jane 20;
Medors J.55;Richard B.20;
Selona 90;Wm.R.90,123;
FERGIE,Daniel K.5;Rhoda 5;
FERGUSON,Alfred A.107;Guy 90;
Joshua 90;Julia 90;Mary
90;Susan S.107;Wilmoth Ann
107;
FERREL,Chas.Price 5;Lucy H.5;
Milton P.5;Temp.72;Henry
C.72;
FERRELL,Edw.Royal 107;Henry C.
James M.107;Lucy H.107;
Mary 107;Mary Jane 107;Mit-
ton P.107;Samuel Huff 107;
Temp 107;
FELLERS,Angeline M.21;Mary O.
21;Peter 21;
FALLS,Cornelius 73;Cynthia
56;Chas Henry 72;Daniel 56;
Emily M.72;Garland 73;Geo.
W.72;Mariah 5;Mary E.56;
Luisa 5;Winny 5,73;Jane 73;
FIELD,Eliz.20;John B.20;Virg-
inia 20;Virginus 20;
FIELDS,Daniel W.20;Fannie F.C.
123;Louisa W.123; Matilda
20;Mildred 90;Saml G.90;
Wm.20;Wm.M.123
FISHER,Charlott 123;Chas.Bri-
ght 5;Eleanor 5;Eliz.5;
Fanny 107;James T.5;Mary
Ann 5;Mary Fisher 56;Lind-
say 56;Matthew 123;Mary M.
123;Thos 56,107;Saml 5;
FITZPATRICK,Archer 21;Hiram A.
21;Lucinda 21;Suckey 21;
Thos.21;
FIXER,Isaac 107;mary 107;Sarah
Fanny 107;
FIZER,Abram 55;Chas.55,123;
Chales B.20;Chas.O.90;
Emily 20;Frances 20;Frances
J.55,123;Geo.S.123;John R.
90;Lydia 20;Mary 90;Rich.
20,90;Sarah Frances 20;
Sarah 90;

INDEX

FLESHMAN,Mary A.90;Thos.W.90;
Wm.H.90;
FOLDEN,Jesse Y.4;Mary 4;Mary
Ann Gasper 4;Sarah Eliz.4;
FORGIE,Araminter 73;Daniel K.
5,73,107;Nancy A.107;Nancy
Anderson 5;Rhoda 73;
FOSTER,Alfred P.72;Faris 107;
Joel E.90;John 72;John
Edw.107;Mary S.107;Martha
A.90;Mary m.72;Nancy 56,123;
Patrick L.56;Rich.123;Rich.
A.56;Rich.123;Saml H.123;
Saml T.90;
FOUTZ,Green B.55,90;Martha 90;
Martha A.55;Mary A.90;
Yelverton L.55;
FOWLER,Emily 107;John Henry
107;Matilda 107;Nelly 107;
Wm.D.107;
FRAILING,Daniel 123;Geo.123;
Ladelia W.55;Nancy O.E.
123;Priscilla 123;Robt.A.
55;Robt.123;Sarah F.55,123;
FRANKLIN,Abner H.20;Angelien
D.20;Arch'd 123;Benj.H.72;
Eleas J.123;Elena 20;Elias 21
,90;Gilly A.F.123;Henry C.21;
James C.20,123;James H.123;
James T.123;Jane 123;Jesse
H.56,123;John W.123;Locky
56;Locky Ann 123;Louiza A.
123;Martha 123;Martha B.55;
Mary Ann 20;Milton W.90;
Molenzo 123;Saml 20;Sarah
G.90;Sarah J.123;Sarah Jane
123;Wm.55,Wm.Abner 20;
FRAZIER,Catista 20;Robt.20;
Wm.20;
FREEMAN,Edwin H.5;Eliz.Frances
5;Garlan H.73;Garland H.5;
James O.5;Lucian Overton5;
Ninerva 5;Marinda 73;Sarah
5;Thormutis 5;Thermuthis 73;
FUQUA,Benj.123;Benj.B.55;Ber-
melia J.55;Caleb 56,90;Eur-
etta 123;Eliza 56,123;Eliza
B.55;Granville 55,90;Jane
123;John H.20,56;Joshua 55;
Julia A.123;Martha Ann 90;
Martha J.20;Martha jane 55;
Martha M.55;Martin 20,123;

FUQUA,Cont.
Martin L.56;Mary E.56;Mary
S.123; Saml F.56;Thos.56,
123;
GARNER:James W.91;Martha E.91;
Sarah E.91;
GARRETT,Absalon 56;Elijah 56,
90;Edw.G.73;Emma C.56;
Fanny F.73;Henry Daniel 73;
Henry 90;John Bunyon 73;
John J.124;John R.124;Mar-
garet 90;Margaret B.56;
Mildred J.124;Sarah C.56;
Wm.90;
GIBBS,Andrew 90;Angeline 40;
Asman A.21;Betsey 21;Betsey
Ann 124;Betty 56;Celia 56;
Eliz.21,124;Esman A.56;
Frances A.56;Geo.90;Geo.L.
21;Geo.W.124;Ginny 124;
Henry 90;Jesse R.56;Joel 56;
John 90;John Edwin 40;
Matilda 21;Marinda 124;Mar-
tha 124;Mary 56,90,124;
Mary A.56;Mildred L.21;
Nancy 21;Paschal B.124;Pas-
chal N.56,124;Rob Henry 56;
Sarah 56;Wm.A.56;Wm.H.90;
Wm.W.40;Wyatt 21;
GIGHLEY,James T.21;John 21;
Mary 21;
GILES,Catherine 91;John S.91;
John S.91;
GILL,Alex 21;Chas.56,90;Chas.
W.21;Harriet 21;jenny Lind
56;Lucinda 90;Monroe 90;
Sarah 21;Scott 21;
GILLS,Asa 21,124;Angeline 107;
Aba 73;Caroline 21;Caroline
E.124;Eller 107;Sarah W.40;
Susan Henryetta 40;Wm.73;
Wm.H.40;Wm.W.107;
GILLISPY,E.B.40;Mary Frances
40;
GILLASPIE,E.B.107;Mary F.107;
GILWATER,Geo.W.91;Preston 91,
124;Sarah J.E.91,124;
GOAD,Davis 124;Eliz.56;Frances
124James G.21;James M.56;
Julia Ann 21,124;Lewis 21;
Lucinda 124;Martha F.56;
Rich.P.56;R632...

145

INDEX

GOAD,Cont,
   Rich.P.56;Robt Wm.124;
   Wm.R.56,124;Uriah 24;
GOFF,Jane E.107;
GOGGIN,Eliz.21;Eliz.L.21;Eliza
   L.21;Hrnretta 91;Heinretta
   21;Jane 21;James 21;Martha
   56;Martha C.56,91;Pleasant
   21;Stephen 57,91; Wm.L.21,
   56;
GOOD,Ann 5;Ann Mary 5;edmund
   5;John 5,40;Kitty 40;Rob-
   erta Ann 5;Sally 40;Violet
   5;
GOODE,Ann M.73;Edmond 107;
   Edmund 73;Lucinda 73;Mariah
   73;Mary Ann 107;Mary V.73;
   Milly 21;Stephen 21;Susan
   Agnes 21;
GOODMAN,Amanda 40;Frances 107;
   Henry 107;John 40,107;Mar-
   tha 40;Martha S.107;Mat-
   ilda 107;Mary 107;Nancy 107;
   Wm.Edw.107;
GOODWIN,Geo.O.107;Jane 56;Jane
A.E.107;Jesse B.56,107;Wm.56;
GOOLEY,Alfred 91;mary 91;Melton
   H.91;
GLASS,James E.40;Mildred Mar-
   tha 73;Lucy 40;Sarah Ann
   73;Thos.W.73;
GRAVES,Ellen 107;John P.107;
   Lucy 107;
GRAHAM,Eliz.21,124;Geo.H.124;
   Lawsom 21;Lawson 124;
   Nancy Jane 21;
GRAY,Ann H.56;Alex 56;Ginny
   124;James 124;James A.56;
   Judia 124;Lucinda 56;Rachel
   56;Sarah E.124;Sarah S.124;
   Wm.124;
GRISBY,Cary 56,91;James 56,91;
GROSS,Abram 124;Lydia 124;Mary
   124;Rich.H.5;Selinda 5;
GULPIN,Ann Minerva 21;John O.
   21;Wm.G.21;
GWATKINS,Caroline 5,73;Frank
   73;Isaac 5;Mary 5;Mary J.
   5,73;Mildred 73;Saml H.5;
   Wm.5;
GWALTNEY,Albert 21,57,124Eliz.
   91,124;John P.91;John 124;
   Julia E.57;Lydia Ann 124;

GWALTNEY,Cont.
   Mary 21,57;Mary Ann 21;

HACKWORTH,Arackna Maude 23;
   Betsey Ann 57;Columbus 91;
   Malinda 23;Martha 57,91;
   Wesley 57,91;Washington 23;
HAGEN,Eliza 92;James 92;Mary F.
   Mildred 91;Nancy 92;Thos.91;
HALE,Harvey 22;Lucy Ann 22;
   Betsey 23;
HANCOCK,Betsy A.22;Betsey 92;
   Jesse 22;John H.58;Martha
   Jane 58;Simon 22,92;Victoria
   91;Saml 91;Wm.D.58;Chris 22;
   Martha 22;Royal 22;
HANNABAS,Ambrose 124;DAvid 22;
   David M.124;James 22;Marce-
   lla 22,124;Nancy E.22,124;
   Thos.A.22,124;Thos.G.22,109;
HARDY,Amanda 7;Eliza Jane 6;
   James A.6,7;Capt.Jos.S.6;
   Lucinda 6;Major Rieley 7;
   Mary 124;Nancy 124;Paulina
   Ann 6;Robt.124;Wm.Henry 6;
HARRIS,Amamda 7;Ann 40;Betsy 6;
   C.J.40;Cassandra 40;Dr.Hec-
   tor 6,7;Frances 6;Geo.Washi-
   ngton 22;Hanibal 6;Harriett
   7,22;James 7;James W.6;Jim
   Henry 6;John Albert 6;John
   E.23;Judy 6;Mack 22,92;Mary
   7;Patsy 6,7;Polinah 6;Polly
   6;Rev.Wm.40;Saml 22,23,92;
   Sarah 40;Wm.Wirt 40;
HARRISON,Emily 109;James 109;
   Robt.109;
HASTEN,Margaret 6,92;Martha
   Christenah 6;Mary M.92;Wm.92;
   Wm.M.6;
HATCHER,A.P.40;Alex.5;Alex M.6;
   Angeline 40,109;Anna Hurt 40;
   Caleb 5,Caleb H.40;Calista
   109;Edw.Perkins 40;Eliz.Noel
   6;Emerline 5;Florintine 40;
   Granville 109;Henry 75;Jame
   109;Jeremiah 40;Jeremiah G.
   40;Joannah 50,92;Jesse Ore-
   lla 40;John C.40;judson Long-
   wood 40;Malinda Ann 40;Mary
   5,40,75,92;Mary Amanda 6;
   Mary L.58;Mary M.40;

INDEX

HATCHER,Cont,
    Pleasant 75;Rebecca S.40;
    Robt.Marion 6;Selene 109;
    Spencer 58,92;Thos.6;Thos.
    H.40;
HAWKINS,Adeline 6;Ann Eliz.73;
    Charlott 6,73;Edw.W.6;Eva
    73;Elvira 109;Geo.W.6,73;
    James 109;Peachy F.109;
    Spencer 6,Sylvia 73;
HAWKINS,Adaline W.75;Alford 6;
    Berry McDaniel 6;Celina Ann
    6;Eliz.6;Edw.E.75;Mary F.75;
    Mary Frances 6;Robt.C.6,75;
    Willie Chapman 75;
HAWLEY,Eliz.Ann 42;L.J.42;Mary
    Emmily 42;
HAUP,Geo.A.91;Saml M.91;Susanna
    91;
HAYNES,Adaline 57;Braxton 6;
    Jacobs 57;Mary Ellen 75;
    Sara Catherine 6;Susan 75;
    Writter M.6;
HEADEN,Eliz.91;Flora 91;
HEARDY,Eaney J.92;Henry C.92;
    Jos.92;
HECK,Eliz.40;Daniel 40;
HENDERSON,Rebecca 6;Rubin D.6;
    Sallie Elvira 6;
HENSLEY,James A.57;Joel 109;
    Luvenia E.109;Mary A.57;Saml
    W. 57;
HEPENSTALL,Caleb 57,91;Celia 91;
HENRY,Betsy 7;Edw.Mournin 7;
    Milly 7;
HERNDIN,Ally 57;Eliz.57;
HICK,Eliz.73;Daniel 73;
HICKS,Bill 91;Charlotte 22;
    Eliza Ann 22;Wm.22,57,91;
HIGGENBOTHAM,Altha 5;Angeline
    Eliz.5;Jos.C.5;
HIX,Ann Henry 23;Drewry 23;
    Judith 23;Phillip 23;Prince
    Albert 23;
HOBSON,Benj.N.6;Claibourn 42;
    Edditha 42;Edna 42;Edw.6;
    Editha Susan 6;Ellen 42;
    Emily 42;Fanny 42;Harriet
    42;Mariah 42;Mary 42;
HOBSON,Allice 109;Caleb 109;
    Emily 109;Eady 109;Ethalina
    109;Fanny 109;Isabella 109;

HOBSON,Cont.
    Julia 109;Mary 109;Reir 109;
    Samuel 109;
HODGES,Andrew D.5;Benj.W.5;
    Ferlander Jefferson 40;Har-
    Riett 73;Judy A.5;Mary 22;
    Milton 22;Samuel 40;Sarah
    Ann 22;Sarah E.40;Thos.C.73;
    Wm.Eldred 73;
HOFFMAN,Allis 7;Angeline Augus-
    tus 7;Frances L.57;John 7;
    Mary F.57;Saml 57;
HOGAN,Geo.W.58;Nancy J.58;Wash-
    ington 58;
HOLDREN,Abram 23,91;Chas.C.23;
    Frances 23,91;Geo.C.22;Geo.
    S.91;Jackson B.22,57;John
    57;Mary 22,57;Patsy 57;
HOLLY,Elijah 5;Eliza T.40;Mar-
    iah 5;Rich.B.40;Sarah E.40;
HOLLAND,Chas.91;Greenberry 91;
HOLLER,James 73;Minerva 73;
    Reubin 73;
HOLT,Eliz.F.42;Emily 22;Fanny
    S.22;Fillis 7,109;Frank 109;
    Jane 109;John 109;John W.7,
    109;Josiah W.42;Lucy 7;Lewis
    7;Mary 22;Mary Allis 42;
    Nancy 7;Sally 109;Sarah Ann
    22;Wm.22;Wm.L.22;
HOPKINS,Alice 7;Amelia 22;Char-
    lotte 22;E.S.6;Edw.73;Frances
    G.22,57;Jesse T.6;John 6;
    Malinda 73;Margaret 7;Marinda
    6;Mary Ann 23;Nancy 22;Rob.
    K.23;Rose 22;Tilghman 23;
HORSLEY,Eliz.L.40;Nicholas Cab-
    ell 40;
HORN,David 23,John 23;Sophia 23;
HOWARD,Cleopatra 109;John A.109;
    John Walker 109;
HOWELL,Amanda 23;Alex W.58;Geo.
    W.91;Martha J.91;Martha Jane
    23;Pleasant 58;Salina 58;
    Washington 23,91;
HOWSER,Daniel 92;Elij.92;Wm.B.
    92;
HUDSON,Birchy M.91;John S.91;
    Sarah 92;Wm.92;
HUELL,John 58;Malinda 58;Wm.C.
    58;
HOMES,Betsey 73;Geo.Walter 73;

INDEX

HACKWORTH,Malinda H.125;
    Saml F.125;Washington 125;
HALLEY,Richard B.108;Sarah
    E.108;
HAMBRICK,A.S.125;Charmain 125;
    Rebecca 125;
HAMMER,Chas.W.125;Edna J.125;
    John D.125;
HANCOCK,John H.125;Martha 125;
    Samuel E.125;
HARDY,Adah 74;A.M.74;Henry 74;
    James A.108;Jos.S.74;Lissa
    Christian 74;Lucinda 74;
    Lucinda D.108;Mariah 74;
    Mary Fletcher 108;Sarah
    E.74;Vina 74;Wm.A.74;Wm.
    Dabney 74;
HARRIS,Doc Hector41;C.J.108;
    C.H.108;Chas.41;Eliza 125;
    Emily 41;Fanny 74;Hanibal
    41,108;Harriett 41,108;
    James 41;James M.41;James
    W.41;James Walter 41;
    Ludwell 41;Louiza 41;Mar-
    iah 41,108;Malinda 74;Mary
    Ann 108;Mary Eliza 41;Mary
    Cole 41;Margaret 41;Nancy
    41;Polina 41,108;Queen 74;
    Rev.Wm.74;Sarah Lewis 108;
    Sulvia 41;Saml M.125;
    Uriah 74;Wm.125;
HARRISON,Patrick 41;Paulis 41;
    Rich.P.41;Sophia 41;Virg-
    inia 41;
HATCHER,Albert M.41,74;Allen
    D.41,108;Alex M.41;Ava
    Alice 41;Albon 108;Benj.
    Brown 41;Betty 108;Caleb
    41;Caleb H.108;Celista 41;
    Eller Jane 108;Eliz.74;
    Eliz.E.41;Fanny 41;Floren-
    tine McD.108;Ginnie 41;
    Ginny 74;Granville 41;Hani-
    bal W.108;Henry 41;James
    74;James Harvey 108;Judy
    74;Julius H.74;Martha 41,
    108;Mary 41,108;Mary C.
    108;Mary Ann 41;Mary E.108;
    Nelly 74;Polina 41;Sophiah
    108;Stephen 108;Sue Fanny
    108;Thos.41;Thos.A.108;
    Uriah 108;Warrick 41;Rob-
    Berta Lewis 41;

HAWKINS,Alfred 108;Alis Ann 41;
    Eliz.108;Ellen Boles 108;
    Eller 74;Fleming 41;Isaac
    74;John F.74;Malissa 41;
HAWLEY,Elawizer 125;Eliz.125;
    Eugenia 125;James B.125;
    Jos.C.125;Julia F.125;
HEWITT,H.H.108;Henry H.41;James
    108;Lucy 41,108;
HOBSON,Clara 74;Edla 74;Emily 74;
    Ethalinda 74;Isabella 74;
    Luiza 74;Martha 74;Mary 74;
    Samuel 74;SArah 74;
HODGES,Benj.W.108;Judy Angeline
    108;Milton E.125;Missouri Al-
    lis 108;Samuel Thos.108;Samu-
    el J.108;Sally 125;Sarah 108;
HOFFMAN,Angeline 74;Chas.74;John
    74;
HOLT,Wm.S.125;
HOPKINS,Matilda 74;Price W.74;
HORN,Cornelius 125;Hudley 125;
    James B.125;
HORSLEY,Benj.Wilks 108;Eliz.108;
    Nicholas 108;
HOWARD,Cleopatra 41;74;John W.41;
    John A.74;Jos.WM.74;Louiza A.
    41;Martha E.74;Samuel 74
HOWELL,A.M.108;Ann 108James Wm.108;
    Milly 125;Pleasant A.125;Salina125;
HUBBARD,Ann 125;Burr 125;Stephen
    125;Stephen S.125;Lydia A.125;
HUDDLESTON,Ann 125;Chas.125;Eliz.
    125;Nancy 125;Richard 125;
HUDSON,Chas.74;Martha 74;Wm.74;
HUDNALL,Frances 125;Jane 125;
HUNT,James 125;Sophia 125;Thos.125;
HUNTER,Aenias 41,108;Harvey 41;
    Mariah 41,108;Robt.108;
HUTTER,E.S.108;Lydia 108;Peggy 108;
HURT,Betsy 108;Charlott 108;Eller
    108;Elijah C.108;Joel 108;John
    P.108;Josephus 108;Matilda 108;
    Mary 108;Narcissa 108;Sally
    108;Sarah M.108;Sophia 108;
    Wm.L.108;

INDEX

HOMES,Cont.
Robt.J.73;
HUBBARD,Bangaland 57;Emsy 58;
John 58;Mary F.57;Sarah 57;
HUGHS,Caroline 22;Daniel 57;
Saml 22,57;
HUDDLESTON,Ann 22;Ann Maria 22;
Bethena 92;Eliza 22;John 58,
92;Richard 22;
HUDNALL,Asa D.92;Eliz.92;Jabey
S.92;
HULL,Octavia 58;Pleasant 58;
Samuel 58;
HUNDLEY,James W.91;Peter M.91;
Sarah 91;
HUNT,Chas.K.22;Frances 22;Geo.
C.22;
HURT,Betsy 6;Ellen 57;Henry 22;
Joel 22,Joel L.57,91;John P.
6;John Wesley 22;Leroy 22;
Mary 6;matilda 91;Narcissa
22;Joshua 22;Sally 57,22;
Sarah 22;Simon Peter 57;
HUTTER,Coleman 6;Emma C.75;E.S.
6;Edw.S.42;Edw.W.75;Frank 75;
Harriett 6,75;Hunter 75;
Jos.42;Lydia 42;Matilda 42;
Phil Anderson 42;Solomon 6;
Susan 6;

IRVINE,Alex 24,58,92;Andrew
126;Benj.H.126;Carter 58;
Dick 92;Felicia 24;Henry 58,
92;Julia 126;Susan 24;Tissy
92;Willis 92;Mary 24;

JACOBS,Aaron 59;Elisha 92;Kiz-
iah 95;
JAMES,Adaline 23;Agness 58;
Elias 58,92;Harrat S.23;
Isaac 23;Joel P.92;Matson
58;Sally 92;Sarah 23;Virg-
inia L.23;
JARROTT,John 92;Mary 92;Polly
92;
JENKINS,John Thos.75;Jos.92;
Louizat 75;Obediah 23,92;
Catherine 23;Tabitha 23,92;
Thos.S.75;
JENNINGS,Eliz.75;Dilcey 110;
Harvey 42;James W.75,110;
James C.42,110;James Edw.
109;Judy A.109;Lucy A.109;

JENNINGS,Cont,
Lucy M.75;Marcella 110;
Rachel J.M.75;Rachel J.N.
110'Vina 42,110;Wm.James
75;Zachariah Benj.110;
Zachariah E.109;
JETER,Amanda 58;Ann B.24,93;
Beverly R.59;Chas.7;Capt.
Jesse 7;Chelvessa 23;Eliz.
126;Emily 75,110;Fielden
24;Fielding H.110;Geo.Harr-
ison 42,93;Henry E.23,58;
Henry J.92;Horace 42;James
7;Jane 92;Jesse 7,42,75,110;
John H.126;Julia 7,110;Lou-
iza 7,75;Martha 42;Mary 75;
Mary A.59;Moses 110;Rose 42;
Smith 75;Susan 59;Wilbert
Thisco 75;Wm.75,110;Winston
75;Wittshire 42;
JONES,A.A.42;Amstead 75;Antho-
ny 58;Alex Lafayett 7;Arre-
nce 24;Benj.75;Daniel 58;
Ed.C.126;Edw.C.23;Ed.W.126;
Eliz.7,24,58,75;Eliz.Ann 7;
Eliz.F.126;Eliza Jane 7;
Eliz J.109;Ellen 126;Ellen
Catherine 7;Eliza 42;Emerl-
ine 7;Emily E.58;Frank 7;
Franklin Pierce 7;Fletcher
58;Geo.7,58,75;Harriett 8;
Harriett Allice 110;Harvey
42;Henry 58;Jackson 24;
Jesse 7;John W.7,109;Lewis
58;Lucinda 109;Lucy 24,Lucy
A.24;Lydia 58;Martha 23,109;
126;Mary Ann 8;Mary Va.7,
110;Milligan 58;Milly 7;
Minerva 109;Molly 42;Oscar
W.58;Pleasant 59;Pleasant
Green 75;Rob.E.58;Robt C.8,
58,59;Rob.Wm.23;Sally 8;
Sally P.109;Samuel Lee 7;
Samuel P.110;SArah 42;Sarah
Jones 75;Syloy 7;Sylvia 75;
Thos.M.7,42;Tillis 7;Wm.7,75;
JOHNSON,Charlott 8;Drury H.126;
Edw.J.59;Emerline F.126;Flor-
entine 23,14;Geo.23;Geo.W.59,
126;Henry 58;James F.7,8;
John 23,58;Maria E.92,126;
Martha 126;Martin S.126;
Nancy F.126;Nancy Jane 92;

INDEX

JOHNSON,Cont.
Rebecca 92;Robt.92;Ruth Ann
59;SArah 23;Sarah Ann E.59;
Sarah E.7;Susan E.7;Thos.
23,59;Wm.58,92;Wm.H.126;Wm.
Henry 8;Wm.W.59,126;Wm.
Witton 7;
JOPLING,Antony 7;Emily 42;Fanny
7,75;James W.42;Jane 7;Jesse
Spottswood 109;Julia Ann 7,
110;Julia Anna 7;Mary 7;
Morton 8;Peter 75;Robt Kelso
42;Samuel Emmet 110;Sarah E.
92,109;Thos.109;Thos.B.75,78;
Wm.W.7,110;
JORDAN,Alex 23,58;Andrew 126;
Ann 23;Ann E.58;Anni 23;
Booker 23;Jane 23;John 58,93;
Jubal 23,59;Geo.58;Lucy A.
58;Maria 126;Rebecca 23;
Rhoda 23;Tansy 93;Wm.V.126;

KABLER,Allice 42;Ann 42;Marga-
ret 42;Wm.C.42;
KABBLER,Catherine 8;Malinda 8;
Polina 8;
KARNES,Abraham 110;Alex Hamilton 110;Ann 110;Eliza Turner 110;John J.110;Julian
Owen 110;Michael 42;Nancy
42,110;Salinda Ann 110;Sarah
42;Sarah F.110;Wm.42;Wm.A.
110;Wm.Hudnall 110;Wm.R.110;
Wm.Randolph 42;
KASEY,Adaline 93;Alex 93;David
59;Deborah 93;Eliz.93;eliza
Ann 93;Elvira F.59;James C.
59,93;James G.59;James S.59;
Jane 126;Jerry 126;John G.
126;Lelia 93;Mary 59,93;Mary
F.59;Mary Louiza 59;Mary N.
93;Nancy J.V.126;Newlon 59,
93;Rhoda 126;Scott 93;Tex-
annah 59;Thos.59,126;Thos.A.
93,126;Virginia M.93,126;
Wm.W.93;
KEATS,james 59;Sallie w.59;
Saml H.59;
KELLY,David W.93;Lydia C.93;
Sarah M.93;
KEITH,Colin B.76;Eliza Jane 76;
Selest hadee 76;

KELSO,Andrew 8;Ann 8;Annah 43;
Betty 43;Benj.110;Emily 76;
Henry 8;Jack 43;John 43;
Judy 43;Kitty 8;Lucy 8,110;
Julia 43;Mariah 110;Mary 43,
110;Nancy 8,76,110;Robt.8,
43;Robt.M.8;Robt.N.43,76,
110;Susan B.8;
KENEDA,Eliz.76;James Pleasant
76;John L.76;Mary 76;Wm.76;
KENT,Chas.H.75;Frank Russell
110;John D.110;Lucy W.75;
Mary O.110;
KERNES,Abraham 8;Ann 8;Frances
Ann 93;Jacob 93;Mary 93;
Spottswood Lee 8;
KEY,Chas.H.110;Chas.marion 110;
James H.8;James Madison 8;
Mildred F.110;Mildred Fran-
ces 8;
KEYS,Cessola A.75;Chas.75;Davis
Leonidus,75;Mildred F.75;
Missouri Catherine 75;Thos.
H.75;
KIDD,Eliz.93;Henry D.42;John A.
93;John Jefferson 42;Mary C.
42,126;Pamela 93;Paulina P.
126;Henry D.126;
KIDWELL,Eliz.59;Hezekiah 59;
Jane Ann 93;John 59;Mary J.
93;Rich.93;
KIRBY,Eliz.93;Magdaline 59;Mary
Jane 93;Thos.93;Wyatt 59;
KIRKPATRICK,Margaret Ann 8;
Phillip 8;Samuel 8;
Kisler,David C.93;Jane 93;Wm.H.
93;
KNIGHT,Fanny 76;Geo Herbert 76;
Henry 42;J.J.42;John J.110;
John Q.76;Nanny leigh 110;
Susan C.110;

LACKIE,Emmelie S.8;Harriett 8;
Jeff 8;
LACY,Alvira F.60;Anderson F.127;
Susan M.127;Thos.J.60,127;
WILSA Ann 60;
LANCASTER,Esther 127;Frances
127;James 127;
LAUGHLIN,Eliz.59,127;James 59,
127;John 59;Lockie L.127;

INDEX

LAUGHON,Ann B.24;Alonzo 25;Chas.
    E.24;Eliz.60;Eliza 24,127;
    Isham 24,93;Joshua 25,127;Jos
    127;Landona 60;Mary E.25;
    Mary Jane 24,93;Misouri 93;
    Noah 60;Paulina 24;
LAWLESS,Betsy Ann 111;Eliz.A.76;
    Eliz.Virginia 111;James 111;
    James R.76;Sarah Martha 76;'
LAZENBY,Annis B.127;Anni E.24;
    Attilia 24;Bettie 126;Edw.
    24,126;Jane 126;Mary 24;
    Minerva 24,126;Rebecca 24;
    Rizen 126;Robt.24;Wm.R.24,
    127;
LEFTWICH,Alex 25,76;Alfred D.
    25,59;Ann 25;Candice 25;
    Caroline 77;Casseius L.60;
    Charlott 25,76;Ellener 76;
    Eliz.43;Etchison G.24;Eve-
    line 60;Evaline 93;Everline
    77;Frances 25;Granderson 24;
    Gray 25;Geo.W.127;Hannah 111;
    Ida 77;James 25,59,93;Joel
    43;John S.43,76;John Wm.25;
    John Q.25;Julia E.24;Laura
    25;Lucinda 43;Lucy Ann 24,25;
    Mark 24;Mary 25,76;Mary Ann
    25;Martha 25;Missouri Emmer-
    line 43;Moreah 24;Massey 24;
    Nancy 43,76;Nelson 76;Octa-
    via 24;Patsey 24;Sallie W.43;
    Sarah 25;Susan 25;Thos.24;
    Thos.W.76,111;Tina 25;Valin-
    tine 60;Wm.25,76,77;
LEE,Ellen 110;Deannah 43;Dinah
    77;Frances Susan Jane 8;
    Garnet 93;James G.60,127;
    John 43;Mary Jane 25;Margar-
    et 93;Roberta Virginia 8;
    Robt.110;Richard A.25;Samuel
    Clay 43;Susan 60;Susan A.43;
    Susan Lee 127;Thos.93;Thos.
    N.8,43,110;Tom 77;Wm.43;Wm.
    H.43,77;
LESLIE,James D.126;Latherat 126;
    Mary J.126;
LINDSAY,Eliz.8;Flora 76;Jenneta
    8;Jenette 76;Robt.8,76;Sarah
    76;
LIPSCOMB,Clara Ellen 126;Geo.G.
    126;Margaret 126;

LOCKARD,James 93;Martha 93;
    Rufus 93;
LOCKIE,Alfred 111;Emily 111;
    Harriett 111;
LOGWOOD,Alex 111;Ann 43;Anna 76;
    Alexander 76;Alex.H.43;Eliza
    76;Ferdinand 111;James Edward
    111;Mary 111;Mary E.43,76,111;
    Rob R.76;Robt.43;Robt.R.111;
    Theodocia Ann 43;Thos.Burrell
    43;Walter Henderson 43;
LOWRY,Allice 111;Ann 111;Bettie
    76,127;Betsy 43;Caroline 43;
    Celia 25;Cephas 111;Cicely M.
    76;Chas.B.76;Clary 111;Eldy
    111;Eliza 8;Ellen 93,111,127;
    Elliott 25,127;Emerline 43,
    76;Fanny 76;Fillis 8;Flora
    111;Irvine 25;John 8,43,110;
    John H.76;John W.111;Junisus
    Daniel 76;Jinisus 76;Lilburn
    111;Lucy 8,76,110;Lucy A.M.76;
    Lunceford 8;Lunsford 76;Marg-
    aret 43;Martha 110;Matilda
    43;Matilda C.8;Mary 110;Milton
    43,111;Minerva 43;Moses 76;
    Nelson 43,76,111;Payton 43;
    Phillis 43;Price 110;Rich.W.
    76;Sarah 43,111;Susan 8;
    Willie 76;Wm.Austin 110;Wm.H.
    43;
LOYD,Chelsey 24;Deanna 25;Eliz.
    126;Henry Jr.24;John Anthony
    24;John A.25;James 59;Jos.G.
    25,126;Lewis 59;Margarett 25;
    Margaret 126;Mary S.25;Mason
    25;
LUCAS,Ann Eliza 8;Martha 8;Robt.
    8;
LUCUS,Chlow 26;Jos.26;
LUCK,Clora 43;Geo.P.8,43,76,110;
    Hillary 43,76;Janies Paschall
    110;John Bumpass 8;Laura 76;
    Laura Lee 43;Mary 43,76;Nancy
    8,110;
LUGAR,Thompson 60;
LUMPKIN,Charetta 127;Fox 127;
    Harry 127;Robt.W.60,127;Rac-
    heal 127;Taswell 60;
LYLE,Judah M.60:Lucinda 60;Wm.60;

INDEX

THE FOLLOWING NAMES WERE OVER_
LOOKED

LANDSDOWN,Lucian 94;Mary 94;
LANTZ,Henry S.94;Peter 94;
LAUGHON,Ardena E.94;Elizabeth
    94;Elizabeth P.94;Jarrott 94;
    Joshua 94;John 94;Lewis 94;
    Louvinia 94;Lydia 94;
LAYNE,Harriett Ann 94;Joseph
    B.94;Martha V.94;Paulina 94;
    Patrick Henry 94;Taswell 94;
    Thompson 94;Thompson H.94;
LAZENBY,Charles 94;Edward 94;
LEFTWICH,Alex 94;Ann B.94;
    Ellen 94;Etchison 94;Gran-
    derson 94;Ider 94;James 94;
    Lucy Ann 94;Lynch A.94;
    Mahala 94;Margaret A.94;
    Mary Ann 94;Massa Ann 94;
    Priscilla 94;Walter E.94;
LOYD,John H.94;Mason 94;Mary
    S.94;Saml G.94;Sarah F.94;
    William T.94;

MAJOR,Alley 44;Catherine K.44;
    Cleotria 44;Edna 112;Emmet
    Dudley 44;Harwood 44;Kitty
    112;Mary Jane 44;S.A.112;
    Spottswood 44;Wm.44;Walter
    Pendleton 44;
MAKEPEACE,Alvin S.44;Ruhamah
    44;Sarah Eliz.44;
MANSFIELD,Ann E.26;Berry S.95;
    Margaret 26;Nancy 25;Wm.25;
    Wm.S.95;Thos.S.26;
MANSON,Mary 9;R.E.9;Sophiah 9;
MANUEL,Jeremiah E.26,95;Martha
    A.95;Martha Ann 26;Mary C.
    26;Thorton E.95;
MARKHAM,Jacob S.96;Lucy 45,111;
    Martha A.96,111;Nancy 96;
    Patsey 45;Tobt.45;Roland 111;
MARTIN,Chas.26;Cynthia 62,128;
    Daniel J.26;Eliz.25,128;
    Emily 27;Frances 27,95;Green
    B.61,127;Green M.61;Gilly
    Ann 62;James 27;James A.95;
    James F.95,127;Jasmine 127;
    Jobe 62;John 27;Job 128;
    Lucy 127;Lydia 26;Mary 27;

MARTIN,Cont.
    Naomah C.61;Neomi C.127
    Samuel 25,128;Thos.J.128;Wm.
    27;Wm.D.27,95;
MARSH,Ann Jane 77;James Robt.77;
    Leona 77;Lydia C.111;Martha
    111;Marion 77,95;Mary Lawra
    111;Mary Permelia 111;Robt.A.
    77;Robt.B.111;Rob.95;Thos.E.
    111;
MARSHALL,Ann M.9,77;Edw.9;Elzera
    111;Gilbert 60;John A.111;
    John R.60;Mary E.60;Mary Jane
    25;Mary J.E.128;Nancy A.25;
    Ossa Ann 77;Poindexter 25,128;
    Robt W.9,77;Sarah Samantha
    111;
MASON,Eliz.112;Geo.E.112;John J.
    9,77;Lucy Eldridge 112;
    Mahala 77;Mahaly 9;Saline 9;
    Thos.Henry 77;
MATTON,Martha M.60;Mary Jane 61;
    Medora T.61;Michal T.61;Robt.
    A.60;Robt.P.60;
MATTOX,Henry D.95;Martha M.95;
    Mary J.96;Michael 96;Robert
    95;Susan J.96;
MATTHEWS,Eliz.R.129;James M.129;
    Mildred S.27;Thos.J.P.129;
    Wm.H.27;
MAUPIN,Carr M.128;Carrenia 128;
    Frances 128;
MAXEY,Eliz.61;Isaac 61;Victoria
    F.61;
MAYHEW,Margaret Ann 26;Rebecca
    26;Wm.M.26;
MAYS,Adline 26,128;Dickerson 26;
    Jos.M.128;Jos.W.26;
MCBRIDE,Emily 95;Frances R.95;
    Wm.95;
MCCABE,James 127;James Harvey 62;
    Jesse 127;John Robt.62;Malinda
    62,127;Salona 127;
MCCARTY,James M.77;Mary 77;Mary
    Eliz.77;
MCCLAIN,John L.61;Lettitia 61,127;
    Pleasant 61;Wm.61;James 61;
    James D.127;Jesse 25;Jane Sarah
    127;Henry C.127;Leroy 127;
    Marcia 25;Mary 127;Mary Ann 25;
    Wm.127;

INDEX

MCCLINTOCK,Amanda 71;Catherine 3;
    Lee 3,77;Wm.Lee 3;
MCDANIEL,Agness 128;Addison 9;
    Albert 111;Allen 9;Betsey 9,
    77;Eliz.128;Eliz.Craig 3;
    Eliza S.77;Eller 77;Fill 9;
    Geo.9;Genetta 77;Jesse W.111;
    Laura 61;Loudon 61;louisa 9;
    Lucinda 128;Lydia 111;Mary
    111;Maria 128;Matilda 128;
    Martha 9;Mrs N.77;Moses 77;
    Nancy 9,78;Nella 9;Nilly 9;
    Patti 128;Rich.W.3;Rose 77;
    Samuel 9,77,78;Tazewell 111;
    Winston 25;Wm.9;
MCGHEE,Albert 77;Burwell 9;David
    R.95;Frances 44;Henry F.128;
    Jack 95;James B.S.95;Louvi-
    nia 95;Martha 9,128;Patsy 9;
    Parthena 9;Samuel H.9,128;
    Sarah Eller 44;Susan 95;
    Silla 95;Thos.95;Wm.I 44;
MCMANAWA Chas.H.96;James M.96;
    Nancy A.96;
MCMANAWAY,Ann 127;Lella 127;
    Nancy 127;
MEADOR,Agnes A.25;Agness E.60;
    Allice 44;Ann 60;Edw.A.25,60;
    Eliza 44,111;G.S.112;Hack 95;
    Job Calvin 44;Jobe W.111;
    John J.44;John W.44,111;
    Mary 96;mary G.25;Mary F.96;
    Meredith 96;Reece 95;Rosa-
    nnah 60;Obediah 96;Peyton 96;
    Sarah A.60;Susan E.44;Whit-
    Field A.60;
MEAD,John 95;Oxanna 95;Virginia
    60;Wella 60.Wm.60;
MEEKS,Eldridge 112;martha Va.112;
    mary Wiatt 112;
MELTON,Isabella 44;Josiah 78;Jos.
    Morton Thos.111;Mariah W.44,
    111;Samuel 44,111;Susan 78;
    Susan Agness 44;
MEADOR,Catherine 26;Green B.26;
    James 127;John O.26;Martha E.
    26;Mary Ann 26;Sparrel H.26;
    Susan 127;Thos.C.26;Thos.R.
    26;Wilson 127;
MELSON,John D.60;Mary 60;
MENNIS,Emer 78;Lucy 9;Mary Eliza
    9;Martha 78;Wm.C.9,78;
MERRIMAN,Edw.95;Neoma Ann 95;

MERRWETHER,Berinda 44,78;Betsey
    44;Betsey Ann 78;C.J.112;
    Chas.I.44;Chas.J.78;Dilsey
    78;Ellen 78;Geo.44;James 112;
    James A.44,78;James Addison
    78;Jane 78;Lucille 78;Marga-
    ret Douglas 78;Polina 44;
    Polly 112;Rachel 78;
MERRYMAN,Elenor 128;Jane 128;
    Malinda 128;
METTS,Eliz.128;Geo.F.128;James
    R.127;John R.60;John W.60;
    Lucy 127;Matilda 127;Matilda
    V.60;
METCALFE,Caroline 112;Dolly 9;
    Easter 78;Eliza 44;Ginny 112;
    James 9,44,78,112;John 9;
    Laura 9;Landonia 44;Martha 78;
    Mary 9;Steven 78;Thorton 78;
MILES,Caleb 95;Emma N.128;Fanny
    77;Henry W.77;James S.27;John
    27;Jos.R.95,128;Malinda 77;
    Sarah 27;Susan G.128;Susan J.
    95;
MILLER,Amanda M.96;James W.61;
    Sarah Jane 61;Mary E.96;Wm.
    96;Wm.S.61;
MILLENER,Albert G.44;Chas.44;
    Martha 44,111;Nancy 44;
MILLNER,Albert G.111;Catherine
    9,77;Eliz.44,111;Eliza Marg-
    aret 9;Geo.111;Jeremiah D.9,
    77;Madison F.44,111;Wm.Jasper
    77;
MINNICK,Catherine 112;Elvira
    Emily 112;Geo.W.112;
MINNIS,Martha 44;Wm.44;
MINOR,Alis C.27;Rob.C.27;Susan 27;
MINTER,Billy 25;Frances 25;
MITCHELL,Ann 61;Billy 61;Caroline
    26,27,128;Catherine 27;Danl
    128;Dr Thos.P.95;Edw.O.P.61;
    Elly 26;Eliza 26,27;Elvira 128;
    Frances 26,95,96;Gustavus J.
    61;Hannah 27;Harriett 95;James
    27;James W.127;Joel D.26,96;
    John 61;John A.128;John G.128;
    John P.25;Jordan 27;Lucy F.96;
    Lucy M.26,120;Malina 26;Martha
    E.61;Mary Jane 26;Mary Susan
    77;Mildred E.61;Mildred Ann 61;
    Milly 27;Parthena 61;Rob.C.
    27,95;Robert 61;Sallt 61;

153

INDEX

MITCHELL,Cont.
Sam161,128;Saml R. 26;Sarah
27,128;Sarah A.77;Stephen
A.77;Summerville 27;Thos.C.
61;Wm.C.26,61,96,128;
Martha Jane 25;
MONROE,John M.27;John T.27;Mary
Jane 27;
MOOR,Catherine 111;Goodridge
111;Susan Martha rebeckah
111;
MOORE,Arrina 26;Catherine 44;
DAvid Wm.44,Eliz.Price 77;
Goodrich 44,77;Jubal A.26;
Susan 77;Wm.M.26;
MOORMAN,Ann 44;Betsy 44;Beverly
77;Eliza 112;Gilbert 77;
Granville 96;Judy 77;Lodo-
wick 77;Malinda 44;Martha
Ann 112;Mary 112;Mary Jane 96;
Otielanna 96;Permela 77;
Toney 44;
MOOSELEY,Edw.Winston 77;Geo.C.
77;Mary D.77;
MORGAN,Alex 26,61,95;Adaline 26,
95;Ann 61,128;Bacum A.95;
Catherine 95;Chris.128;Chris-
topher 61;David C.27;Fie 26;
Jesse 61,128;Jesse Dell 95;
Julia 61;Julennea J.128;
Medora S.95;Marcella W.128;
Nancy 26,95;Pleasant 95;
Taswell 61;Rich.27;Solo M.26;
Susan 27;Whitfield 61;Wesley
95;Wm.B.26,95;
MORIMAN,Charlott 26;Saml R.26;
MORMAN,Ann 112;Betsy 112;Henry
Clay 112;Lodowick 112;Wm.
Dabney 112;
MORRIS,Joshua 96;Lively M.128;
Lydia 96;Mary 78;Mary Ann 112;
Mary A.96;Mary Eliz.112;
Micajah 128;Micajah G.61,128;
Sarah S.61;Wm.78;Wm.H.112;
MOSBY,Bettie M.77;Margaret E.44;
Mary Alli 77;Mary Frances 44;
Powantan 44;Sally 78;Sinor 78;
Thos.4,78;Thos.Y.77;
MOSELEY,Geo.C.44;Julia 44;Louiza
44;
MOTLEY,John 26;Martha 26;
MURPHY,Elijah F.96,128;Emily 96,
128;Jeremiah 96;Jeremiah E.128

MUSGROVE,D.P.27;Demetrus 95,128;
Filmore 61;Julia A.27;John
H.61;Lucy A.95;Margaret 95;
Martha 27;Martha Ann 128;
Wm.W.128;
MOULTON,Benj.60;Mary 60;Mary
Ellen 60;

NANCE,Albert 62;Albert F.129;
Edwin 129;Eliz.62;Eliz.J.129;
Henry 62,92;Jane 62;Jane G.
129;John A.129;John W.96;
Sarah 129;Sarah E.96,129;
Sarah M.62;Thaddeus 96;Thorp
H.62,96;Thos.W.62,129;
NEIGHBORS,Anderson 62;Chris 62;
Eliz.27;Eliz Ann 62;Henry
27;Lucy Ann 62;Mary Ann 62;
Samuel Henry 45;Susan 27,45;
NELMS,Chas.D.62,129;Chris C.27;
Eben 96,127,129;Ester 27;
Florilla 62;Henrietta 96;
Idelia 129;Jane 27;Joe Ben
62;Leroy E.129;Louisa 27;
Lucy Ann 27;Mary E.62,129;
Mary Lucy 27;Suckey 27;Wins-
ton 129;
NELSON,Caroline 45,78;Doct.Thos.
H.9;Emily 45;Edw.9,78;Edwin
Matthews 78;Hannah 9;Julia 9;
Julia Ann 45;Lewis 45,78;
Martha 9,45;Mary Ann 78;Nancy
9,Nanny 78;T.H.78;Thos.H.45;
NENIMS,John N.96;Madison 96;
NEWMAN,Bailey 27;Betsy 28;Call-
ohill 129;Callahill M.96;
Elias 129;Elisha 96;Harriet
27;James W.62;Jesse 112;Jos.
W.129;Julia A.96;Martha 129;
Mary 112;Mary Ann 62,129;
Mildred 27;Mildred Key 112;
Rosea Wm.112;Robert 112;
Sally D.28;Sarah J.27;Sarah
P.112;Wm.28;Wm.C.129;
NEWSOM,Ann 62;David M.96,129;
Edw.B.96;Eliz.62;Frances
Ellen 28;John H.28;John W.96;
Lelia O.96;Lucy Ann 62;Mary
F.28,96;Nathaniel 62;Susan E.
96,129;Wm.H.129;

INDEX

NICHOLS,Betsey 129;Bersheba 129;
   Caroline 129;Griffin 129;
   Isaac H.27;J.L.129;Julia
   Ann 27;Marinda 27;Rhoda V.
   129;Sandy B.27;Saml W.129;
   Sarah J.129;Thos.F.129;Wm.27;
NIMMO,John W.129;Josiah H.129;
   Mary Starr 129;
NININGHER,Caroline 96;David S.
   96;Ellen 96;
NOEL,Abner 112;Adah 45;Alex 9,
   45;Alex J.78,112;Amanda 78,
   112;Angeline 112;Ann Eliza
   112;Arrenia 45;Catherine
   112;Catherine A.45;Catherine
   J.78;Caleb R.78;Caleb Corne-
   lius 78;Chas.112;Eliz.112;
   Emmaly 9;Eramus 45,112;
   Frances 112;Hillary Alexan-
   der 45;Jeffrey 96;John 45;
   John C.45,112;Landona 78;
   Luvenia 45;Marge 112;Mar-
   garet 78;Martha 45;Pales-
   tine 112;Palestine W.45;
   Rachel 45;Robertine W.78;
   Robert Hall 112;Stephen 9;
   St.Paul 45;Virginia 45;Wm.96;
NORCROSS,Frances 9,113;samuel
   9,113;Wm.Nelson 9;
NOWLIN,James H.28,62;Jane 28,62;

OAKS,Rice L.28;Susan 28;
OAHS,Amanza 63;Rice T.63;Susan
   63;
OGDEN,Amanda 79;Annah 113;Cat-
   herine Starr 9;Cornelia 113;
   Charlott 79;Elisha E.9;Henry
   M.10,79,113;Harriett 10,113;
   Jane 10,113;John 10,79;Julia
   10;Luiza 113;Margaret 79;
   Malinda 79;Martha 79;Mary 10,
   79;Mary Frances 9;Polina 113;
   Rhoda 10;Rhody 79;Sallie
   Robert 45;Susan 45;Walter 10;
   Wm.45,113;Winny 10;
OGLESBY,David 113;Joshua 113;
   Joshua B.45,79;Mariah 45,113;
   Malinda 79;Martha 45;Wm.79;
OGLSBY,Dick 10;Eliz.10;Ledowick
   10;
OLLIVER,Derritt N.113;Frances
   79;James W.113;John K.79,113;

OLLIVER,Cont.
   Lueresey 113;Lumbia Ann 113;
   Margaret 113;Mitton Derret
   79;Tabitha A.113;
ONEY,Isabella Edgar 10;James W.
   10;Mary Frances 10;
ORRANGE,Ann Eliz.113;Burwell S.
   113;Edw.N.45,113;Eliza I.45;
   Eliza Jane 113;James Wm.113;
   Sarah Eliz.45;Tilman S.113;
ORE,Aleline 28;America 28,97;
   Elinda 97;J.97;James A.28;
   Mary 28;Sarah 97;Spicer P.
   97;Geo.28;Wm.28,77;
OTEY,Ann 79;Austin 79;C.C.79;
   Catherine 45;Chas.C.45;Doct
   John A.10;Fanny 10;Frances
   Wm.10;John W.9;Julia Ann 10,
   113;Kitty 9,113;Leonder
   Harrison 9;Malinda 78;Mary
   C.78,113;Mary Wm.10;Polina
   45;Sarah P.79;
OVERACRE,Emily 113;Emily N.45;
   Geo.45;Geo.W.45,113;
OVERSTREET,Addison 129;Alex 62,
   129;Ann 129;Ann E.62;Bars-
   heba 97;Benj.28;Catherine
   62,129;Chas.28,97;Chas.A.113;
   Chas.Lewis 113;Ellen 129;
   Eliza A.U.28;Frances 129;
   Granville 28;Hiram N.96;Hiram
   W.129;James Harrison 45;Jam-
   es R.28;Jasper A.97;Jeremiah
   129;Jesse 62;John G.62;John
   S.62;Joshua 28,97;Lillia Ann
   96;Lucy 62;Maria V.62;Martha
   28,97;Mary 28,96,129;Mary J.
   129;Mary Jane 28,97;Nancy F.
   45,97;Phebe Ann 113;Robt.W.
   62;Stephen 129;Tabitha 62,129;
   Thos.62,129;Tilman I.45;Wm.
   129;Wm.B.62,97;Wm.H.97,129;
OWENS,Agnes Harriet 10;James F.
   M.10;Martha Frances 10;Mary
   Agnes 10;
OWNBY,Catherine J.113;CHas.P.
   113;Elvy 45;Hillery 45;Nancy
   45;
OWNSBY,Catherine J.62;Chas.L.62;
   Chas.P.62;

INDEX

PAGE,Ann 10;Eliz.46;Erastus
80;Edm.G.46;Frances Ann 80;
John G.10;Mary Reynolds 10;
Parthena 10,46;Robt.10;
Robt.W.46;Selia 46;Thos
Garland 46;Wm.Jasper 80;
PAGET,Ann Booker 46;Beverly 46;
Jane 46;Mary Jane 46;Polly
46;Rich.46;
PAGITT, Beverly 10,46,113;
Eliz.M.46;James A.10,113;
James Melvin 10;Jane 113;
John R.10,79;John William
10;Lucy 10,113;Mary Eliz.46;
Mary Frances 79;Permelia 10;
Rebeckah Jane 113;Sarah F.
79;Sarah Frances 10;
PALLESON,Martha 11;nelson A.11;
Priscilla 11;
PALMER,Caroline 113;CHas.113;
Robt.J.113;
PARKER,Ammon H.97;Banks 64;
Caleb D.63;Calvin F.130;
Catherine E.130;Geo.C.10,80;
Hester Ann 10;John 130;
Julia A.130;Martha D.64,130;
Mary Arnold 10,80;Phebe 28;
Plunkett 63;Racheal 130;
Sarah Catherine 28;Sarah
Claburn 80;Virginia 97;
PATE,Alex P.97;Amanda 130;Betty
97;Ed.130;Cornelius C.63,97;
Hannah 130;Mary 130;Martha
130;Corneluis 130;Wm.130;
PATTERSON,Clara H.63;Eliz.63,
114;John M.97,130;Jon Niickson 97;Lizzie Letton 114;
Maltree 29;Matthew 29;Moultry 63;Mary Eliz.114;Phebe
Jane 63,114;Robinette 130;
Susan 29,63;Sophia 97,130;
Thos.63,114;Thos.W.97;Wm.114;
Wm.T.97;
PAYNE,Ann 29;Charlotte 97;Eliz.
131;Frances 98;James H.29;
John B.131;John R.63;Jesse
P.97;Lewis 97;Martha 29;Mary
A.63;Octavia 131;Thos.M.98;
Thos.Q.63;Thos.R.98;
PEARCE,Amand C.29;James F.T.29;
Josiah 29;
PEARCY,Ann E.63;Ann Eliza 29;
Betsy 29;Frances O.29,63;

PEARCY,COnt.
Henry 63;Livlla 130;Maria E.
130;Mary Frances 11;Mary
Jane 29;Wm.29,63,130;
PECK,Edw.45;Eliza 45;Jos.Thos.45;
PENDLETON,Ann 98;Ann H.63;Eliz.
28;Henry 28,63;James 98;James
M.29;Jane 29;Mildred 98;Nancy
28,63;Nancy E.29;Rhoda J.98;
Rufus 98;Thos.98;Wm.H.98;
Wm.J.98;
*PENN,Harriett 10;Moses 10;
PERCELL,Phillis 28;Thos.28;
PERKINS,D.A.114;Jane 10;Jos.10;
Mary 114;Pleasant 114;Robt.
Emmit 10;
*PENN,Adaline 80;Eliza 46;Harriett
46;Jefferson 80;Jesse 80;
Lucinda 80;Mary 46;Mary C.114;
Moses 46;Paul S.80;P.S.114;
Sanford 46;Wm.Cornelius 114;
PERROWS,Andrew 79;Andrew J.79;
Cornelia 79;Eliz.80;Henry -
Jackson 79;Henryetta 79;James
S.10,80,114;Martha A.10,79;
Nancy 114;Sarah 114;Urania Va.
80;Vina 80;
PHILLIPS,Alice Spottswood 11;
Catherine Frances 11;Lindsey 11;
PETTICREW,Ann 114;Matthew 114;
Rufus 114;
PETERS,Clifton C.28;Isham 28;
James H.63;Mahala J.130;Martha
Ann 46;Mathina Ann 46;Mary
Bell 130;Mildred M.28;Mosa 63;
Paulina S.63;Sally 28;Susan 28;
Wesley 130;Wm.46;
PHELPS,A.M.97;Ammin 28,30;Emeline
97;Frances 97;Harriett 130;
Jos.97;James M.130;John Booker
63;Louisa 130;Malinda P.63;
Mariah 46;Mary 28;Matilda 46,
114;Peter W.46,114;Phill 114;
Rachel 28;Sandy 130;Thos.J.63,
97;Wm.R.63;
*PENN,Ellen 29;Fanny 29;Letta 29;
Lucinda 29;Maria 29;
PIERCE,Eliz.46;John Pleasant 46;
Elizabeth 113;Moses 46,113;
Robt.Lee 113;
PLATT,Andrew L.29;Frances 29;
Morton S.29;

INDEX

PLOTT,Andrew S.97;Frances 97;
    Frances Rebeckah 114;lewis E.
    114;Martha E.114;
PLYMALE,Mary C.29,130;Perry L.
    130;Saml 29;Samuel P.130;
    Wm.T.29;
POINDEXTER,Agnes 11;Agness 80;
    Anderson 11,79;Angeline 79;
    Alla 114;Aylsey 79,114;Ann
    Eliz.114;Dabney 63;Davis D.
    114;Dosha 46;Elijah Dabney
    80;Eliz.M.79,80;Eliza 79;
    Eliza D.46;Emilly 79;Frances
    10,79;Frances Susan 114;
    Frank 11;James 46,114;James W.
    63,130;Jane 79;John S.11;
    Judy 11;Killie 11;Louisa 11;
    Lucinda 79;Lucy 79;Matilda 11
    Marrianna 130;Martha 46,114;
    Martha G.46;Mary 80,114;Mary
    Whitlow 10;Milton 11;Morris
    79;Rich.W.10,46,80;Sam 11;
    Sarah 11;Sophia 63,79;Sophia
    A.130;Susan 11,46,114;Sylva
    46;Thos.11;
POLLARD,Adaline 98;Ann Eliz.29;
    Frances 98;John A.29;Mary
    28,29;Saml C.131;Sarah C 28,
    131;
PONTON,Emily 114;John F.114;
    John James 114;
POWELL,Charlott 45,79;Cisaley
    113;Edwin 45;Frances 10;James
    98;John H.98;Laura Ellen 10;
    Lucinda 45;Lucas 10;Mary 98;
    Morris 45;Polly 113;Sarah
    113;Thos.98;Wm.45,79;
POWERS,Angeline 29;James A.29;
    James S.29;Lafayett 29;Mariah
    29;Mary 29;Sarah 29;Wm.29;
PREAS,Alex 63;Cecilia 98;Eliz.
    29,131;Henry 63,131;John R.
    98;Jos.29,131;John Henry 63;
    Mahala 29,98;Mary Jane 29,98;
    Thomas 63;Wm.H.29,98;
PREBLE,Geo.W.46;Nancy 46;Wm.46;
PRESTON,Adline 130;Ammin 131;
    Caroline 130;Chris 64;Chris-
    topher 29;Clay 64;Eliz.29,97,
    131;Fletcher 64;Harriett 130;
    Henry 97;James S.97;Jane 130;
    Jesse A.64;Jesse B.29;John A.
    97;John F.64,97,131;John L.
    131;John S.63;Lucy 63;Mariah
    97;Martha 131; Martha A.97;
    Mary 63,131;Mary Ann 64,131;

PRESTON,Cont.
    Milly 130;Polly Ann 97;Sarah
    130;Scott 29;Seanna 97;
    Sophia 29;Thos.J.130;Wesley
    29;Wm.63,97,130;Wm.J.29;
PULLEN,Caroline 63;Charlott 28,
    63;Dicy 28;Fanny 130;Gran-
    ville F.63;Granville R.97;
    Jane 63;Jesse 130;Jonah 97;
    Julia Ann 28;Maria 28;Mary
    28;Robert A.130;Sally 63;
    Susan 28;Thos.Henry 28;Wm.F.
    63;
QUARLES,Abram G.136;Caswell 64;
    Cornelia 30,64;Edw.B.64;
    Eliz 30,46;131;Eliz.A.30;
    Eliz.R.46;Frances 131;Flora
    64;Giles T.30;Henry W.30;
    James M.131;John 30,64,131;
    John B.30;John W.64;Mary
    30;Mary Cameron 30;Mary F.
    131;Samuel H.46;Susan 64;
RADFORD,Ann M.115;Chas.11;David
    115;Eliza 11;James 11;Jane
    131;Lydlla 115;Mahala 115;
    Matilda 80;Marshall 115;Mar-
    tha 115,131;Mary 131;Mina
    Jordan115;Munford 30;Minford
    M.131;Nathan 115;Octavus 115;
    R.C.W.80;Rozetta 11;Sally
    131;Susan 115;Wm.115;Winston
    11,80,115;
RAINS,Mary E.30;Mary M.30;Rich-
    ard 30;
RAMSEY,James M.30,131;Lilly Lee
    131;Margaret 64;Marinda 30;
    Martha 30,131;Eliz.131;Pow-
    atan 131;Sarah C.131;
READ,Edw.T.47;E.T.114;Eliz.30;
    Eliza A.114;Eliza Amanda 47;
    Lelia Jane 114;Sylvia 115;
    Wm.A 115;
Reece,Anna 47;Ben 47;Daniel 115;
    Geo.Washington 11;Jane 131;
    Jim 131;Jos.T.11,47,81,115;
    Lucinda 47;Lucy 11,81;Mariah
    47,115;Mary 30;Richard Lewis
    81;Wm.W.30,131;
REYNOLS,Chas.B.47;Louiza 47;
    Nelson 47;
REYNOLDS,Ann Eliz.81;Catherine
    11,81;Chas,B.81;Chas.D.80;
    Don Henry 80;Edw.J.81;Emmet
    Baxter 81;Gene 81;Geo.Winfrey
    80;Hubbard Spinner 81;Jane M.
    80;Joel P.11,81;John 81;

INDEX

Reynolde,Cont.
    Luallen J.81;Mildred Albany
    11;Martha 80,81;Robt.81;Sarah
    Ann 81;Theodore 80;
RICE,Amanda Va.115;Amanda Vir-
    ginia 47;Ann Eliz.115;Bailey
    47;Leannah 47;Lewis 47;
    Mary Frances 47;Wm.C.47,115;
RICHEY,John Rich 11;Harvey F.11;
    Sarah Jane 11;
RITCHERSON,Clinton 131;Daniel
    131;Nancy 131;
RILEY,Eliz.46,114;Geo.46,114;
ROACH,Harvey P.98;John A.98;
    Sally B.98;
ROBERTS,Albert 131;Alex.131;
    Amand 30;Ann A.64;Ann B.131;
    Buca 30;David 131;Frances L.
    30;Geo.F.64;Harriett 131;
    John 131;John G.64;Josiah B.
    64,131;Littleberry 30;Mary
    F.131;Nancy 30,131;Reva 131;
    Victoria 64;Winny 30;Wm.H.30,
    131;
ROBERTSON,Celia Ann 64;Cindar-
    illa 131;Dennis 64;Emily 34;
    Fanny 98;Frances W.30,64;
    Geo.W.98;James 64;jeffrey 34;
    Jom Henry 34;John J.30;Nich-
    olas N.98;Nicholas W.64,131;
    Milly 30;Phillis 30;Pleasant
    131;Sally 64;Sarah E.64;
ROBINSON,Ann E.47,80;Benj.N.11,
    47;Benj.T.47;Doctor 47;Edw.
    N.11,47,115;Ellen 47;Ellen
    Grace 115;Eliz.47;Henry 11;
    James H.47;James W.47,80;
    Jane 47,80;John 47;John H.47;
    Lelia Allice 47;Malinda 47,
    115;Mariah 11,115;Martha M.
    47,115;Mary 47;Mary Ann 47;
    Missouri 80;Mrs Angeline H.80;
    Roderick 80;Vina 11;Virginia
    47;
ROSE,Catherine 11,114;James M.
    98;John Edw.11;John T.Alex
    115;Keziah 115;Martha E.30;
    Martha J.30;Nancy Jane 47;
    Sarah Ann 47;Sarah Frances
    114;Thos.E.114;Uriah 47;
    Wm.H.30,98;
RORER,John J.98;John Q.98;Sally
    B.98;

ROSEBROUGH,Ann 11,80;Artha 80;
    Henry 80;John 11;Mariah 80;
    Robt.80;Robert 11;Sally 80;
    Tom 80;
RUCKER,Amanda 11,115;Ambrose
    30;Anthony 98;Burnard 80;
    Emily 80;Hanibal 115;Har-
    riett 11;James 115;James M.
    11,80,115;Jos.30;Julia Ann
    115;Lucinda 80;Mahala 30;
    Mary 80;Natt 115;Sarah 80;
    Sarah E.80;
ROUTON,James Henry 81;Lucy A.
    81;Samuel 81;
ROY,David M.46;Eliz.114;Fill
    114;James Henry 114;John
    114;Mariah 46;Sally 46,114,
    Wm.W.114;
RUFF,David 47;John James 47;
    Nancy 47;
RULE,Adam 11;mary 11;Mary Rebe-
    ckah 11;
RUSHER,Ann 114;Giles 114;Jesse
    T.46;James 114;Judith Ann E.
    46;Martha Susan 46;
RYAN,James Henry 80;Julia 80;
    Phillip H.80;Sarah 80;Sarah
    E.80;

SALE,Albert 48;Lindsay 48;Mal-
    inda 12;Mary 48;Milly 12;
    Nancy 81;Rachel 48;Rev.Nel-
    son 48;Rich.A.81;Sally P.12;
SAUNDERS,Ailsey 133;Angeline
    100;America 100;Ann 99;ANzo-
    letta 47;Aylesey 12;Ava 31;
    Burwell 30;Catherine 81;
    Cordelia 12;Eliz.101;Eliza
    31,81,99,100;Eliza Ann 65;
    Eliz.Morris 81;Eleanor 64;
    Emma D.100;Fanny 133;Flor-
    entine 65;Danl 133;Frances
    30;Geo.C.30;Geo.G.100;
    Harriett 99;Henry 65;James
    A.99;James C.100;James D.99;
    Jane 133;John E.81;Jos.31,
    101;Judy 31;Julius 65,133;
    Kenay 99;Mariah 101;Martha
    32,47,65,81;Martha J.100;
    Mary 100;Mrs A.M.81;Nancy 31;
    Phillip 64;Preston W.99;Pru-
    dence 65;Sabra 32;Saml R.101;
    Susan 133;Texanna 31;Thos.32;

INDEX

SAUNDERS,Cont.
Thos.100;Thos.D.32;Thos.F.133;
Thos T.65,99;Waddy 65;
Winston 47;Wm.65;
SAUNDERSON,Eliz.A.48;Emmet J.100;
Geo.E.48;Mary Jane 100;Thos.
N.100;
SCHIMED,Bernard 99;Catherine 99;
Chas.A.99;Eliz.99;Gothlieb
99;Henry A.99;
SCOTT,Arthur 48;Caroline 47,116;
Cooper 47;Eliza 82,116;Eliza
M.116;Eller 82;Geo.82;Harriett
116;Hariott 48;Jane 48;Mariah
48;Mrs E.R.48;Patsy 48;Saml M.
47,116;Samuel 82;Sarah M.65;
Spencer 116;Thos.W.65;
SCRUGGS,Cuthia 31;Eliz.32,100;
Eliza 31;Fanny 133;Henrietta
31;Huophilis C.31;Henry 66;
Jane 133;John 31;Lucy 31;mary
133;Nancy M.66;Theophilus 66;
Toby 99;Rachel 31;Reeves L.133;
Reeves S.31;Throphilus 133;
Virginia 32;Wm.31;Wm.B.66,99;
SEAY,Amanda 81;Amanda N.12;
Amanda M.116;David P.12,81,
116;Harriot 81;Mary Eliz.116;
Sarah Ann 12;
SELDON,Mary E.99;Sarah 99;
SETTLE,Barbary 31;barberry 66,100;
John 100;John S.66,31;Jos.100;
Littleberry 100;Sarah Ann 31;
Wm.S.100;
SHARP,Capt.Samson 12;Charlott 12;
Jim 12;Patsy 12;miltchal 12;
SHELTON,Adaline 133;Chas.115;
Catherine 12;Chester 48;Geo.
W.133;John 133;Jane Watts 12;
Nancy 48,115;Eliz.Margaret 12;
Rich 12;Wesley 12,48,115;
SHEPHERD,B.H.F.47;
SHOAN,Ann 66;James K.66;
SIMS,Judith 65;Wm.B.65;Wm.T.W.65;
SINER,Jonathan 31;Julina 31;Lavi-
nnia 31;Lucy 31;martha Ann 31;
Susan 31;
SKINNELL,David P.65;Eliz.A.E.99;
Eliz A.65;Fannie 99;Geo.E.65,
99;James 66,132;Lucinda 65;
Missouri H.65;Nathaniel 132;
Rebecca G.66,132;
SLAUGHTER,Archer 115;James C.115;

SLAUGHTER, Cont.
Mariah 115;
SLEDD,Ann 12;Arabella 12,82;
Betsey 12,82,116;Mary 12,
82;Mary Ann 47;Milly 12;
Moses 82;Sarah 12;Wesley
82;Winny 12;WM.E.12,47,82,
116;Wm.Robt.12;Yarmer 47;
SMELSOR,Catherine 31;Chas.W.
66;Frances 31,66;Henry K.
100;Mary Jane 31;Nancy 31;
Paschal 31,66;Rhoda E.100;
Wm.H.100;
SMITH,Alex 66;Alex B.66;Alex.
A.66,98;Catherine 115;
Celine 32;Emmer Lewis 115;
James A.115;Julia 32,65;
John A.66;John Calvin 12;
Geo.W.66;Lucy J.66;Mahala
66;Martha 30;Martha F.115;
Martha Jane 98;Mary E.98;
Minerva 132;Paulina 98;
Priscilla 66;Rob.98;Robt.
12;Stephen 30,66,99,132;
Ursula 66,98;Wm.C.32,65,98;
Wm.Jr.115;Wm.Thos.115;
SMOOT,James Thos.116;Mary F.
116;Wm.H.116;
SLUSSER,Edw.Jonas 81;Henry 81,
Jane 81;
SNEAD,Caroline 115;Geo.W.115;
Virginia Ann 115;
SPENCE,Andrew 81;Lucy 81;Wm.
Andrew 81;
SPINNER,Ailsey 81;Amanda 81;
Doc.Jesse F.81;Doct.J.F.12;
Jesse 12;Martha Ann 12,81;
Wm.Sherman 81;
SPRADLIN,Chas.H.100;Chas.R.100;
Franklin 30;James 30;Luci-
nda 30;Martha 64;Meador Jr.
64;Sarah 64;
STALEY,James S.12;James Booker
12;Martha Marshall 12;
STAILEY,David 65,99;Harriett
E.99 Martha 65,99;
STANLEY,John N.115;Martha 115;
Virginia 115;
STEPTOE,Doc.Wm.81;Emmer 81;
Frank 12;Henry C.132;Ida
132;Isabel 81;John 65;John
65;John R.65,99;Louisanna
132;Louiza 81;Malinda 81;

INDEX

STEPTOE,Cont.
   Martha 48;Mary 12,81;Mary E.65;
   Matilda 81;Molly 115;Lucy 12;
   Noah 115;Rhoda 12,48,81;Robt.
   C.12,81,115;Robt G.48;Sarah P.
   99;Violet 12,81;Watt 12;
STEPHENS,Frances O.31;Mary E.31;
   Wm.99;Wm.H.31;
STEVENS,Agnes 100;Daniel B.100;
   Eliz.J.65;Genevery 133;John M.
   65,101,133;James F.100;Lucy Ann
   E.100;Mary E.100;Susan 65,133;
   Susan D.101;Wm.H.100;
STEWARD,Berry 32;Mary Ellen 32;
   Parthena 32;
STEWART,Estill A.W.98;Littleberry
   99;Mary A.E.J.98;Martha M.99;
   Saml G.98;Parthena 99;
STCLAIR,Bird L.132;Burwell C.31;
   Drucilla 132;Eliz.Frances 116;
   Emily 132;Harry F.132;Frances
   31;John D.132;John P.31;John F.
   132;Margaret 132;Martha Ann 116;
   Martha F.132;Mary C.31;Rhoda 66;
   Robt.66,132;Roda 132;Rich.F.132;
   Ruhanna A.66;Samuel 116;Sarah
   Frances 31;Sarah J.132;Thos.L.
   132;Wm.F.132;
STIFF,Bur 100;Burwell 66;Geo.W.65;
   James M.65,132;Julia Ann 100;
   July Ann 66;Lucy A.132;Lucy Ann
   65;Mary L.132;Wm.H.100;
STINETT,Eliz.66;Pleasant E.66;
   Tandy 66;
STINNETT,Alex 31,99;Catherine 31,
   99;Eliz.99;James M.99;John J.32;
   John L.31;Judith 31,99;Leanner
   31;Lindsay 31,99;Margaret 32;
   Martha Jane 31;Pleasant 99;Sarah
   F.99;Tandy 99;Wm.R.31;
STILLER,John 65;John P.65;mary
   Ann 65;
STONE,Alice Lee 132;Catherine 132;
   Eliz.32;Everett 132;Geo.32;James
   F.132;Jane 66;Martha 30,99;
   Micajah 132;Paulina B.132;Perm-
   elia 132;Spencer 132;Thos.66;Wm.
   D.32;
STRATTONEliz.26;Frazier O.26,31;
   Jack,99;Milly 31;Sarah 99;
STRONG,Clifton 12;Laura 12;Patsy
   12;
STUMP,Martha Ann 65;Sarah B.65;
   Wm.B.65;

SUBLETT,Edmund 65;John Irvine
   65;Wm.Henry 65;Nancy 65;
   Sarah 65;
SWAIN,Admire 132;Callahill
   M.66,99;Charlotte E.99;
   Elijah 31,64;Eliza 65;
   Ellen 66,Emily 65,132;Jeff-
   rey 66;Nancy 8,65;Permelia
   99;Pleust P.132;Patricia
   Ann 65;Pleasant 65;Robt.65;

TANKISLEY,Anderson 16;Mary
   Jane 13,116;Paulis Good 13;
   Rich.A.13,116;
TANNER,Almeda 82;James Rogel
   13;Joel 13;Jos.82;Rhoda
   Jane 82;Rhada 13;
TARDY,Martha Ann 48;Paul J.48;
   Thos.Elihue 48;
TATE,Ann Eliz.32;Caleb 32;Henry
   F.32;Hugh A.133;Hugh H.32;
   Julia P.133;Malissa 32;Mary
   P.32;Mary D.133;
TAYLOR,Adam 13;Albert H.48,82;
   Elisha B.66;Eliza 82;Emily
   82;Frances Jane 13;James
   Peterson 13;John R.82;Mar-
   tha Jane 48;Mary Jane 48,
   82;Marshall P.Scott 48;
   Sarah 66;Sarah B.66;Thos.
   Henry 82;Wm.N.48;
TERPIN,Emerline 82;Julia 82;
   Ned 82;Pocahontas 82;Roland
   G.82;
TERRY,Amanda 133;Chaney 133;
   Elisha 33;Frances 32;Henry
   33,67,133;Lucy Ann 67;Mary
   Jane 32;Sam 67;Sanford W.
   32;Sally 33,133;Vina 133;
THACKER,Harriett 133;Melissa
   133;Samuel 133;
THAXTON,David F.12;David T.83;
   Emily Susan 83;Ginny 12;
   Harriet 48;Harriett 116;
   Mariah 83;Milly Ann 12;N.F.
   116;Nathaniel 48;Sophia 32;
   Wiatt 116;Wm.32,48;
THEMBS,John B.13;John Frederick
   13;Sarah Ann 13;
TINSLEY,Adaline 16;Alfred 49;
   China 32;Lucy 49,82;Milly
   49;Mourning 82;Saml G.32,66;

INDEX

THOMAS,Amanda Pope 12;Amanda P.
82;Anderson 82;Cahs.F.101;Eld-
eridge 67;Elisha B.66;Eliza
33,82;Eliza Ann 48;Eliza
Brookin 13;Frances Julia 116;
Fleming 66,101;Geo.W.49;Har-
vey 33;Henryetta 49;Isaac 48;
James 13,48;John 66;John C.
13,82;John Stele 82;Laura 67;
Laura V.66;L.H.48;Louisa 33;
Mary Charlott 12;mary Eliz.
13,48;Mary F.82;Mary Jane 48,
66;Nancy Me 48;Napoleon Bonapart 82;Nikson 66;Proser P.
13;Prosser P.83;Robt.82;Rosey
66;Rufus N.116;Samuel M.12;
S.M.82;Saml M.48;Saml H.66;
Sally 13,48;Sarah B.66;Sarah
101;Sarah E.66;Sarah Eliz.49;
SarAH L.116;Soniza 48;Susan
66;Susan P.82;Susan Porride
13;Thos.J.66;Thos.M.48;
THOMASON,John N.48,116;Jos.Green
116;Mary D.48,116;Samuel Edw.
48;Thos.J.66;
TOLLEY,Catherine 82;Dabney 82;
Jermine 82;Owen 82;
TOMPKINS,Danl 133;Daniel 32,66;
David 101;Eliz.133;John Taylor
32;Lydia 32;
TOMS,G.W.116;Geo.Washington 116;
Henrietta A.116;
TOWLER,Absalom 101;Mary Ann 101;
Polly 101;
TUCK,Geo.101;Geo.T.101;Geo.W.32;
Mary 32,101;Nancy Ann 32;Sarah
Ann 101;Sarah J.101;Stephen
H.101;
TURNER,Ann 32,133;Admire 32,133;
Charlott 32;Chas.E.32,101;
Chas.H.32;Caroline 101;Comora
O.101;Elijah H.101;Geo.32;
Hardaway 101;Jesse 116;John W.
133;Judy A.133;Lucinda 32;
Margaret 133;Margarett D.133;
Nancy 32,101;Orvilla 133;
Obediah W.133;Parthena 133;
Rev.Jesse H.116;Sarah A.101;
Sallie F.116;Tabitha 101;
Thos.W.101;Wm.A.32;
THOMPSON,Alex.S.116;Amanda 32,116;
Betsey 116;Caroline 116;Char-
lott 82;Chester 82;David E.116;
Dosha 116;Jane 116;Jenny 82;
Jesse S.32;John 13;Lewis 82;

THOMPSON,Cont.
Margaret R.116;Milly 32;
Mildred 116;Nancy 32;Nelson
13,82,116;Rhoda M.32;Sally
116;Susan 13;
THURMAN,Adeline C.133;Austin 66;
Austin L.32;Anna Maria 32,66;
Alex.L.32,133;Aug.S.101;Emma
F.101;Jerry 133;Jim 133;John
32;Judua 133;Mary 33;Mary
Ann B.32;Nancy 32;Robt.J.32;
Sophia 32,133;Susan 32;Susan
M.133;
TURPIN,Amanda 48,116;Davy 49;
Elisha G.48,116;Eliza 13;
Eliza Susan 82;Elmira 83;
Emma Veloria 49;Genetta 49;
Flora 49;Henry Ann 116;Jesse
13;John 13;Joshua 13;Julia
116;Laura Riverta 116;Louiza
49,83;Luchtta 82;Madison 116;
Margaret 48,83;Mariah 13;
Martha 13;Mary E.49;Nancy 83;
Natt 83;Phillip 48,83;R.G.116;
Roland G.13;Robt.H.116;Sally
Ann E.116;Spottswood 82;Thos.
48,49;Willis C.49;
TYLER,Jos.W.33;martha 33;Tilgh-
man 33;

UPDIKE,Anson 33;Avon 101;Caroline
33;Caroline F.101;Chrls.101;
Lohsa 101;Mary Jane 33;Saml33,
67;Sarah C.101;Thos.J.33;

VARNER,Fanny Bell 117;John W.49,
117;Mary F.49,117;Wm.Frances
49;
VAUGH,Bedford 49;Jos.Wingfield
49;Mary J.49;

WALDREN,Thos.D.35;
WADKINS,James A.134;Lelia L.134;
Martha J.134;
WADE,Adline 135;Alex 34,69,103.
135;Calista Ann 50;Callahill
M.101;Chas.68;Davls P.34;Eliz.
R.50;Eliza 135;Geo.34;Irvine
135;Isaac 69;James M.33,134;
James T.69;Judith 34;Judy 135;
Lucinda 69;Martha 68;Mary 34,
68,102;Mary E.68,135;Nancy 33,

INDEX

WADE,Cont.
Nancy 134;Nancy A.68;Saml 103;
Sarah 134;Silas G.33,134;Squin
68;Thos.33;Virginia 101;Wm.68,
102;Wm.A.34,102;Wm.H.50;Wm.W.
68;
WAGGONER,J.R.102;Martha 102;Wm.
0.102;
WALES,Rich.M.102;
WALKER,Andrew 3;Caroline 33,102;
David H. 33,102;Dosha 67;Edgar
33;Edw.T.101;Ellen 35;Eletha
H.102;Frederick 102;Henry Clay
102;Henry S.33;James 102;James
A.33,102,134;Jesse 67;Joe 68;
Joel 34,135;John W.67;Kinissa
33;Louisa 33;Maria 134;Mary E.
135;Nancy Ann 34,135;Polly Ann
33;Rufus 102;Saml P.67,68;
Saml T.34;Stephen 33;Thos.67;
William Gillmon 101;Wm.J.35;
WALROND,James 68;Moses 68,103;
Nancy 68,103;
WATSON,Armonia Sale 118;Barnett
A.49,83;Benj.R.118;Catherine
49,117;Chas.Jos.14;Green 103;
Henry Mitchell 83;Hubert Flo-
rain 117;Jame P.103;John 83,
49;Jordan 117;Jos.D.83,118;
Mariah L.50;Martha 117;Mary
Ann 83;Mary E.83,118;Mary Ann
R.117;Mary Jane 103;Mitton Clark 13;
Nancy 49,117;Permilia 83;Reb-
eckah Jane 118;Rozetta Jane
117;Sarah Jane 13;Stephen Rich.
50;Tenah 49,83;Uriah A.14,117;
Wiatt 49;Wiatt J.50;Wm.83;Wm.
D.13,83;Wm.Mitchell 83;
WATTS,Allice 49;Eliza 14;Eliza
Jane 84;Elvira 14;Elvira F.84;
Harvey 49;Isabella 14;Isabelle
49;James D.84;James W.49;Jane
49;Mary 84;Nancy 14;Rich.D.14;
Sallie Lee 84;Sophia 49;Susan
14;Wiatt 14;Winny 14;Wm.14;
Wm.P.84;
WEBB,Lucy 33;Sallie 33;Wm.33;
WEBBER,James B.14,84;James Edw.
14;Nancy 14;Nancy E.84;Oliver
Perry 84;
WEEKS,Ellen 34,135;Mary L.135;
Sarah S.34;Wm.D.34;

WELLS,Alice R.135;Ann 135;
Catherine 135;Chris.C.68;
David G.102;Ellen 135;
Fanny 135;Florentine W.
!02;Harriet 68,Harriett
34,135;Harvey A.135;Malinda
35;Martha 68;Rob.A.102;
Rich.135;Rich W.34;Rich.M.
34,68,135;Wm.135;
WEST,Chas.G.35;Joel 35;
WHEAT,Eliza 83;Emerline 83;
Hazel 83;Phillis 83;Sarah
83;Zach J.83;
WHEELER,Eliz.69;Gabrial Jr.
135;Gabriel T.69;Geo.68;
Gilly E.135;John A.135;
Lettilia 68;Mary E.67;Nancy
67;Saml T.69,103;Sarah 103;
Sarah E.69;Solomon 69;Solo-
mon J.135;Thos.103,135;
WHERELY,Emily 135;John 135;
Maria 135;
WHITE,Alex 68.135;Alis 103;
Addison 134;Albert 49;Ann14,
50;Alfred 84;Allice Mason
118;Catherine 67,134;Cathe-
rine Jane 34;Catherine S.117;
Chas.Henry 83;Clara 49,83;
Daniel Edgar 83;Dilsey 50;
Eliz.P.84;Eliz.118;Eliza 84;
Etlebert 84;Elvira W.118;
Eliz.P.83;Francis 84;Geo.35,
135;Gilla 103;Henry A.84;
Henry D.134;Henry Edw.84;
Henry M.49,83,118;James 84;
James M.135;James Becknett
83;Jacob 117;Jacob S.14,50;
Jacib S.84;Jane 68;Jeremiah
C.118;Jesse 68;John 84;John
E.103;John M.50,84;Jos.F.134;
Julia 68;Leek 118;Major
84;Malinda 49;Martha 49;
Martha Jane 34;Mary A.84;
Mary Ann 134;Mary Catherine
84;Mary V.84;Maysa 84;Nancy
84;Rosser 49;Sarah 49,50,
83;Sarah Ann 84;Sarah Fran-
ces 84;Sarah Martha 83;Sam-
uel 34,67,134;Sophia J.135;
Susan 14,35,135;Wiatt 50;

INDEX

WHITE,Walter 117;Wm.Henry 68;
WHITELY,Ann C.14,50;Eliz.14,Eugene
    14;John 50;Watsey 50;
Whitley,Ann 49;Ann C.14;Duke 14;
    Elbert 14;Eliz.49;Ginny 14;
    Phill 14;Ransum 49;Sarah 14;
    Sylva 14;
WHITTEN,Ben 101;Catherine 34;
    James 134;Jane 134;Jane P.68;
    John D.68;J.H.117;Jos.34,68,
    101;Martha A.134;Mary 117;
    Matilda 34;Mildred 33;Milly
    117;
WHORLEY,Eliza 67;Francis 67;
    Frances W.67;Louisa 67;Virgi-
    nia M.67;
WIGGENTON,Alfred 84;Benj.14,50,84;
    Calidonia 103;Caroline 103;
    Chas.A.103;Clara 84;Cora 14;
    Cornelia Scott 84;Creasy 14;
    Eliz.103;Frances 34;F.M.84;
    Ginny 84;Isral 34;James Munroe
    103;Jenny 14;John J.134;Leanna
    84;Martha 84;Moses 50;Nancy P.
    134;Orrange 84;Polina 14,84;
    Polina Morning 14;Robert 103;
    Rose 50;Susan 34;Sylvia 84;
    Wm.103;
WILCH,Adaline 49;James 49;John
    Wesley 49;
WILDMAN,Elisha S.33,102;Mary 33,
    102;gideon 102;
WILKERSON,Aggy 50;Agness 117;Ann
    50;Betsey 50;David M.34;Dibrel
    50;Early 50;Geo.Washington 117;
    Holcomb 83;Hugh Brown 117;
    Isaac 117;Jacob 84;Jos.68;Jos.
    B.117;Juliett B.117;Keziah 13,
    117;Lucy 83;Magdalen 117;Marg-
    aret 50;Martha J.34;Nancy 118;
    Nicholas 13;Owen 84;Patsey 50;
    Polly 50;Rachel 50,84;Sam 68;
    Sally 118;Sarah 83;Sarah Cath-
    erine 13;Susan 117;Tabby 13;
    Thos.M.50;Virginia 34;Wm.50;
    Wm.L.13,117;Wm.0.50,117;Wm.
    Oliver 13;
WILKS,Ann Eliz.84;Benj.50,84,117;
    Burwell 117;Eliz.67,84,102;
    Eliza 50,117;Harry 68;Henry 68,
    84;Henry C.134;Henry S.67;
    James 50;John 50;Lucinda 50,
    117;Malinda 117;Nancy C.102;

WILKS,Cont.Sarah 134;Saul H.
    134;Sophiah 50,84,117;
    Wm.G.67;
WILLARD,Margaret 134;Nicholas
    Winfrey 134;
WILLIAMS,Albert 13;Brackenr-
    idge 13;Caroline 50,103;
    Cary 117;Chas.M.68;CHas.W.
    135;Cornelia 33;Edm.34;
    Edw.103;Emmer 49;Frances
    83;Hannah 50;Henry O.135;
    J.M.103;James F.33;James M.
    50;Jinretta 34;John A.49;
    John J.68;Josafine 68;Mat-
    ilda 49,83,117;Marsella 13;
    Martha J.68;Marvella 83;
    Saml 34;Samuel 50;Sarah 49,
    117;Sarah A.49;Sarah F.103;
    Sep.103;Susan 68,103;
    Susan A.135;
WILLIAMSON,Caleb 117;Dillard
    S.34;Eliz.13;Geo.117;Jos.
    A.134;Mahalia A.34,133;
    Mary 134;Moses 117;Nancy
    13,117;Polly 117;Rich.A.P.
    133;Solomon 13,117;Thos.J.
    133;
WILKS,Eliz.J.13;Leyburn 13;
    Roena 13;
WILLS,America 67;Edw.M.67;
    Fanny 135;Harvey A.135;
    John B.67;Mary 67;Robt.67;
    Wm.135;
WILSON,Amanda 84;Bettie Fran-
    ces 50;Betsey 14;Edw.D.35;
    Eliz.13,49,50;Eliz.S.117;
    Elijah 34;Elijah C.102,135;
    Eliz.Frances 14;Eliza 33;
    Eliza Ann 14,117;Emaline
    35;Evalina 67;Eveline 103;
    Geo.H.50;Geo.W.14,117;Geo-
    rgianna 117;Henry 14;James
    33;James M.35;James R.67,
    103;James W.13,83;John N.
    35,135;John Thos.49;John R.
    135;Jesse P.84;Judy Emer
    50;Julia A.F.135;Martha S.
    34,102,103;Mariah 103;
    Mariah Jane 117;McHenry 33;
    Mary 83;Mary E.117;Martha
    L.135;Mary J.34,135;Minerva
    35;Nancy E.102;Nelson Ross-
    er 83;Peter H.14;Polina 50;

WILSON,Cont.
Roderick 84;Samuel 13;Susan
13;Susan Webster 13;Thos.J.
117;Thos.C.50;Vincent 13;Wm.
117;
WINGFIELD,Ann E.103;G.A.35;
Harriett 103;Letty 35;Louisa
35;Milis 67;Nelson D.67,103;
WITT,Albert M.101;Albert R.67;
Alex 34;Alis 67;Ann Booker
103;Biddy 34;Eliza Jane 102;
Engeline 102;John E.67;Lucy
Ann 101;Louisa 102;M.A.103;
Margaret 101;Maria 134;
Martha 34;Mary 34,134;Nancy
33,102;Queen 102;Roland 102;
Reubin 102;Susan 68;Wm.68,
102,134;Wm.W.33,102;
WOOD,Almara 68;Almary 134;
Bennett L.134;Chas.A.13;
Chas.W.67,133;Genette 49;
Harriott 83;John 49,83;John
B.68;John T.83;Jenetta 68;
Jenette 83;Jeremiah 67;Julia
Ann 68;Laura 67;Lydia 13;
Malissa E.134;Martha Ann 67;
Mary A.134;Mary Ann 67;Mary
Eliz 83;Patra 68;Rebecca 101;
Rebeckah 13;Saml T.101;SArah
Ann 49;SAlly D.68;Sarah
Margaret 83;Terrissa 67;
Talitha Florentine 13;Thos.
101;Thos.C.13;Tilghman A.68;
Wesley C.68;Wm.H.68;Wm.O.68;
WOODY,Martha Jane 117;Mary Ann
117;Rich.R.117;
WOOLFOLK,Geo.117;Julia 117;Wm.
117;
WORLEY,Ann Marie 34;Catherine M.
118;Eliza 34,134;Eliza V.34;
Emily 50;Frances W.34,134;
Henry A.118;John 50;Lewis
Calvin 84;Mariah Catherine
118;Mary 84;Rich.A.84;Samuel
L.Goggin 50;Sidney 34;Sarah
Virginia 83;Susan 83;Wm.83;
Wm.Tell 134;
WRIGHT,Agness B.50;Albert 135;
Amy 134;Bartley 102;Chas.102;
David Henry 50;Ellen 134;
Fanny 102;Gairy 135;Geo.W.102;
Hannah A.V.102;James 67,102,
134;James M.35,103;James O.33,
102;Gustavus 50;Jane E.50,84;

WRIGHT,Jim Henry 34;Joel 135;
John D.50,84;John Q.A.34;
Jos.P.34,134;Jos.69;Jubal
67;Jubal J.67;Judith 134;
Leanor 135;Lettitia 67;
Major 103;Maria Louise 33;
Mariah S.102;Martha 34,134;
Martha E.67;Martha P.134;
Mary 103;Mary G.34;Mary L.
35;Mary S.35;Nanny Edgar
84;Nicholas 67;Peter M.35,
102;Peter Sr.103;R.F.Ellen
134;Robt.134;Robt.S.33;Robt
W.135;Saml T.102;Sarah A.
102;Sarah J.102;Sarah E.102;
Sarah Jane 35;Stephen 134;
Susan S.E.35;Walter C.102;
Wesley Martin 50;Wm.64;Wm.
P.103;Wright H.34;
YOUNG,Catherine 118;CHristian
51;John 51;John H.118;Lucy
51,118;
ZIMMERMAN,Adaline 103;Rob.B.
103;Wm.103;

www.ingramcontent.com/pod-product-compliance
Lightning Source LLC
Chambersburg PA
CBHW081645280326
41928CB00069B/3051